The Media and
the War on Terrorism

The Media and the War on Terrorism

Stephen Hess
Marvin Kalb

EDITORS

Cosponsored by the
Shorenstein Center on the Press, Politics
and Public Policy, Harvard University

Brookings Institution Press
Washington, D.C.

Copyright © 2003
THE BROOKINGS INSTITUTION
1775 Massachusetts Avenue, N.W., Washington, D.C. 20036
www.brookings.edu

All rights reserved

Library of Congress Cataloging-in-Publication data

The media and the war on terrorism / Stephen Hess and Marvin Kalb, editors.—1st ed.
    p. cm.
"Cosponsored by the Shorenstein Center on the Press, Politics, and Public Policy at Harvard University."
Includes bibliographical references.
 ISBN 0-8157-3581-2 (pbk. : alk. paper)
 1. Terrorism—Press coverage. 2. War—Press coverage. 3. Terrorism and mass media. I. Hess, Stephen. II. Kalb, Marvin L. III. Brookings Institution. IV. Joan Shorenstein Center on the Press, Politics, and Public Policy.

PN4784.T45M38 2003
070.4'49303625—dc21   2003007527

9 8 7 6 5 4 3 2 1

The paper used in this publication meets minimum requirements of the American National Standard for Information Sciences—Permanence of Paper for Printed Library Materials: ANSI Z39.48-1992.

Photographs of the Brookings/Harvard Forum sessions
by Jennifer Kurz and Jennifer Whitman

Typeset in Minion and Clearface Gothic

Composition by Circle Graphics
Columbia, Maryland

Printed by R. R. Donnelley
Harrisonburg, Virginia

Remembering

Daniel Pearl

*"Killing him so brutally,
in front of a video camera,
marked a new low in
man's inhumanity to man."*

JUDEA PEARL, FATHER

The Media and the War on Terrorism

CONVERSATIONS WITH

Jill Abramson
Hafez Al-Mirazi
Peter Arnett
Alex Arriaga
David S. Broder
Margaret Carlson
José Carreño
Victoria Clarke
Yasemin Çongar
Ceci Connolly
Candy Crowley
Lloyd N. Cutler
Susan Dentzer
Karen DeYoung
Thomas A. Dine
E. J. Dionne Jr.
Thomas Donilon
Joseph Duffey
Lawrence S. Eagleburger
Glenn Frankel
Michael Getler
Michael Gordon
Lee H. Hamilton
Toby Harnden

Peter D. Hart
Mark Jurkowitz
Bernard Kalb
Stanley Karnow
Kevin Keane
Jeane J. Kirkpatrick
Claus Kleber
Andrew Kohut
Mort Kondracke
Ted Koppel
William Kristol
Thomas Kunkel
Rudiger Lentz
James M. Lindsay
Steven Livingston
Joseph Lockhart
Michael McCurry
Harry C. McPherson
John McWethy
Jean-Jacques Mevel
Carol Morrello
Alan Murray
Dee Dee Myers
Ronald Nessen

Geneva Overholser
Susan Page
Todd Purdum
Lois Raimondo
Tom Rosenstiel
Christopher W. S. Ross
Warren B. Rudman
James Sasser
Bob Schieffer
James R. Schlesinger
Daniel Schorr
Alicia C. Shepard
David Shipler
Robert Siegel
Andrei K. Sitov
Tom Squitieri
Jonathan B. Tucker
Sanford J. Ungar
Kevin Whitelaw
Judy Woodruff
R. James Woolsey
Robin Wright
Barry Zorthian

Contents

Foreword

As a former reporter and diplomat, I feel a special connection with a book that brings together sixty-nine journalists, government officials, and scholars to examine reporting, policymaking, and the connections between reporting and policy in this time of crisis. The issues and perspectives aired in the pages that follow seem all the more immediate to me, since I'm writing this foreword with the television in my office tuned to CNN, which is providing live reports from reporters "embedded" in U.S.-led units fighting their way toward Baghdad.

The history of *The Media and the War on Terrorism* underscores the special convening role that institutions like Brookings play. Shortly after September 11, Jim Lynn, a former U.S. budget director and member of President Ford's cabinet (and a Brookings trustee as well), called Mike Armacost, my predecessor, to ask whether Brookings might be helpful in clarifying what was sure to be a confusing, complicated, and very important question, namely that of the relationship between the press and government in the multidimensional campaign against terrorism. Mike turned the question over to Steve Hess, a Brookings senior fellow known for his five-volume "Newswork" series about Washington journalism in general and especially coverage of international news. Steve asked Marvin Kalb, a distinguished former network diplomatic correspondent who was running the Washington office of Harvard's Shorenstein Center on the Press, Politics, and Public Policy, to join in planning a conference.

Steve and Marvin soon concluded that the subject was a moving target and therefore should be approached as a continuous dialogue. That was the origin of the Brookings/Harvard Forum on the Media and the War on Terrorism, which held twenty sessions from October 2001 through September 2002 with participants that included a former secretary of state, a former secretary of defense, a former CIA director, TV anchors, and some of the world's most renowned war correspondents.

The response to the forum was heartening: large audiences at Brookings in Washington; extensive press coverage, particularly in the Middle East; and enthusiastic comment from C-SPAN viewers. A quick posting of the transcripts on the Brookings website became the grist for classroom discussions. Two of the programs were beamed around the world by the State Department from its Foreign Press Center and another program came from the National Press Club. The next step was to prepare this edited version of the conversations in a form designed to be student-friendly.

Adding to the importance of this undertaking at this time is that the media are entering a period that is both troubling and potentially liberating. I used to work for a company, Time Inc., which was in the business of publishing magazines. It then joined with a motion picture company, Warner Communications, and became Time Warner, until it merged with an Internet company, AOL. It now is AOL Time Warner. Media giantism is a cause of worry for many of us who care deeply about journalism. There are now fewer *Time* correspondents stationed outside the United States than there were when I left the magazine a dozen years ago. Over the same period, ABC, owned by Disney, cut its foreign bureaus from twelve to eight, and the amount of time that network news devoted to foreign dateline stories dropped by two-thirds until it was forced up by September 11 and the war in Afghanistan.

Yet there's a paradox. Because of satellite TV and radio, cable, and the World Wide Web, if you have the right technology, you can scan the airwaves, surf the channels, and cruise the Internet to find news and analysis on virtually any subject, from any perspective, in any language, at any time of day or night.

In this brave new media world, with increasingly capable VCRs and with the combination of high-speed data lines and the exponential growth in the speed and memory of personal computers, knowledgeable information consumers can order a la carte from a vast menu and arrange for home delivery, at specified times and in formats of their choosing. They will be able, in effect, to program their TVs to produce a customized evening news show and to program their home computers to spit out personalized daily newspapers or weekly news magazines.

But it will take quite a while for most Americans to get into the habit of actively designing their own daily window on the world, meaning that for some time to come, well-informed viewers and readers will be an elite—those who care enough to invest time, money, and skill in keeping themselves informed—and that's not a good thing in a democracy.

Moreover, if indeed we are heading into an age in which we fully exercise the freedom technology gives us to be the editor-in-chief of the news we consume, that will push us more in the direction of atomized and perhaps in some cases antagonistic subcommunities, exacerbating our differences along cultural, partisan, and ideological lines.

Managing—and minimizing—these dangers will require a much more systematic effort to include education about the world—geography, culture, history, current events—in the American school curriculum. It shouldn't take a September 11 for Americans to know where Afghanistan is or to learn that there's something called the Koran.

To take full advantage of the potential of these wide-ranging new information systems, however, we need more than passive, catch-as-catch-can news habits—a headline here, a weather report there, and a political rant while we're driving home. To understand this dangerous and fascinating world in which we must live, Americans need to become *active* consumers. We at Brookings hope that *The Media and the War on Terrorism* is a worthy contribution to this cause.

STROBE TALBOTT
President, Brookings Institution

Washington, D.C.
April 2003

With thanks . . .

Creating the Brookings/Harvard Forum on the Media and the War on Terrorism, the coming together of two great institutions to produce an exciting series of panel discussions that led in turn to this book, was a collaborative effort of many people, from those who authorized the project and raised the money to those who placed the chairs in the auditorium, publicized the events, arranged the tapings, supervised the transcripts, checked facts, suggested topics and participants, provided personal and logistical support to the moderators, and edited the manuscript and designed the book. In addition to our thanks to the panelists, Stephen Hess and Marvin Kalb wish to thank the following people (listed in alphabetical order):

Michael Armacost, Michael Barre, Edmund Berkey, Jefferson Brown, Rebecca Clark, Lawrence Converse, Robert Dabrowski, Frederick Dews, Robert Faherty, Michael G. Freedman, Andrew Glass, Carol Graham, Gary Harding, Lindsey Hench, Eileen Hughes, Colin Johnson, Alex S. Jones, Bernard Kalb, Christopher Kelaher, Peter Kovach, Paul Light, James Lynn, Robert Mason, Elizabeth McAlpine, Marcia McNeil, Sean Meehan, Ronald Nessen, Joseph S. Nye Jr., Nicole Pagano, Nancy Palmer, Adrianna Pita, Daniel Reilly, Stacey Rosenstein, Harry Schwartz, Walter H. Shorenstein, Susan Stewart, Strobe Talbott, Mike Wallace, Janet Walker, Jennifer Whitman, Paul D. Wolfowitz, Susan Woollen, and four anonymous reader-reviewers.

The Media and
the War on Terrorism

Introduction

For a generation, until the collapse of the Soviet Union, American news organizations reported on the world largely through the prism of the cold war. Particularly on the TV networks' evening news programs, where stories have to be short and preferably dramatic, the East-West conflict was a useful framing device.[1] Moreover, the epicenter of the struggle was in Europe, the part of the world that most Americans care most about and whose cultures American journalists were more apt to understand and whose languages they were more apt to speak.

But after the Berlin Wall came down in 1989, international news seemed to lose its urgency for many Americans. Media enterprises turned their attention to domestic matters, which were of greater interest to their consumers. News businesses were not displeased to shut down expensive foreign bureaus. At the same time, without the threat of a rival superpower, U.S. foreign policy makers searched for new defining themes. Revolving attention turned to such topics as human rights, trade, the environment, and regional hot spots; when necessary, news organizations simply parachuted journalists into war zones or other disaster areas. Although the Associated Press, CNN, and a handful of major newspapers—notably the *New York Times, Washington Post, Los Angeles Times,* and *Wall Street Journal*—continued to maintain a substantial presence abroad, by the morning of September 11, 2001, the world outside the United States had become of only modest interest to the rest of the American

---

1. As defined by Kathleen Hall Jamieson and Paul Waldman in *The Press Effect* (Oxford University Press, 2003), p. xiii, "The metaphor of a frame—a fixed border that includes some things and excludes others—describes the way information is arranged and packaged in news stories. The story's frame determines what information is included and what is ignored."

journalism establishment.[2] That day's horrendous events instantly created a new focus of American national purpose, forcefully articulated by the president, and a new framing device for the media: The War on Terrorism.

What was most immediately apparent about covering this war was its breadth, the vast scope of what had to be included. Take coverage between January 1 and April 5, 2002, on the ABC, CBS, and NBC nightly news. While there were strong competing stories, such as the Enron scandal and the Winter Olympics in Salt Lake City, 28 percent of total stories still related to terrorism. There were accounts of the battle of Gardez in the eastern mountains of Afghanistan, Israeli-Palestinian violence intensifying in the Jenin refugee camp, airport security testing, the kidnapping of *Wall Street Journal* correspondent Daniel Pearl in Pakistan, a crackdown on terrorism in Yemen, legal charges against John Walker Lindh and Zacarias Moussaoui, feature stories on how people were coping, and business stories about the impact on the stock market.[3] It was a foreign story and a domestic story. It was a military story, of course, but also a diplomatic and economic story. Coverage of the anthrax scare encompassed health and science. The creation of the Department of Homeland Security was to be a major story about governance and politics.

A complementary impression was the complexity of the circumstances that the United States had been thrust into: a worldwide terrorist network of al Qaeda operatives; the tragedy of Afghanistan; the conflict between Pakistan and India over Kashmir; Russia's President Putin and his war in Chechnya; the aftershocks of the terrorist attacks in the U.S. that would be felt in East Africa, Indonesia, and the Philippines; the unresolved crisis of Palestine; an unfinished agenda in Iraq. All related. And always at root was the need for knowledge of Islamic culture and the Muslim religion, which generally had not been of interest to most Americans.[4] A simple fact: in a 1992 survey of 774 foreign

2. For a brief summary of media efforts to explain international affairs in the post–cold war period, see Everette E. Dennis and others, *The Media and Foreign Policy in the Post–Cold War* (New York: Freedom Forum Media Studies Center, 1993), with annotated bibliography.

3. See Tom Rosenstiel and others, *The War on Terrorism: The Not So New Television News Landscape* (Project for Excellence in Journalism, May 23, 2002). The war on terrorism was the top story of 2002, with 2,092 minutes on the network evening news programs compared with 1,756 minutes for "economy, finance, business," according to *Tyndall Report* (New York: ADT Research, 2002).

4. See Jenny Baxter and Malcolm Downing, eds., *The Day That Shook The World: Understanding September 11th* (BBC News, 2001), for short essays on how these changes were interpreted by BBC correspondents.

correspondents working for U.S. news organizations, only ten said that they could conduct an interview in Arabic.[5]

To explore a conflict "unusually complex both to wage and to report," in the words of former Brookings president Michael Armacost, the Brookings Institution joined with Harvard University's Shorenstein Center on the Press, Politics, and Public Policy to create the Brookings/Harvard Forum on the Role of the Media in the War on Terrorism. There were twenty sessions—from October 31, 2001, to September 19, 2002, essentially spanning the first year of the war—made up of informal conversations among past and present government officials, foreign and domestic journalists, and scholars. This book of edited transcripts tries to capture the flavor of their discussions.[6]

The book is arranged in six sections. The first, "The Media and the Government: World War II to the End of the Twentieth Century," includes four panel discussions that look back on past crises. In the first discussion, journalists and the spokesman for the U.S. embassy in Saigon during the Vietnam War review press coverage of conflicts from World War II through the 1991 Persian Gulf war. They reflect on changes in technology, changes in the government's attitude toward the press, and economic changes that affect their work.[7] In the second, four former presidential press secretaries explain how they handled national security questions at the White House. Was it ever appropriate to withhold information from the media? Or to leak information to favored reporters?[8] In the third, a former secretary of defense, a former CIA director, and a former U.S. representative to the United Nations remember the media as an obstacle to getting their jobs done, yet in the fourth discussion, a former secretary of state tells how he used the media to promote policies he favored. The

---

5. See Stephen Hess, *International News and Foreign Correspondents* (Brookings, 1996), p. 86. Besides the language skills and demographics of foreign correspondents, other chapters explain the locations and subjects of international coverage.

6. This book reproduces about one-third of the spoken text. The original transcripts, along with biographical information about the participants, are preserved on the Brookings website: *www.brookings.edu/gs/projects/press/Press.htm* [January 21, 2003]. Many of the programs also are available from the C-SPAN archives.

7. For additional analysis of war coverage, see Barrie Dunsmore, *The Next War: Live?* Discussion Paper D-22 (Shorenstein Center, Kennedy School, Harvard University, March 1996); Everette E. Dennis and others, *The Media at War: The Press and the Persian Gulf Conflict* (Gannett Foundation Media Center, June 1991); Frank Aukofer and William P. Lawrence, *America's Team, The Odd Couple: A Report on the Relationship Between the Media and the Military* (Freedom Forum First Amendment Center, 1995).

8. See Stephen Hess, *The Government/Press Connection: Press Officers and Their Offices* (Brookings, 1984). Chapters cover leaks, briefings, and reactions to crises; also see Elie Abel, *Leaking: Who Does It? Who Benefits? At What Cost?* (New York: 20th Century Fund, 1987).

press, as seen by high-ranking government officials: obstacle or opportunity? And to what extent was the so-called CNN effect—the impact of instantaneous, worldwide TV coverage—responsible for President George H. W. Bush's decision to send American troops to Somalia in 1992 and President Clinton's decision to withdraw them the next year?[9]

Relations between the Pentagon and the press during the early stages of the war in Afghanistan is the subject of the second section, "War in Afghanistan: The Early Stages." At a November 2001 meeting at Brookings between Washington news bureau chiefs and top Defense Department information officers, the journalists outlined their needs for information and access and the information officers let them know how much the department was willing to provide. Another panel of media critics offered a three-month assessment of the Pentagon's press policies in January 2002. Could the government have been more cooperative in providing reporters with information and access? All agreed that geography and security concerns in Afghanistan made the operation particularly difficult to cover, yet wasn't the problem, one journalist argued, that the press and the government have conflicting institutional positions that cannot be reconciled?[10]

In section three, "The Journalist's Dilemma: Three Stories," the panels turn to the media's coverage of—or disinterest in—three terrorism-related stories to look for clues to why some things that are important (at least in retrospect) do not get much attention. A report by the blue-ribbon Hart-Rudman Commission predicted events much like those that occurred on 9/11, but it was barely noticed when it came out in January 2001. Was that because of competition from other newsmaking events, or was the report too scary, or was it not promoted sufficiently by the commission?[11] The anthrax scare, on the other hand, got plenty of attention.[12] The media's problems lay in deciding what to report in the absence of hard evidence, dealing with scientific uncertainty, and striking the proper balance between being necessarily informative and need-

9. See Steven Livingston, *Clarifying the CNN Effect*, Research Paper R-18 (Shorenstein Center, Kennedy School, Harvard University, June 1997); also see Johanna Neuman, *Lights, Camera, War: Is Media Technology Driving International Politics?* (St. Martin's Press, 1996).

10. See Michael Getler, "Challenges: The Press and the Pentagon," *CJR* (November–December 2001), p. 26; Stanley W. Cloud, "The Pentagon and the Press," *Nieman Reports* (Winter 2001), pp. 13–16; Nina J. Easton, "Blacked Out," *AJR* (March 2002), pp. 36–40.

11. See Harold Evans, "Warning Given . . . Story Missed," *CJR* (November–December 2001), pp. 12–14.

12. See David Murray, Joel Schwartz, and S. Robert Lichter, "The Anthrax Feeding Frenzy," in *It Ain't Necessarily So: How the Media Remake Our Picture of Reality* (Penguin Books, 2001), pp. 197–212; and John Schwartz, "Efforts to Calm The Nation's Fears Spin Out of Control," *New York Times*, October 28, 2001, section 4.

lessly frightening. The third story concerned dissent. In the months following 9/11 there was wide support for the antiterrorism campaign and very few stories about dissent. How much attention should the media pay to dissent when it is a marginal aspect of the national mood?[13] These are the daily dilemmas of journalism.

News gathering in Afghanistan, the Middle East, and Washington is the focus of section four, "Reporting from the Field: Three Sites." In the first discussion, journalists who had just returned from Afghanistan explain the new technologies of war coverage and techniques for surviving in a war in which journalists often were targets. Their vastly different experiences range from being caught in the crossfire of competing Afghan warlords at Tora Bora to being tightly controlled by the U.S. military at Kandahar airport.[14] How do war correspondents assess personal risk? In the second discussion, correspondents covering the conflict between Israel and the Palestinians also touch on reporting in a dangerous environment, but they focus more on sorting truth from propaganda, changes in a conflict with a long history, differences between American and European reporting, and the problems in covering shuttle diplomacy.[15] The third conversation, about news gathering in Washington, takes place among foreign correspondents, who explain the news angles that are especially important to their audience; relations with their editors, who often get breaking news from the United States before they do, through the Internet; their treatment by the U.S. government; and how they deal with their audiences' stereotypes of Americans.[16]

"From Different Perspectives," section five, includes a discussion of the U.S. government's public diplomacy program and whether it differs from

---

13. See Laura Flanders, "Why Is Dissent Not Fit for Coverage?" *Extra!* (The Magazine of FAIR—The Media Watch Group) (November–December 2002), pp. 10–11.

14. Commentary on reporting from Afghanistan includes Sherry Ricchiardi, "Dangerous Journalism," *AJR* (April 2002), pp. 28–33; Pamela Constable, "The Conflict in Covering the War," *Washington Post*, December 2, 2002, Outlook section; Robert G. Kaiser, "Already, Too Many Pieces Are Missing," *Washington Post*, December 23, 2001, Outlook section; Matthew Rose, "In War's Early Phase, News Media Showed A Tendency to Misfire," *Wall Street Journal*, December 24, 2001.

15. Aspects of Middle East reporting are discussed in Sherry Ricchiardi, "Bullying the Press," *AJR* (May 2002), pp. 26–31; and Sharyn Vane, "Days of Rage," *AJR* (July–August 2002), pp. 32–37.

16. The most controversial news outlet has been the Arab language network al Jazeera. See Fouad Ajami, "What the Muslim World Is Watching," *New York Times Magazine*, November 18, 2001; Sharon Waxman, "Arab TV's Strong Signal," *Washington Post*, December 4, 2001, Style section; and "Judging al-Jazeera," *Communicator* (published by the Radio-Television News Directors Association), December 2002, pp. 8–9.

propaganda,[17] an assessment of the role of Congress in the campaign against terrorism, an analysis of American public opinion during 2001–02, and the perspectives of four Americans with distinguished careers in public service who were asked to place the war on terrorism and the government's response in a broader context.

The book concludes with section six, "9/11 and Beyond," in which a panel of journalists returns to the beginning, to the remarkable story of how American news organizations covered the events of September 11, 2001. The panelists review relations between the government and the media in the first year of the war on terrorism, and they turn finally to the factors that may account for the dramatic rise and fall in public support for the media that occurred over the year.

Here is an opportunity to eavesdrop on interesting conversations among men and women who have had unique experiences. There is new information—and good stories. The notes to this introduction are meant to constitute a selective bibliography for those who wish to delve deeper into the topics in each section. Certain currents or themes keep popping up, and they are worth further attention.

Technology: Journalism and War Respond to Change

What becomes clear from the first comment in the first panel discussion is how aware journalists are of how changes in technology have affected their work. Daniel Schorr begins by explaining the technology of radio reporting from Omaha Beach on D-Day in 1944, and Ted Koppel joins in: "Let me pick up where Dan Schorr left off, because there is kind of an evolutionary scale here in terms of the technology and how the technology has had an impact on the way that things are covered." He compares TV coverage in Vietnam in 1967, when "as much as three days might elapse between the time that the story was written and the time it got on the air," and today, when "a journalist has to be prepared to go on the air instantly, around the clock." For the audience, that means knowing about events sooner; for Koppel, it also means less time for correspondents to think about and report the events.

Those responsible for government information policy feel the same pressures. Describing what she called "one new dynamic of warfighting and war

17. See Carla Anne Robbins, "In Attack on Terrorism, U.S. Has Early Priority: Managing Its Message," *Wall Street Journal*, October 4, 2001; William Powers, "Brand of the Free," *National Journal* (November 17, 2001), pp. 3576–79 ; Maud S. Beelman, "The Dangers of Disinformation in the War on Terrorism," *Nieman Reports* (Winter 2001), pp. 16–18.

reporting in the Information Age," Victoria Clarke, the Pentagon's chief spokesperson, has written, "We can be quick, or we can be accurate, but [it] is a challenge to be both at the same time. With news hitting the airwaves or Internet almost as quickly as it happens, journalists are understandably impatient for information. Our challenge is to find a balance between speed and precision—being as quick as we can and as accurate as possible."[18]

The battlefield uses of new technologies—such as small, inexpensive digital video cameras—suggest not only improved ways to relay copy from inaccessible places, but, in the constant tug between military authorities and journalists, the possibility of military field commanders losing control of the story.[19] Michael Gordon of the *New York Times* explains how using new technologies affected his reporting from Afghanistan: "I had no relationship with the American military, despite repeated efforts to establish one. But what I did have was my sat phone, and I had e-mail, and I could kind of call back to the Pentagon and say, 'Look, this is what I see here. How does it fit with what's supposedly happening?' "

And yet in war today there is another type of technology that also may have a profound impact on what is reported and how. Increasingly military technology, the new tools of war, determines how basic information is provided and authenticated. That began to become apparent in 1991 during the Persian Gulf war, when the world learned of bombs hitting Iraqi targets from U.S. military videotapes presented before an audience of journalists playing the part of "extras" in the drama, asking questions that TV viewers often found irritating. The military clearly set out to dominate the news, and it had the equipment to succeed.

Pentagon briefings, often technologically enhanced, reached an apex under Secretary of Defense Donald Rumsfeld during the fighting in Afghanistan. As reported in the *Washington Post* on December 12, 2001: "The Rummy Show has aired two or three times a week since bombs-away on Oct. 7, and it's a direct hit. The best zingers make the nightly news and next day's paper. Members of the public call the Pentagon to find out when Rumsfeld—whose friends call him Rummy—will be on television next. Nielsen Media Research figures that something like 800,000 people watch his appearances live on cable."[20] Note how often conversations in this book turn to Rumsfeld's briefings—

18. See Nancy Ethiel, ed., *The Military, the Media, and the Administration: An Irregular Triangle* (McCormick Tribune Foundation, 2002), p. 140.

19. See *A New Look at the World: Digital Video and International News* (Pew International Journalism Program, 2001).

20. David Montgomery, "The Best Defense: Donald Rumsfeld's Overwhelming Show of Force on the Public Relations Front," *Washington Post*, December 12, 2001, Style section.

sometimes in awe, as when German TV correspondent Claus Kleber reported on the reaction in his country, and sometimes in frustration, as when ABC correspondent John McWethy said of the briefings: "Message control is the way that this administration is trying to communicate what it is trying to do." In short, the government's briefing system is designed to give the public the information that the government wants the public to have, but it is not necessarily designed to meet the demands of the press.

At the same time, the advent of two technological innovations—cable TV with its twenty-four-hour news channels and complicated military weaponry that requires explanation—has produced a new breed of semi-journalists: a corps of retired generals and admirals and other experts whose pointers have been much in evidence on TV screens since the 1991 Persian Gulf war. It is a news formula that often gets mired in making predictions or in rhetorical crossfire, as chemical and biological weapons expert Jonathan Tucker explained to our panel on the anthrax scare: "I would be on shows in which there would be an alarmist and I would be the one trying to tamp down some of the hysteria, and the alarmist would get 90 percent of the attention. So I assumed that it was because he was saying what they wanted to hear."

All of this mixing of wars, technologies, and journalism is nothing new, of course, and dates back in American history at least to the Mexican-American War in 1846, when the newly invented telegraph intensified reporters' competition for battlefield scoops. Still, then as now, the mixing deserves special attention because of the consequences, predictable and unexpected, that always follow.

Globalism: The World Watches Together

As new technologies contribute to shrinking the world, globalism, in the context of the media and the war on terrorism, boils down to the proposition that everything relates to everything else. That interrelatedness comes into focus in the pages ahead when foreign correspondents in Washington talk of their work and their relationships with their editors and their audiences, diplomats and others talk of the role of propaganda, and everyone talks of the so-called CNN effect.

But before there could be a CNN effect, there had to be a Cable News Network. In the opening chapter Peter Arnett relates how Ted Turner, CNN's founder, "introduced the idea of international global images" in the early 1980s and expanded it to include "satellite coverage of the whole world," which led in 1991 to Arnett's being in Baghdad as the United States dropped the first bombs of the Gulf war. He continued to report live from the besieged capital throughout the conflict. The Age of Instant TV War had arrived.

"The CNN Effect," a separate chapter, relates how pictures of starving children led to President George H. W. Bush's decision to send troops to Somalia in 1992. As Lawrence Eagleburger, secretary of state at the time, told our panel, "If there hadn't been television and the reporting on the mess in Somalia we would never have done it, absolutely correct." Had the Age of Instant TV Diplomacy also arrived? And, of course, the brutal pictures on television of the desecrated body of an American soldier being dragged through the streets of Mogadishu forced President Clinton to withdraw the troops the next year. Judy Woodruff, the CNN anchor, suggested one measure of the power of televised pictures when she said that the soldier's body had been seen in CNN's report for only two and a half seconds.

In contrast to globalism's wide-angle view, or perhaps because of it, foreign correspondents in Washington often have to report the world through a narrow lens. In the pre-CNN era, according to a 1979 study, foreign correspondents in Washington concentrated on reporting "cosmic" issues rather than the home angle.[21] Now the panelists spoke of the importance to them of the Turkish angle or the Mexican angle or the Russian angle. When covering the Afghanistan campaign, for instance, the angle for Turkish correspondent Yasemin Çongar was, "What's going to be the second target?"—Would it be neighboring Iraq?—"because this is the only thing Turkey is so much concerned about." The Mexican angle, according to José Carreño, was "the impact of this conflict on the U.S. borders with Mexico in terms of vigilance, in terms of trade, in terms of immigration, in terms of the people that are already here, illegal aliens, most of them are Mexicans." The "biggest story" for Andrei Sitov "was probably the introduction of the Russian presence in Kabul, although it's the emergency ministry's personnel rather than the military."

Foreign correspondents in Washington work within the context of their audience's view of the United States and Americans. For Jean-Jacques Mevel of *Le Figaro*, it's what he calls "the historical French anti-Americanism." "Under the surface," according to Toby Harnden of London's *Daily Telegraph*, Europeans consider themselves "more sophisticated and more thoughtful and more reasonable. . . . Americans eat too much, are very fat, and just make loads of money . . . [They] don't read books, and don't have passports, and don't travel."

But anti-Americanism is rarely the attitude of the foreign journalists who report from America. More typical is that of Sitov, the Russian, who said, "I feel it is a personal and professional privilege to work here," adding, "I also met

---

21. See Stephen Hess, "How Foreign Correspondents Cover the United States," *Transatlantic Perspective* (published by the German Marshall Fund of the United States), December 1983, pp. 3–5.

some wonderful people, made some very good friends." They try to see as much of the country as possible. Harnden, for example, was in competition with a colleague to visit the most states, and he said with pride, "In two years I've actually written stories from thirty-five states." They see themselves as countering the misperceptions of their audiences and home offices.

Rising negative views of the United States throughout the world also disturb those in "public diplomacy," whose job it is to sell U.S. policies to people overseas.[22] But how receptive are those who don't trust the United States to getting a sales pitch from the U.S. government? The view of the United States seen through the eyes of foreign correspondents, although not always flattering, is less likely to be rejected out of hand by overseas audiences.

Everything connects to everything in what we call globalism: a vigorous foreign press corps in the United States creates a healthier bond between America and the rest of the world; and the attention that the U.S. media devote to the rest of the world expands Americans' understanding of why their government has declared war on terrorism—and of how some U.S. policies may have helped to give rise to terrorism.

Yet regardless of how the United States is being forced to feel the consequences of its position as the world's only superpower, there is no assurance that international news in the U.S. media is going to return to its cold war dimensions. Perhaps the contrary. Andrew Kohut's polling found that nine months after 9/11, "There is little indication that the news interests and habits of the American public are much different than they were in the year 2000."[23] If Americans choose to go back to thinking as usual, will American news organizations not go back to business as usual?[24]

The Clash of Responsibilities: Waging War, Reporting War

The major current that runs through these conversations is the clash between those in the government who have the responsibility to provide for the common defense, as established in the Constitution, and those who have the

22. See Adam Clymer, "World Survey Says Negative Views of U.S. Are Rising," *New York Times*, December 5, 2002; for the full report, see the Pew Global Attitudes Project, *What the World Thinks in 2002* (Washington: Pew Research Center for the People and the Press, 2002).

23. Andrew Kohut in John Schidlovsky and others, *International News and the Media: The Impact of September 11th* (Washington: Pew International Journalism Program, 2002), p. 5.

24. For a survey of foreign news in the U.S. press, see Stephen Seplow, "Closer to Home," *AJR* (July–August 2002), pp. 18–31.

responsibility and the right, guaranteed by the same Constitution, to tell the public what the government is doing and where and how well the government is doing it.

Sometimes these conversations became quite heated, based as they were on the past experiences of the panelists. Recalling his years as a war correspondent in Vietnam, Stanley Karnow accuses the military of lying—"or at the very least they will try to keep you from finding out and reporting everything that goes on because in certain cases it's embarrassing and embarrassing to the military means that it serves the interest of the enemy." From the other end of the press-government nexus, former CIA director R. James Woolsey concludes: "I would say that although we did the best we could, my general impression was that with rare and important exceptions like David Broder [*Washington Post*], most of the press that was covering us, including for the national dailies and the like, was not objective about either the CIA's importance or what we did."

When Pentagon officials and Pentagon reporters were brought together at Brookings during the Afghanistan engagement, much of the conversation resembled a negotiation over what the government would and would not permit in covering the war. For instance, when Kirk Spitzer of *USA Today* asked whether "we could not in some fashion cover the Rangers a little more closely than we have now," Colonel Bill Darley replied, "If I understand the question, Kirk, the question is, Can you embed with the Rangers? The short answer, under current circumstances: No."

They were not arguing about abstract principles; their immediate concerns were how to fight and how to report a specific war. There are comparable debates before and after all American military conflicts, debates that often are complicated, theoretical, ethical, judgmental. But at root, they are really about work, about professional soldiers and professional journalists trying to do their jobs.

In this context, to fully grasp the boldness of the Pentagon's media strategy in the second war against Saddam Hussein—encouraging 600 or so journalists from all over the world to embed with coalition troops in Iraq—it is useful to jump back a few wars, to Vietnam. Reporters in Vietnam were free to roam, write, film, and photograph at will. The United States lost the war. "Ergo," the military planners must have thought, "in the next war we will be very cautious about having the nattering press wandering around the war zone."

Fast forward to the Persian Gulf war in 1991, and, sure enough, we see the most restrictive press policy ever: censorship on the battlefield with military officers clearing reporters' copy and information otherwise delivered through the generals' televised briefings. The United States won the war. "Ergo," thought the military, "how much better can it get?"

The brilliance of choosing the embedding strategy in 2003 was that the military abandoned a design that it considered highly successful, realizing that what had worked in Gulf War I might be a poor choice for Gulf War II. Why? Because in 1991 the Americans were universally recognized as the good guys; not so in 2003, when world opinion was hostile and certainly would have been skeptical of information that came through the U.S. government.

Because the military's media strategy permitted reporters to be up front, allowing what Ted Koppel called "a total convergence of access and satellite technology," the war was seen though the eyes of journalists.[25] The press rather than the Pentagon became the messengers. The most obvious consequence of embedding was that people all over the world got more information, faster, than they had ever gotten from a battlefield before. Yet embedding was not without critics. Two major strands of criticism were depicted in a Doonesbury cartoon by Garry Trudeau in which an embedded CNN reporter interviews an army public affairs officer.[26]

Reporter: So how're the embeds working out, lieutenant?

Officer: Well, it's a mixed bag. On the one hand, the TV pictures show us at our best. But they also show the horror of war . . . which our enemies can repurpose as propaganda. I'm not talking about your recent feed, of course.

Reporter: Which one? The soldier giving out Skittles?

Officer: Classic stuff. I smell Emmy.

Criticism number one is a variation of the Stockholm syndrome: the journalists start to identify with the soldiers and lose their professional detachment. The same thing, of course, can happen to reporters covering a police beat or a sports team, and journalists must always guard against the tendency. But the problem is magnified when it is a matter of life or death, as *Asahi Shimbun* correspondent Tsuyoshi Nojima noted while embedded with the 1st Marine Expeditionary Force: "I have asked myself repeatedly whether I can keep a neu-

25. See Howard Kurtz, "The News Veteran," March 28, 2003, *Washington Post*, March 28, 2003, Style section.

26. Garry Trudeau, "Doonesbury," April 10, 2002, *Washington Post*, April 10, 2002, Style section. Among the many interesting articles on the embedding controversy, see Josh Getlin and David Wharton, "With Media in Tow, Does Objectivity Go AWOL?," *Los Angeles Times*, March 22, 2003; Carolyn Lochhead, "It's All There in Living Color," *San Francisco Chronicle*, March 25, 2003; Josh Getlin and Elizabeth Jensen, "Media and Government Make Uneasy Bedfellows," *Los Angeles Times*, March 26, 2003; David Shaw, "Embedded Reporters Makes for Good Journalism," *Los Angeles Times*, April 6, 2003; Douglas MacKinnon, "Embedded Journalists Put Our Troops in Danger," and Christopher Hanson, "Reporting the War," *Baltimore Sun*, April 7, 2003.

tral attitude, because I sleep with [U.S.] soldiers every night and I am always guarded by them. . . . Yesterday, when a bomb hit Iraqi troops, I unconsciously shouted, 'Great!'"[27]

Looking back on the coverage from the battlefield in Iraq, it is clear that the Pentagon chose a risky news management strategy and that it paid off for the U.S. government, the press, and the public: the government got third-party assessments of a war that it was winning; the journalists got what journalists most want—access; and the public got some of the most stunning wartime reportage ever recorded.

Yet it also is clear that the Pentagon had another important reason for choosing this strategy: it expected to conduct a war that would be very short and relatively low in casualties. Yet a future war might be neither. So it is a shaky premise to think embedding will become a permanent fixture of battlefield reporting because it worked well in Iraq.

Ultimately, then, how does a democracy resolve the clash of responsibilities that arises in waging war and reporting war? We think that there are answers in these conversations, especially in the views of two panelists, one from each of the two perspectives, who seem to share a similar approach to problem solving: Karen DeYoung, associate editor of the *Washington Post*, and Victoria Clarke, assistant secretary of defense for public affairs.

"It's a trade-off," said DeYoung, the journalist. "It's a trade-off between our argument that the more information we have the better we are able to reflect the truth and all parts of the truth, and their belief that if we limit the information that's available to you and funnel it through one source, then we have control over the information. And sometimes we lose, sometimes they lose. Hopefully in the end everyone wins."

And the final word from Clarke, the military's spokesperson and probably the prime architect of the Iraq embedding policy: "It is in my interest for the American people to get as much appropriate news and information about this war as possible. If we keep them informed, if we keep them educated, they will stay with us." Turning to the reporters, she then said: "The news media. It's your business. It's your obligation to get out as much news and information as possible. So we have common objectives. There is a healthy tension. What's the level, what's the appropriate information? There are probably mistakes and variations on each side, but I happen to think it's a very healthy tension."

Trade-offs and healthy tension. These are the keywords that best define what the relationship should be between government and the media in the war on terrorism.

---

27. Reported with the permission of Yoichi Nishimura, Washington bureau chief of *Asahi Shimbun*, April 16, 2002.

PART ONE

The Media and the Government

*World War II to
the End of the
Twentieth Century*

2

Lessons of Wars Past

We have no crystal ball to tell us the future, but we can learn from the past. It was in this spirit that we convened a panel of four distinguished war correspondents and one former government spokesman on October 31, 2001, for the first in a series of twenty Brookings/ Harvard forums over the following year. The five panelists were

—**Peter Arnett**, who covered seventeen wars, won the Pulitzer Prize for his reportage from Vietnam and garnered worldwide attention for his live reports from Baghdad during the Persian Gulf wars in 1991 and 2003

—**Stanley Karnow**, who started covering Asia in 1959 as chief correspondent for *Time* and *Life*, won a Pulitzer Prize in 1990 for his book *Our Image: America's Empire in the Philippines*, and wrote a best-selling history of Vietnam that served as the basis for the PBS series *Vietnam: A Television History*

—**Ted Koppel**, who started covering wars in Vietnam but has since covered many others, including the second Persian Gulf war, winning in the process thirty-seven Emmy Awards, six Peabody Awards, and nine Overseas Press Club awards, all while anchoring ABC's *Nightline*

—**Daniel Schorr**, the last of Edward R. Murrow's legendary CBS team still fully active in journalism, who began a twenty-year career as a foreign correspondent in 1946 and now is senior news analyst for National Public Radio

—**Barry Zorthian**, who was the U.S. Embassy's chief spokesman in Saigon during the Vietnam war, a senior official in the U.S. Foreign Service, and later a member of the Board for International Broadcasting before retiring as vice president of Time, Inc.

Although the panelists had covered (or defended and explained) many wars, they spoke mostly about Vietnam, arguably the most searing post–World War II experience in American history until the Bush administration's current

17

struggle against global terrorism. Vietnam spawned many of the now familiar battles between the Pentagon and the press—over access to the front lines, freedom of movement, manipulation of the press, deception—battles that continue today.

Schorr reminded everyone that during World War II American reporters were in uniform and that their relations with the government and the military were close, almost intimate. "They submitted voluntarily to censorship," said Schorr. They were part of the "war effort." Not until halfway through the Vietnam war was that feeling of mutual trust shattered, but shattered it was, for reasons that included the length of the war and rising casualties.

Koppel recalled that Vietnam was not a "live" war. Journalists filmed the war using 16-millimeter cameras and then shipped the film to New York by way of Tokyo or Hong Kong. That took days—for Koppel, a blessing. Those days gave him a chance to think and write a better piece. In his opinion, live reporting, as in Afghanistan, took reporting "a half-dozen evolutionary steps back"; live transmission meant little to no time to think, reflect, call a source, double-check a fact. The new technology of miniaturized cameras, satellites, and videophones has transformed the coverage of war.

Karnow bemoaned the fact that truth often was the first casualty of war, with officials lying to reporters in Vietnam and the public at home about the progress of the war. "They were not being told the truth," he said, even when the truth was obvious. Karnow recalled, for example, that for a time the U.S. military would not confirm the presence of military helicopters in Vietnam. One day Karnow pointed to an aircraft carrier decked with helicopters entering Saigon harbor. "What about that?" Karnow asked an officer. "I don't see no aircraft carrier," the officer responded, with a straight face.

Such attempts at deception created what was later called "the credibility gap," leading many U.S. reporters in Saigon to distrust the U.S. military and ultimately the U.S. government. That gap has persisted in the ongoing war against terrorism, except for a brief period after the attacks on September 11, 2001.

Still, despite its growing problems with the media, the U.S. government did not impose censorship during the Vietnam war. Zorthian explained that there were "no restrictions" on the press; in his view, the government was "not mendacious." The same claim could not be made for the Iraqi government during the 1991 Persian Gulf war. The U.S. government blasted Iraq for lying and worse, but Arnett, who covered the conflict for fifty-seven days, did not feel that it was his responsibility to enter into an argument with the Iraqi government. He was there to cover what he could see and hear and learn; he was there to practice his craft, and he would let others decide whether his reporting was fair and accurate.

What emerged in part from his coverage was a global political/ diplomatic/journalistic phenomenon called the CNN effect, meaning—in 1991 in the context of the Persian Gulf war—that Arnett's reports were seen in the foreign ministries and newsrooms of 193 countries, affecting official and public opinion everywhere.

With keen insights born of experience and interspersed with unforgettable anecdotes, the panelists highlighted key lessons from past wars. If past be pro- logue, read carefully.

Marvin Kalb: *We are going to be talking about what lessons journalists learned from wars past. How can those lessons be applied to the current struggle against global terrorism? I would like Dan Schorr to think back to World War II and find, if you can, what lessons could have been extracted by journalists covering that kind of a war that could perhaps be applied to today.*

Daniel Schorr: On D-Day Charles Collingwood was taken to Omaha Beach to report live on CBS the invasion of Normandy. In those days to do that he had

to carry a sixty-pound battery pack on his back that would transmit a signal for him to one of the ships at sea, which would then boost it to London. The BBC circuit would then take it to New York, and it would go on the air live. But he couldn't have a return feed, because there wasn't enough energy to do that.

So he was told, At this precise moment you start talking and you will be heard live, talk for fifteen minutes, then sign off and go back to Ed Murrow in London. I listened to the tape of this sev- eral years later. The trouble was that he was on a section of beach where there was not very much activity. Yet he had to start at a given moment. He started talking. You could see the planes overhead, ships at sea, boats are landing; you began to feel he was straining to fill time because there wasn't very much action there.

Then you heard Collingwood saying, with a little lift in his voice, "Now, it's very difficult for me to give you an overall picture of what's happening here, but I see a navy officer approaching. Let me find out whether he knows something more. 'Excuse me, Commander. I am Charles Collingwood at CBS News. I wonder if you have any idea of what the whole picture is on this beach.'" The answer to which was, "Beats the shit out of me, Charlie, I'm the NBC correspondent."

The relevance of this is that he was in an army uniform. The NBC correspondent was in a navy uniform. All of this betokened the fact that in World War II correspondents knew which side they were on. They were a part of something called the war effort. . . . They would go and ask, "Would it be harmful if I reported this? Would it be harmful if I reported that?"

And it is important to remember that because that is an era of history where the press and the military worked closely together, being sure of the rectitude of what they were doing and why they were doing it, and that got lost somewhere. It survived some during the Korean War, during the Vietnam War. It began to collapse when they found out that the government thought nothing about managing the news—because they felt that we have to win this and it's our job to manage the news, and if we lie to you that's lying in a good cause—and managed to undermine the trust on which the relationship between the press and the military has to be if it's ever to work. And ever since that time it's been going very rapidly downhill.

Ted Koppel: Let me pick up where Dan Schorr left off because there is kind of an evolutionary scale here in terms of the technology and how the technology  has had an impact on the way that things are covered. When I was in Vietnam in 1967, it was just at the very beginning of satellite technology in terms of its use in journalism. Most of the time, which is to say about 98 percent of the time, we would do a story out in the field on film. We would hand the film bag to anyone who might be heading back to Saigon. In Saigon it would be met by a courier who usually would have to keep it overnight because it would arrive, let's say, at 5:00 or 6:00 in the evening and there wouldn't be another flight out until the next morning. Then it would be flown probably to Tokyo, from Tokyo to Los Angeles, from Los Angeles to New York, where it would be picked up by a motorcycle courier. It would be taken into ABC, NBC, CBS. The film would then be processed, edited, and put on the air. Perhaps as much as three days might elapse between the time that the story was written and the time that it got on the air. So you had to write it with that in mind. It had to be a story that could survive for at least three days.

When young people today are covering—whether it be a war or any event that is deemed worthy of live coverage, which I suppose in the era of twenty-

four-hour cable networks means anything that moves—in these days a journalist has to be prepared to go on the air instantly, around the clock. Now that
may seem like an evolutionary step forward. In point of fact, it's half a dozen
evolutionary steps back, because they rarely have time to go out and do any
reporting. They are almost chained to that satellite relay point, wherever they
may be.

Stanley Karnow: You remember Churchill's remark in wartime: "Truth must
be protected by a bodyguard of lies." If you pardon my name dropping, I was

sitting in the Ritz Bar in Paris with Hemingway one time,
and he said, "Every reporter needs a built-in shit detec-
tor." Let me illustrate a couple of points of how the
reporter begins to learn his niche, his profession—craft, I
should say.

About 1962 Kennedy decided to send helicopters to
Vietnam, but he wanted to do it secretly. It would have
been a violation of the Geneva agreement. I am sitting on
the terrace of the Majestic Hotel in Saigon, which is right on the river, with an
army public affairs officer. And as we're sitting there an aircraft carrier comes
around the bend of the river with its deck covered with helicopters. I say, "Hey
Joe, look at that aircraft carrier." He said, "I don't see no aircraft carrier."

One more. One day we were bombing, secretly bombing, Laos. And one day
I went over to the American embassy because I knew the embassy was targeting the bombing, to find out where the targets were. I saw a source of mine,
and I said, "Listen, can you tell me what the targets are?" He looks at me and
says, "Tell you what the targets are? Come on, I can't even discuss the whole
question of bombing. It's completely off the record." I said, "Come on, everybody knows it's going on. Give me an idea of where these targets are." "I can't
do that." Finally, I wheedled and wheedled, and he says, "All right." He goes to
his safe, he opens it up, he takes out a copy of *Newsweek* with a map of the
bombing targets. It's that secret. He says, "You can't take that out of the
office." The point is that eventually you become skeptical. Skeptical, to put it
mildly.

One of the lessons, by the way, that the military likes to believe they learned
in Vietnam is you can't have a war without censorship. In Vietnam, if you
wanted to go on a military operation you went down to the black market in the
street and you bought yourself a fatigue uniform and boots and a helmet and
everything. You could even buy guns in the black market, although journalists
shouldn't carry guns, and you went out to the airport, you got on a helicopter,
and you went to an operation. Nobody was censoring what you wrote, the

pictures were going out. Actually, you really weren't journalists in those days; you were historians.

Kalb: *Are you meaning to say that when journalists go out to cover something now, [they are] supposed to look back upon the experience of Vietnam and say, "The government is lying to me"?*

Karnow: They're supposed to start off on the proposition that they're not being told the truth, or [that] they're being spoon fed.

Barry Zorthian: Vietnam was what I call an open war. There were no restrictions on the media. The circumstances were such that restrictions could not be  placed on the media. The sovereign power was the Vietnamese government. We had correspondents in Vietnam who were never accredited to MACV, the Military Assistance Command. And there was certainly no pretransmission censorship. So correspondents were free to write, to go where they wanted, write what they wanted, broadcast what they wanted without any restriction.

I reject and protest, at least for the years I was there in Saigon, this picture of a constantly mendacious government and a constantly immaculate press. I don't mean by that that the government was always forthcoming. They did, by and large, project what they believed to be the situation in combat. The press saw it very differently in many ways. There's no monolithic press. There was media with different viewpoints towards the war and different coverage of it, and I do think we ought to recognize that the government, at least in those years in Saigon, tried to project what it thought was the situation in the field.

Now there's a natural tendency on the part of the military as well as the civilian side of the government to look at things in a more positive way than [perhaps, a skeptical press]. But the picture is more gray than black and white, and I do underline that particular point.

Peter Arnett: At the beginning in 1962, there was a general sense that what the United States was doing in Vietnam was absolutely justified. And the early critical accounts came from disenchanted American advisers who were simply trying to improve the war effort. It was a committed press corps. I was from New Zealand, but New Zealanders had troops in Vietnam. We believed it was a worthy cause. To that degree I think in Afghanistan today you have a media that thinks what's happening, government policy towards the terrorists, is a worthy cause.

Now going on to the course of events in Vietnam, it became a question of what was factually accurate and what was politically embarrassing. I don't  think anyone is questioning the accuracy of what the Vietnam reporters put on the air. It was a question of the timing. It was politically embarrassing to the United States. That seemed to me the big issue.

Going on to the Gulf war. You can't think of the Gulf war without thinking of Ted Turner. I know Ted Turner's not thought of very much now because he's sort of pushed out of the media mainstream, but it was Ted who in the early '80s introduced the idea of globalization of information. Television information. Ted introduced the idea of international global images and pushing to get what he saw as both sides of the story. He also saw it as a way to make money. In the early days of CNN, Ted would get a few of us together every now and again for a pep talk, and he would say, We're really going to change journalism. We're going to destroy the networks, and we're all going to get rich doing it. Ted's worth $6.2 billion today.

When we come to the Gulf war, CNN had expanded to the degree that we had satellite coverage of the whole world. A signal could go all over the world. The first time that any television news organization had that capability. In addition, on the ground we had an Iraqi government which, as the Gulf war built up, started attracting journalists. They have pretty sophisticated people within the Iraqi government. When the bombing did start, they looked at CNN as a conduit, an information conduit. We realized that, and we still stayed, even though realizing that we'd have to carefully explain and qualify everything we said.

The pressure of the [U.S.] government was very strong at the time. The Bush administration—Bush I—called up the media. White House spokespeople called up, suggested that we would be unsafe in Baghdad. The backstory was that having a credible American news organization in an enemy capital would be harmful to the national war effort. It got to the point where CNN actually considered closing down, as all the other American news organizations were doing. It was Ted Turner who, in the end, given the option of letting some of us stay or ordering us out, said we could stay.

The point is that CNN globalized television images, and very soon afterwards the BBC went around the clock with news. Then we have Fox, MSNBC, other news organizations. Images were available. The global image is not only accepted, pictures are accepted, but they're everywhere and news organizations are everywhere, so CNN doesn't even have to be in Kabul. Someone is there, and CNN and everyone else is using the images.

Kalb: *The question, broadly speaking, is, Should there now be a new set of responsibilities that the journalists in America must understand and must conform to as you go about covering the current war?*

Karnow: The question sort of answers itself. Clearly there has to be some modus vivendi, otherwise there will be no vivendi. The question is how and when, and how it should be applied, and what it should be. I go back to the war in Grenada. That was the first invasion, the first expedition that I know that was ever launched in which the press was kept out of it totally for the first several days. And I recall meeting a colonel at the Pentagon and arguing how can you conduct an invasion in a democratic country against some island and not let the press there? Isn't that antidemocratic?

Ever since Vietnam I have found that the military feel that they were let down, if not betrayed, by the press. As far as they are concerned, the propaganda part of the war—the psychological, the public relations, call it what you will—is an essential part of winning the war because it has to do with morale back at home. And to try to maintain morale at home is considered to be a positive duty for the military. In order to do that they will have a bodyguard of lies around the truth, perhaps. They will maybe tell real and direct lies. Or at the very least, they will try to keep you from finding out and reporting everything that goes on because in certain cases it's embarrassing, and embarrassing to the military means that it serves the interest of the enemy.

Their trouble now is that they're being defeated today not so much by the American press as by technology. I mean when you get the people appearing on television live over there and issuing their statements about what's wrong with America and so on, or when you get al Jazeera getting interviews, how do you stop it?

It almost started during the Gulf war when a couple of people managed to sneak in towards the very end and get into Kuwait before they were ready to announce that Kuwait had been liberated, because they now had smaller, jeep-mounted dishes and you could theoretically get in even though the U.S. military didn't want you there. Since that time it has exploded.

Koppel: Why don't we focus for a moment on that famous telephone call that Condoleezza Rice made to the presidents of the various news organizations requesting that they not use the images of Osama bin Laden and some of his top lieutenants, with the not unreasonable argument being that perhaps they were conveying some kind of a message to other cell members of the Taliban or of al Qaeda here in the United States. I thought at the time, what a totally stupid argument. Anyone in this country with a satellite dish can get al Jazeera television directly. Anyone with access to a computer can get the Internet directly. And the Internet—and I'm sure most of you gathered here know this—but the Internet was, of course, designed by the U.S. military for one reason and one reason alone: for survivability in the case of a nuclear attack so that commanders would be able to communicate with one another after a nuclear attack. So if the whole purpose of creating the Internet was to survive a nuclear attack, who in his right mind thinks that you are any more going to be able to control information?

I'd like to add one other point. Not since World War II has there been a declaration of war. So to talk about censorship the way that we discuss it in the context of World War II is not relevant to the Korean War, it's not relevant to any of these petty little engagements that we've been involved in since then. It certainly was not relevant to the Vietnam War. War was never declared. So the issue of the military or the government actually imposing censorship in a legal fashion never arose.

Kalb: *How successful do you think the government is right now in conveying its message to the American people?*

Koppel: Not very good at all. And the irony is, to be perfectly frank about it, we don't get a great many senior government people to appear on *Nightline* anymore because they would much rather appear on Larry King; they would much rather appear on a program on which they're likely not to get a tough cross-examination, not to mention the fact that they would much rather appear on CNN and be seen in how many countries is it now, Peter?

Arnett: A hundred and ninety-three.

Koppel: A hundred and ninety-three. And even though they may not be seen by everyone in those countries. I mean one of the great ironies of the CNN mystique is that CNN's average audience in normal times during the day is about 300,000, 350,000. I suspect now in times of crisis the average audience may be up over a million. Any program that appears on ABC, NBC, CBS—any of the regular networks—has that beat by a factor of five, ten, or fifteen. But there is a tremendous value that is perceived by the government in having their spokespeople seen in those 193 countries around the world, in foreign ministries, by intelligence agencies. Not to mention the fact that the presidents and prime ministers and generals and defense chiefs of these various governments, when they appear on CNN, they get to see themselves on the air. When they appear on ABC, NBC or CBS, they do not.

Zorthian: There is only one standard that has historically been accepted as a restraint on media coverage. That is information that jeopardizes an operation or jeopardizes the lives of troops.

Now that goes back to World War I, I believe. The acceptance of that standard was not a problem in Vietnam; as far as I know, it was not a problem in the Gulf. The media, certainly the responsible media, is perfectly ready to accept that kind of a restriction.

What is heavily criticized in the media is output that is not censorable, not in our open society, not in our scheme of life. If we restrict censorship, restriction of information to those two points—jeopardizing operations, jeopardizing the lives of troops—the media has been very, very responsive on that in my experience.

Kalb: *Do you feel that the government has been successful, for the most part, in getting its message out to the American people?*

Zorthian: For the most part it has, because the media so far in our current situation has not been too challenging to the government. It's starting.

Kalb: *What do you mean, challenging?*

Zorthian: Well, they haven't been questioning too much the briefings they're getting daily.

Kalb: *Why?*

Zorthian: Well, I think by and large they've gone along with the feeling that this is a great threat to the United States, patriotism calls for acceptance of the government's viewpoint.

Koppel: We're only six weeks into this. Six weeks into the Vietnam involvement I think you would have found the same kind of thing.

Zorthian: That's right.

Schorr: Let me bring up the question which we've brushed against. I understand your list of where the press should accept troop ships sailing, operations, all the rest of it. What about the responsibility of the press with regard to enemy propaganda? What about these sons of bitches getting on the air and saying they hate America and everybody hates America? Can we not trust Americans to see things like that?

Zorthian: I have no objection to the media covering that kind of information. Remember the target here ultimately is the American public. And I think they should get whatever there is on the other side of the picture, and I trust the American public to take that into account and evaluate it accordingly.

Karnow: I think you have to look at the nature of the war, how long it goes on. I wrote a book about America in the Philippines—we fought a war in the Philippines. As it went on and there was a kind of a quagmire, the public began to turn off on it. It was pre-Vietnam in a way, without television. World War I was short. Everybody waved the flag when Woodrow Wilson went in. But if you look at the period after World War I, there was a tremendous antiwar reaction in the '20s and the '30s. World War II—yes, we knew who the enemy was and so forth. There may have been some carping about particular things, but generally speaking everyone was supportive. Korea—[public support finally eroded] on to the point where Eisenhower has to run on a campaign of "I will go to Korea and end the war."

The press is decried or accused of shaping opinion. I think the press reflects opinion just as well. And when the public begins to get sour on a long, indecisive situation like Korea . . . Vietnam. In 1968, February, Walter Cronkite—in the middle of what was called the Tet offensive, which was a devastating offensive by the enemy—Walter Cronkite did a commentary on CBS in which he expressed doubts about the war and began to indicate that maybe it wasn't going anywhere. The president of the United States, Lyndon Johnson, and everybody to this day said Walter Cronkite changed American opinion. Baloney. If you look at the surveys, American opinion had changed four or five months earlier, and Walter, in a way, is reflecting opinion as much as he's contributing to changing it. I think at this moment there is a lot of patriotism. We are not questioning things. I suspect if this thing goes on long enough inconclusively, you're going to begin to get criticism. The military's not going to like that; the administration's not going to like it.

Kalb: *Peter, you were with CNN, but now that you're free of the constraints of CNN, I ask you the following question: Today we learn that there is a major new guideline at CNN, and that new guideline says that when you report on, say, some American military activity in Afghanistan—a Red Cross installation gets bombed—that you quickly point out that this is all in response to the fact that on September 11, 3,000 Americans were killed. In other words, this is now part of the journalistic mantra that is being ordered upon CNN reporters. Your view?*

Arnett: It is ill advised. Certainly on CNN, it is perfectly capable of balancing any report that appears from Afghanistan or anywhere else. When I was in Baghdad I would try to tell the anchors, I am credible because anything I report out of Baghdad is either denied or refuted by the Pentagon or there is a balancing comment from a briefing or from some other source outside. Often the reporter on the scene, certainly in Baghdad, I hadn't a clue what was happening outside Iraq. It was hard enough to know what was happening inside Iraq. So I was in no position to do any balancing. I think it's asking too much for the reporter to do it. Sometimes it was told by anchors: Saddam Hussein in 1988, he used germ warfare on the Kurds. I said, Okay, but you say it, not me. My professional sense said that I don't have to complain about Saddam Hussein; George Bush is complaining about Saddam Hussein more than I could ever do. So I felt justified in presenting my segment of information to be evaluated in the context . . . it came from, and I thought that was good enough, and I think that's how we should evaluate material from Afghanistan.

Schorr: My sense of this new [CNN] ruling is it reflects the kind of defensiveness which we've already displayed in the reaction to Condoleezza Rice's warning to not use all this propaganda. Not only because it might contain coded messages, which was really rather silly, but also because it conveyed propaganda and might affect the American people adversely. Once we begin to see that the government will try to involve the press in playing a positive role in whatever it is that the government wants to transmit, we are in trouble if the press is willing to accept that.

Koppel: When a camera is trained on a live event, that is a miracle of technology when it's broadcast all around the world. It has nothing to do with journalism. Journalism is the process of editing and sifting. It is the process of selecting and prioritizing. It is the job of putting into context. In other words, if Walter Isaacson [president of CNN] had said, "We have to be careful about . . . just putting cameras on people and allowing them to talk for half an hour on CNN without putting it into some kind of context, . . . putting them on live without knowing what they're going to say, without knowing whether it has any importance, whether it should be a part of a news broadcast," I have no trouble with that.

Our job, our function as Americans is to create that sense of context, to give people as much of a sense of how it is that something is happening, why it is that something is happening, of putting it into as much of a frame as we possibly can. I don't believe that I am being a particularly patriotic American by slapping a little flag in my lapel and then saying, Anything that is said by any member of the U.S. government is going to get on without comment, and anything that is said by someone from the enemy is immediately going to be put through a meat grinder of analysis. Our job is to put it all through the meat grinder of analysis.

Kalb: *Does that mean that there really is, in your mind, a capacity for journalistic neutrality?*

Koppel: I don't happen to believe that's a function of neutrality. I believe that's a function of applying . . . intelligence, as much as the good Lord gave us, to putting events into context as clearly as we possibly can.

Karnow: I object to the word "neutrality." I just want to remind you when Admiral Felt [Admiral Felt was commander in the Pacific in 1962] came up to Peter and said, "Okay, Arnett, get on the team." That's what the military wants you to do. They want you to get on the team. They want you to do the reporting the way they want the reporting done.

Koppel: [E]very one of our networks, every one of our parent organizations has just rediscovered for the first time in a few years how valuable a news organization that looks beyond its own boundaries can be. And we didn't do very well for the last few years on that. We really had not done a particularly good job at covering foreign news in large measure because it's expensive, it's time consuming, and the American public, by and large, seemed to prefer endless coverage of the O. J. Simpson trial to what was going on in Saudi Arabia or Egypt or Japan or anywhere else in the world.

When I joined ABC in 1963 I believe the news budget was approximately $5 million annually. The news budget today for any one of the three broadcast networks—ABC, NBC, CBS—is about half a billion dollars. And they still make a profit. Not much of one, but they make a profit.

The fact of the matter is that what has changed over the last thirty-some-odd years is that network news organizations, which were never regarded as profit centers back in the early '60s, these days are. They are expected to make money. So to the degree that there is any adverse pressure from these large corporations that we all work for, it's for economic reasons, not political. Politically—I don't think that Michael Eisner [president of Disney] is subject to political criticism either from the Clinton administration or the Bush administration. Economic pressures? You bet.

Schorr: The media spent the last twenty or thirty years cutting out its coverage of foreign affairs. Bureaus one after the other were closed because who needed them? If there had been more of a sense of the duty of the media to remain au courant with what's happening in the world—[with] what was happening in Afghanistan not today but five years ago, what was happening in Pakistan not today but five years ago—had we followed these changes as they were happening gradually, I don't think we'd be in the fix we are today trying to understand it all.

3

Presidential Press Secretaries

D id you know that lies come in several flavors, none of them tasty to the official liar or the press? Did you know that leaks come in many shades and varieties, all woven into the very fabric of Washington's running game of press-and-politics? And did you know how difficult it is even to define a leak?

For the one person in Washington with the distinct pleasure—and pain—of speaking officially for the president of the United States, namely, the presidential press secretary, no day passes without the double temptation of lying or leaking, in one form or another. Most press secretaries try desperately to get through the daily briefing without yielding to either. They appreciate the simple fact that telling the truth is the highest form of professionalism; anything less damages their credibility with the press and the president's ability to lead the nation.

We invited the following former press secretaries on November 11 and 28, 2002, to discuss the challenges of their job, especially during a time when national security was the central issue:

—**Joe Lockhart**, who worked for President Bill Clinton from 1997 to 2000

—**Michael McCurry**, who also worked for President Clinton, from 1995 to 1998

—**Dee Dee Myers**, yet another Clinton spokesperson, from 1993 to 1994

—**Ron Nessen**, who worked for President Gerald Ford from 1974 to 1977.

Whether working for a Democratic or Republican president, the spokesperson has only one client and therefore only one overarching priority: to make the president look as wise as Solomon, decent, practical, and farsighted; and to deflect and if possible demolish all criticism of the president. No easy task.

Nothing is more important to the press secretary than having access to the president, or at least the appearance of access, such as through being listed on his daily schedule. "The single most important quality for a good press secretary is access," said Nessen. "Unlimited access is important," echoed Lockhart, "both in its practical and symbolic values." A spokesperson must always appear to be close to the ultimate source of information and power, namely the president. No daylight must ever be allowed to be seen between the two of them. Myers maintained that "you're only as good as the access you have." In her view, "access and information are everything. Without those, you really can't function effectively."

That is especially true during times of national crisis. When the spokesperson speaks, the press hears the president. So does the public. Information can be conveyed directly through a press conference or indirectly through a leak, which is difficult to define and almost impossible to isolate or manage. For example, Lockhart recalled the famous story of President John Kennedy, outraged over a sensitive story he'd read, summoning press secretary Pierre Salinger to his office and demanding an investigation into who leaked the embarrassing detail. A few days later, Salinger returned to the Oval Office, pointed to the president, and said, "You did, sir."

Clinton, like Kennedy, loved going outside of channels; he talked with friends, who then talked to reporters, or he talked with reporters himself. Either way, "leaks" magically appeared in the press. Myers tried to list the types of leaks. There are, first, selective leaks, either to a reporter known to be sympathetic to the administration's policy or to a newspaper or network that can deliver an important audience. Then there are "trial balloons," leaks lofted into the Washington stratosphere "to see how [they] play." Such leaks have the capacity to destroy a pending policy shift or launch it into history—it depends on how they influence the Oval Office, Congress, or the editorial and op-ed pages of the *Washington Post*, the *New York Times*, and the *Wall Street Journal*, the three most influential newspapers in the country.

Lockhart explained that not all leaks are deliberate instruments of policy or press manipulation. Quite often it is downright difficult to define a leak: a story is published or broadcast, and even Washington insiders quickly but mistakenly assume that it is a leak when it actually is the result of hard work by an investigative reporter or official bungling or a combination of the two.

Whether analyzing leaks (or manufacturing them), the press secretary must make certain that they enhance the president's position and policies. In modern times, that calls for sophisticated management of the flow of news. In effect, says Lockhart, the press secretary has to become a kind of "television programmer." He underscored the importance of our "media culture," marked by a steady, unbroken, obsessive preoccupation with news and information. "If you don't program," noted Lockhart, "that leaves this incredible void." Somebody, something must fill it.

Nessen did not disagree with this line of analysis, but on the basis of his Vietnam experience, he concluded that nothing was more important than public support, especially in wartime. "No president can pursue a war for very long without public support," he stressed. The press secretary's job—now in a 24/7 news environment and tougher, trickier, and more subtle and challenging than ever before—is to encourage the media, and through it the public, to support the president's policies.

Stephen Hess: *A little history: The first president who had a full-time press spokesman was Herbert Hoover. The press secretary's job really came of age under Steve Early, Franklin Roosevelt's press secretary. But the modern White House press office as we know it today was invented by James Hagerty, Eisenhower's press secretary. As of this date, . . . twenty-three men and one woman [have] held this august post. If I counted correctly, fourteen of them are still alive, and our conversations include three of the thirteen men and 100 percent of the women.*

Marvin Kalb: *We are all consumed now with the war in Afghanistan. My question to each of you concerns national security. What was the single most pressing, most important, most challenging national security or foreign policy issue that you had to deal with?*

Ron Nessen: Well, I guess there were two in the Ford administration. One was the capture of the American merchant ship Mayaguez by the Khmer Rouge in

the Gulf of Siam [in 1975]. The interesting part was that there was anarchy in Cambodia at that time. Nobody was really in charge; there wasn't any government. The United States didn't know how to communicate its demands that the crew and the ship be let go because there was nobody running a government in Phnom Penh. So we thought, maybe there are some news tickers still active in Phnom Penh. So we sent the message via the press. We held a briefing and read this statement, which was meant for the Khmer Rouge. I remember I was reading this statement and reporters wanted to go very slowly, at dictation speed. But that was the only way to get in touch with the Khmer Rouge. It was to do it through the press.

Kalb: *So you were using the press as a kind of middleman to the enemy in this case?*

Nessen: Correct. But the real security episode that we had in the Ford administration was the end of the Vietnam War. The Vietnam War ended in April of 1975, when the remaining Americans in the embassy in Saigon were airlifted out by helicopter, and the helicopter lift lasted a lot longer than expected. Finally it was over, and all the Americans who had been in the embassy were evacuated. Some of the Vietnamese who had helped the United States were evacuated. [Secretary of State Henry] Kissinger and I went to the Old Executive Office Building to do a final briefing. I read a statement from President Ford, and Kissinger did a detailed briefing. The thrust of it was, of course, all the Americans have been evacuated from Saigon; our role in the war is over.

So we came off the stage of the Old Executive Office Building and Brent Scowcroft, who was then the national security adviser, said, "I have bad news. All the Americans are not out of the embassy compound in Saigon. There are twenty-four marines still there." Not left by accident, but left as a rear guard. Get all the civilians out of the embassy, and then the helicopters were going to come back for these twenty-four marines. So the question was how do you tell reporters that you told them all the Americans were gone, and now, a half-hour later, you're telling them there are twenty-four marines there? So there was a debate about if we should say anything. What should we say? How should we say it? After all, they're going to be gone in an hour anyhow. Don Rumsfeld, who was then the defense secretary and is again the defense secretary—and I'll never forget this because I can still hear the words echoing in my head—Rumsfeld said, "This war has been marked by so many lies, let's not end it with one last lie."

We put out a statement saying whoops, we made a mistake, all the Americans are not out of Saigon. There are twenty-four marines there. They'll be gone in an hour. I always thought it was a very admirable thing for him to do, and I think it was the right thing for us to do.

Kalb: *It's a fascinating story. Thank you very much. Joe Lockhart, your moment and how did you handle it?*

Joe Lockhart: Well, I think probably as far as volume went, we spent more time on the Middle East peace process than any other issue. But as far as intensity, the most difficult communications challenge we had was the conflict in Kosovo. It's interesting, because we generally thought we were pretty good at communicating and understanding the different challenges and understanding in our political tradition the need to be awake and aware twenty-four hours a day and stay ahead of a story. We learned in the first couple weeks of Kosovo that we weren't as good as we thought.

At the start of a day I'd get a recap from the national security people of what had happened overnight, including presidential phone calls. I remember one morning talking to the person I used to get me that information, and [I] asked, "What did he do last night?" He said, "He had a thirty-minute conversation with Tony Blair." I said, "Well, what did they talk about?" He said, "Mostly they talked about you, what a miserable job you're doing."

So that sort of brought home that this was a real problem as opposed to a perceived problem. The problem was, we were doing an okay job of communicating here in Washington, but we forgot the idea that in a NATO-led conflict, there are nineteen capitals, each telling its own story. That's a reporter's dream. You just line up the nineteen stories, find the differences, and you can go all day on that. We quickly realized how we had not planned for that and very quickly set up an operation.

There was a very professional gentleman in NATO named Jamie Shea [NATO spokesman from 1993 to 2000], who used to do two briefings a day, and I always marveled at his ability to get up and talk. But he was a little slow sometimes in getting back to a reporter when you asked him something. So one day, I [said], "Well, you know, just get some of your staff to do it." I then realized that he had only three staff people and was doing the work [that] nineteen governments had hundreds of people working on.

We made the decision to move a lot of people over to Brussels. For political reasons, we couldn't become the primary spokesperson for this conflict, but we had to have an influence in how it was talked about. I'd say three weeks into this, we had our act together. But it was a very steep learning curve and very painful as far as what our performance was.

I think the interesting thing is there's a certain parallel to what's going on now. I don't know any more than what I read in the newspaper, but if what I read in the newspaper is accurate, some of the same growing pains happened and have been addressed in quite the same way. My only hope is that Ari [Fleischer, White House spokesman] doesn't come into the office one morning and find that President Bush and Tony Blair were talking again, about him.

Kalb: *Dee Dee Myers, your sense of the major moment and, looking back, how do you think you handled it?*

Dee Dee Myers: This is not a fun story to tell. You know, the first years of the Clinton administration were marked mostly by small foreign policy problems.

There were no major conflicts ongoing, certainly nothing on the scale of what we're seeing right now.

 Very early in Clinton's term, President Bush—the former President Bush—had gone back to Kuwait to mark an anniversary of the liberation. While he was there, there was an assassination attempt on his life that was foiled by the FBI. Of course, an investigation began immediately into who was responsible, and there was tremendous interest both here and around the world. The immediate suspect was Baghdad, that the Iraqis had been involved.

I would regularly get asked about the situation at my briefings. The guidance that I would give, which I had gotten from the National Security Council, the national security adviser, was that the FBI is investigating; when they've reached a conclusion, they'll forward that to the president, and he'll make a decision on how to respond. Well, one Friday, in preparing for my briefing, I went through the usual steps, checked the status of the investigation—they said no change; I was told no change.

I went out to my briefing. I gave the usual response: The FBI's looking into it; once they've reached a conclusion, they'll forward it to the president, and he'll make a decision. Unbeknownst to me, the FBI had forwarded the decision to the president on Wednesday night; the president had decided, and the conclusion was that the Iraqi government was indeed involved. The president had made the decision to retaliate, to bomb the defense ministry in Baghdad using cruise missiles launched from ships in the Gulf. I didn't find that out until Saturday.

Not only by that point had I given the wrong guidance—that the president hadn't received the conclusion—we put a lid on. A lid, for those of you who don't know, is at the end of the news day, when the president isn't going to make any additional statements or be seen; put a lid on means no more news. A bunch of White House reporters had gone to an Orioles baseball game and were en route when we had to beep out and say not only is there no lid, but you better get back here as quickly as possible. By then the missiles had already landed in Baghdad; we were waiting for a bomb damage assessment to be able to brief on what was happening. The bombing went pretty well. My credibility bombed in the process.

It was an incredibly difficult moment for me. To this day, I believe it was more a sin of omission than commission. I don't think people were trying to keep me out of the loop.

Kalb: *Dee Dee, the relationship that the spokesperson has in the White House, access to the president, access to the national security adviser and all—access, it would seem to me, as an outsider, would be absolutely crucial. Ari Fleischer, for example, the current spokesman at the White House, is said not to have that kind of access to the president.*

Myers: I think you're absolutely right, Marvin: that you're only as good as the access that you have. Information is everything. Having current information, knowing the president's thinking, knowing the conflicts that are developing around him and how those might shape up and affect or be affected by his thinking. Access and credibility are everything. Without those, you really can't function very effectively. I think my access was at times better than others, but often not as good as it needed to be. The example that I just gave being sort of exhibit A. That was by far the worst moment that I had in the White House.

Kalb: *Was it because it was a national security issue? Let's say it was a domestic political issue. Would you have been brought into the loop more?*

Myers: Probably. I mean, certainly more. It would have depended upon the shifting tides and staff structure that we went through in the early years. I think it got a lot better. I think the structure got institutionalized in a way that was much more effective. I think the Clinton administration worked through a lot of the early bugs, a lot of the early wrong attitudes about the press and what the press's role was. Of course, I was a part of all that. I'm not trying to point fingers. It's just something that I think got a lot better. You can't do the job without the information. I think that was certainly one of the problems I had.

Part of it was born in the structure that we came to the White House with. My title was press secretary. I had a lower rank, smaller office, and a smaller salary than all of my previous male predecessors. I reported to George Stephanopolous. I didn't initially do the daily briefings; George did those. After a few months, he moved on to a more protected job and I took over the daily briefings, just in time for this Iraq incident.

So there were a lot of problems in that. There were a lot of people who had responsibility for talking to the press in the early days. We had a lot of overlapping responsibilities. The press had access to just about everybody that worked in the West Wing, and it made for very difficult situations, not just for the press secretary, not particularly for me, but also for the president, because he wasn't able to speak with one voice.

There was myself, David Gergen, George, who continued to be a very senior administration official, and Mark Gearan, who was the communications director. All of us had overlapping responsibilities. By about eighteen months into it, that was fixed, but after much damage had been done to the White House in general and to my credibility in particular.

Lockhart: I think the idea of unlimited access is important, both in its practical and symbolic values. The ability to get in and see the president at a moment's notice is an important part of doing the job, because there is a certain quality to the information you can get from the president that you can't get from anyone else. I think the ability to know you can allows you not to overuse the privilege or the privileges you're given to do it. I think more important, and it's why the job of press secretary is very similar to the job of a reporter, is understanding the structure of the building. There are lots of people, and they all look important and they'll all tell you they're important, but you quickly find out who is and who isn't. You find out where decisions are made. And I had the benefit of coming into the Clinton administration for the second term, where a lot of the problems Dee Dee has alluded to were solved.

Not that we didn't have problems, but during my tenure there we had both a very strong national security adviser and a very strong chief of staff. So it was very easy for me, sort of one-stop shopping, to make sure I knew almost everything that was going on.

Kalb: *Did you feel that they were leveling with you?*

Lockhart: Sure, because I think they understood. And if you had asked me before I was going out to my daily briefing—if you'd given me the choice [of] five minutes with the president or . . . five minutes with John Podesta, the chief of staff, most days I'd take it with the chief of staff. Because in the structure of the White House that I worked in, that was where all roads led to. I could, in three or four minutes, find out what was going on throughout the government—all the things that were likely. Whereas half of these decisions hadn't made it to the president's desk yet.

So I guess my conclusion is you need to be able to work like a reporter within the administration, knowing where decisions get made; and secondly, you need to know which questions are the right ones to put to the president and which are the right ones to put to other places.

Kalb: *Ron, you had worked for many years as a reporter. Did the people around the president trust you as a totally reliable guy, that you were not going to leak things to the reporters?*

Nessen: Well, people in the White House never trust the press secretary. It's one of the reasons why the single most important quality for a good press secretary is access. To get the information first hand, so you don't have to ask somebody how should I answer this question. That is the most important quality. And I think there's this sense among other White House staff people, Gee, if we don't tell the press secretary, he won't accidentally blurt it out when we don't want anybody to know about it, or not right now, anyhow.

When I went to talk to President Ford—and he offered me this job—I had been a White House correspondent for NBC and I had seen all the press secretaries back to [Pierre] Salinger [Kennedy's press secretary]. I knew that . . . the one quality that you had to have was access. I said that would be the only way that I would be able to take the job. I want to be in on all the meetings and all the discussions and all the decisions and hear what's going on . . . [T]hen you can decide what to say and when to say it, but you need to know the information.

Then Helen [Thomas, of UPI] or somebody will always ask, did you see the president today? In the Ford White House, I always had an official appointment on his calendar every morning. But you also have to know who else in the building you can get a lot of information from.

Kalb: *But you did see the president every day?*

Nessen: I did see the president. When you're traveling, there are many more opportunities to see him—or go up after work, have a drink. I was somewhat naive. Having been a White House correspondent, I thought, this is sort of like the same job, I'm like a pool reporter of one. I was going to go and find out what was going on and then I was going to come back and tell the other reporters. That was, in the long run, naive, but that was my original concept. I think it was harder to make sure you knew everything that was going on in foreign policy, security issues, because Kissinger was the national security adviser and the secretary of state. He had his own ideas about the uses of information.

When Bill Plante of CBS asked Larry Speakes [Reagan's press secretary from 1981 to 1987] one day about rumors that the United States was going to invade Grenada, Larry Speakes had never heard of this before. So he went down to the National Security Council and asked [NSC director] John Poindexter whether we were going to invade Grenada. Poindexter said, That's preposterous, knock it down hard. Larry went out and said, No, we're not going to invade Granada, and we did. It undermined Larry's credibility.

Hess: *It brings up the rather important question of lying, since these are the voices through whom most Americans will learn the government's position on the war. It strikes me that there are four types of lies in this regard. There are honest lies.*

Kalb: *Honest lies?*

Hess: *This is Jody Powell being asked about the rescue mission in Iran and he knocks that down and reporters seem to allow that as an honest lie. [Powell, Jimmy Carter's press secretary, knew of the hostage rescue plan in advance, yet purposely gave false information about it to a reporter.] There are inadvertent lies that come up all the time. The inadvertent lie is things are happening so fast that you just sometimes are wrong; you—*

Kalb: *But that's different from a lie.*

Hess: *Well okay, there are certainly half-truths. I think that's what Mike McCurry would have called telling the truth slowly. Then there are damn lies, which would be Joe McCarthy saying there are 205 communists in the State Department. But they all don't have to be about great questions. The Nixon White House gave out the recipe for Tricia's wedding cake, which was an old family recipe, they said. It wasn't an old family recipe. So you gotta watch it. Will any of you guys admit to lying to the press?*

Lockhart: Well, it depends on how you define it. I'll admit to being wrong. I'll give you an example. The president went up to the UN. Castro was there, and there was a luncheon, and only the heads of state and their personal aides were allowed in. There were no photographers, no cameras. There was a lot of speculation . . . [W]ould the president talk with Fidel Castro? Would he shake his hand? It was the only thing about that lunch that I cared about.

The president's personal aide at the time had a different set of things he cared about. So I called him, and I said, Did anything happen? He said no. In his mind, nothing had happened, because the president got in on time, got out on time, and got to the next event. To him, it didn't matter that Castro came up from behind, tapped him on the shoulder, and shook his hand. Castro's aides told the press, and they came to me and they said, Did it happen? I said, No, it didn't happen. Then a reporter came up to me and took me aside and said, You really should check again, because I have this from a very good source—another leader who had been in the room and had seen it. He said that they had no reason to lie to me about this. So I called the guy back up and said, Did they shake hands? He said, Of course they did. I said, Well, why didn't you tell me? He said, You didn't ask me that. So under the inadvertent lies, I lied and I cleaned it up as quickly as I could.

Myers: I think it's very rare that you have to lie. Lying destroys your credibility, unless lives are genuinely at stake. And I think Jody Powell agonized over having to tell a direct lie, but he believed—and I think he was right—that it would have put Americans' lives at risk if he told the truth.

I think that what that sets up is a difficult dynamic, which is, Jody was totally in the loop, he knew everything that was going on. The press wants a press secretary that knows everything that's going on. There occasionally—and very, very occasionally—are times when that forces the press secretary to lie. The press has to give the press secretary a pass on that, as hard as that is, because it's the price of them being in the loop even on the most sensitive, high-risk, national security types of missions. And I don't know if the press will ever give us that wink and nod, but that's absolutely required.

Kalb: *Dee Dee, what would have been wrong with the spokesman saying simply, I can't answer that question?*

Myers: To say nothing creates the suspicion that there's something going on. In order to knock down that suspicion, he had to give an unqualified no.

Nessen: I've had this argument with Jody over the years, and I really believe— and more so as time goes by—that what you lose in credibility through the deliberate lie is so damaging that you shouldn't deliberately lie. I think every press secretary has a different formulation, and, after all, you have to remember that this was a very good friend of his who asked the question, Jack Nelson [of the Los Angeles Times]. I think you have to say, "I'm sorry, Jack, I can't talk about that right now—I don't have anything for you on that right now." Because I think the damage is too great for lying.

Kalb: *Did you lie or didn't you?*

Nessen: No, I never did, but here's what I did do. I think the closest I ever came was out of an oversensitivity and protection for Ford. He wanted to go to Florida to play—he loved golf and he wanted to go and play in the Jackie Gleason Pro-Am golf tournament in Florida. For some reason, I was too protective to say, Hey, the president wants to go to Florida and play in the golf tournament. So we cooked up some HUD housing conference as an excuse for him to go to Florida because I was too sensitive to just say, Hey, he's going to Florida to play golf. So that's the closest I came.

But there are other reasons. Helen [Thomas] came to me one time when I was in the White House, and in her own inimitable way said, "Is Bill Simon going to be fired?" William Simon was the treasury secretary in the Ford administration. Bill Simon wasn't the most popular guy, and there had been talk about him moving somewhere else or moving on. Obviously, I couldn't say yes and I couldn't say no. So I was trying to think of just the right formulation that would wriggle me off the hook. It took me half a second longer to answer the question. Helen took my silence as acknowledgment that he was going to be fired and wrote a story. I think she quoted, "White House sources suggested tonight that William Simon would be fired as treasury secretary." You know, he wasn't; we were both wrong.

Hess: *Well, these folks never lie, not even a little white lie. But how about a leak? Do they do any leaking? Is treatment of the press Orwellian: all animals are equal, but some are more equal than others? Dee Dee, how do you deal with the press in that regard?*

Myers: Well sure, press secretaries leak, selectively leak, for a lot of different reasons. It's selective placement. It depends on how you define a leak. There's a lot of different leaks. There's the kind of leak where you give a story to a particular news organization that you think will either get maximum coverage in a way you think will be helpful to you, or you think a particular reporter has a particular understanding or sensitivity to the issue; maybe they have a particular background in it so you think you'll get a fairer hearing.

There's the kind of leak where somebody says something . . . to see how it plays. A trial balloon. There's a leak that happened all too frequently in my experience with the White House, which is people trying to push the president in one direction. The executive branch of the government is a cauldron of competing ideas. Everybody wants the president to come down on their side. A lot of times, people will leak that he's further along towards a decision— those can be very damaging kinds of leaks. Then there's the anecdotal leaks, which are innumerable. People want to tell little stories, usually to let everyone know that they were where the thing was happening and that they know. Those can also be very damaging kinds of leaks. What else am I forgetting, guys, of variety of leaks?

Lockhart: Mistakes, people who say things by mistake.

Myers: It can either be right or it can be wrong. And it doesn't matter if it's right or wrong, the damage can be devastating either way. So I think press secretaries engage in a lot of different kinds of leaks to try to further the president's agenda. It's always in the name of righteousness and good, of course. But it's part of the game. It's part of the way the game is played. Part of it helps you build chits with certain reporters. You're giving them a little inside information; you're telling them something; you're steering them off of a story. There's a lot of different reasons that you do it. There's planting a little anecdote to make the president look good.

Kalb: *Have you been involved in anything where the president asks you to put out this particular bit of information and give it to "Y" newspaper?*

Nessen: There are certainly pieces of information that the president will say, "Make sure that people know this."

Lockhart: I think President Clinton definitely had an opinion about reporters, although the vast majority of reporters he had no opinion of because he didn't know them very well. But he had a group of people who he thought very highly of, another group of people who he didn't think so highly of. You know, on leaks, it's amazing how there's really two kinds: One is the one you do yourself, which you think, What a great story! You don't think of it as a leak because it's sort of a pejorative phrase. Then the something that you didn't want out, which is the damn leak, which there are a lot of.

Reporters will judge me on this, but I didn't myself leak a lot of stories. I found that it was easier to have a relationship with the broadest group of reporters you could, and that caused occasionally some problems.

I was actually more sort of the referee, made sure that it was done somewhat on a fair basis, that we didn't sort of—in an uncoordinated fashion—four days a week give a story to one newspaper, leaving everyone else out.

Nessen: My attitude towards leaks was that the press secretary ought to be the one who puts his name on the story. And not to leak—but I mean, obviously, everybody does. The most famous leak story about the White House was during Kennedy's time, when he called Salinger into his office one morning, pointing to the paper, and there's a story in there with some anonymous source, some leak, and he's raging about it . . . and gives Salinger the order to go out and investigate and find out who's responsible for this leak. Couple days later, Salinger comes back and says, I found out who the leaker was, Mr. President. It was you. Because Kennedy did have a closer relationship with some reporters than later presidents.

Lockhart: A lot of the things that happen are not deliberate attempts to leak information. One of the issues that we faced is the president had a lot of friends and he loved to talk to them. He would have a work schedule, he'd work fifteen-, sixteen-hour days, and his way of unwinding at the end of a day, whether it be 9:00 or 10:00 or 11:00 at night, was to get on the phone and talk to people, not people in Washington—people around the country. In that very large group of friends of the president were lots of people who liked to communicate to reporters how friendly they were with the president. So literally, he'd hang up and they'd pick up the phone and call their favorite reporter and say, guess what he just told me?

You sometimes sit and wonder. You'd look at a story and you'd say, how could they possibly have gotten it that wrong and that distorted.

The reporting community will probably disagree with me, but there is a sense, sometime, of not always [doing] the due diligence that should be done on particular sources. I think we've dumbed-down sourcing here in political reporting in Washington. It's almost anybody who says it, the press secretary could say it or the cab driver who took the deputy assistant secretary for transportation logistics from point A to point B; it doesn't matter. And the only quote that is more valuable than the one from someone who will put their name on it is [the one] from someone who won't put their name on it, which is sort of inverted logic, but it's the way that this town works.

Hess: *Dee Dee had talked about the problems of coordination, overlapping jurisdictions. Getting back to the present situation, that seems to be part of the problem of this administration, at least in the last two months. There seem to be so many different voices, and they've added a new one with Tom Ridge and the Homeland Security. Tell us how you folks coordinated with the State Department, the Defense Department, and so forth. What's the right system?*

Nessen: I think one of the key rules, particularly during a national security or wartime situation, is to have one spokesperson. And I think today there isn't one spokesperson for the current antiterrorism campaign. And I think that one of the problems is that there isn't one spokesman. And to the extent that there is a main spokesman, it's Rumsfeld, which strikes me as not a good use of a defense secretary's time in the middle of a war, to be doing the daily briefing.

But in terms of coordination, I think the arrangement was probably more informal in the Ford administration than it has become over time. But it was, basically, a phone call around in the morning to coordinate what we're going to talk about and what the story of the day was.

Lockhart: I actually think there's a new element in this. We live in a media culture now that's on twenty-four hours a day. So as a spokesperson and communicator, you've become almost a television programmer. Because CNN, MSNBC, and Fox are on all day long. You can sort of sit back and say, No, we're just going to do one briefing a day, and then we'll let them chew on that. That I think is counterproductive because, although maybe only 1 million people are watching at any given time, if you look at one important subset of that million, it's other journalists who keep one of these stations on all the time.

Just like they used to read the wire every five or ten minutes, now they have wire copy with pictures; it's much more entertaining. You have to program. You have to because if you don't program, if you don't have the Transportation

[Secretary] out at 10:00, the Pentagon at 11:00, the State Department at 12:00, the White House at 1:00, the Homeland Security guy at 2:00, that leaves this incredible void, where less informed people get to tell the American public what's going on. So I think you've got to think of this almost as a programming person who's got to fill up the time. I don't know that it's the White House press secretary, but somebody's got to—it depends on the structure of the building. I know that during Kosovo, this was something that we got very involved in.

But more important than the programming, actually picking the times and the spokespeople, is the quality of the information. I think that we have, in the current situation, a recognition of the first piece—and it took some time—but we now have a recognition that you really need to keep people out throughout the day because there is a rhythm to the story. You have to feed it at different times in the day. Otherwise the story will get out of control, or you will lose your ability to shape the parameters of it.

But the quality of information doesn't seem as consistent. It's one thing to tell the American public that you have someone who is now speaking for homeland security, but if he can't speak to the essential question the people are concerned about, then it's not going to be an effective briefing; it's not going to be an effective part of the information show that is going on. So I think there needs to be at least as much or more emphasis on trying to get at the information that people want to know about or feel they need to know. I think the great dichotomy over the last six weeks has been how well the Bush administration, from the Pentagon to the White House to the State Department, has described what we're doing in Afghanistan and why we're doing it. Then on the other hand, how they've come up short in explaining what we're doing at home and why we're doing it and what the real threat is.

I think ultimately, with all your messengers deployed, there are times when there's only one messenger and that's the president himself. If you look at the last four or five weeks, I think some of their trouble stems from the fact that they have been reluctant to put the president in a situation where the answers aren't as clear, where the issues are murkier. And they've tried to put other people out, and the results have been fairly predictable.

Kalb: *Let me frame what Joe is saying as a kind of concluding question. How do you think the administration is doing? We've been in this war now for a little more than two months, and there have clearly been different phases in this operation. There was the shock of September 11. We didn't start bombing until October 9. Right now, we're in a period of very dramatic change within Afghanistan itself. Ron, do you feel the American people are getting all of the information that they need—and overall, your judgment on the administration's handling?*

Nessen: Well, I think you have to go back to a fundamental decision that was made at the Pentagon after the Vietnam War. I was a correspondent in Vietnam for NBC. We could go anywhere, we could do anything we wanted to. The news bureaus had their own cars, their own motor scooters; they could hitch rides on helicopters and planes. We weren't even accredited to the U.S. military; we were accredited to the South Vietnamese government. You could go anywhere and see anything. The lesson of Vietnam that the Pentagon learned was never [to] let reporters do that again. They never have, including this war, and all the intervening wars. The reason is that—and it's an accurate reason—is that negative reporting affects public support, and no president can pursue a war for very long without public support. So the decision was, We'll keep reporters away from the battlefield. That way, they can't do negative stories; that way, it won't demolish public support. And we'll be able to pursue the war. I think that's the rule that is in place now.

Kalb: *Has it been effective?*

Nessen: It's been effective in keeping reporters off the battlefield. Clearly, Americans have not gotten information about everything that's going on. The justification for withholding information during wartime or military operations . . . used to be two things: You wouldn't give out the information, or if you got it, you wouldn't publish it or broadcast it if it would endanger lives or if it would endanger an operation. I think both sides have misused that rule. Reporters, out of competition, have bent that and have published information that can be harmful. The government has bent or broken the rule to not put out information, not because it would endanger lives or an operation, but because it was embarrassing.

Myers: I agree with a lot of that. It's very clear how much the president hates leaks. I think the culture of the current White House is very tight with information, sometimes to their own detriment. That said, I think they've done a pretty good job communicating about the war in Afghanistan. I agree with everything that Joe said about the way the current media climate sort of forces you to become a programmer. They seem to coordinate pretty well between State and the White House and the Pentagon most days.

The briefers are all very credible. Secretary of defense, General Myers, right down the line. Including, I think, Ari Fleischer's done a good job of just doing his job in that role. I think they've done a less good job, clearly, on the domestic terror, particularly around anthrax. Part of it [was that] it was a new, a whole new ball of wax no one had seen before. There weren't processes in place for dealing with it. But I think that their proclivity to try to control information worked against them. Their desire sometimes to put out reassuring information, which was then incomplete and only served to hurt their credibility down the line. I think they've started to do a better job of that, but until the quality of the information coming out of some of the briefers on the domestic side of the story is more reliable, they're going to continue to have a problem.

I think they recognize that. And that's why last week we started to see the president. We saw him more last week than we've seen, probably, almost in the previous two months of this conflict combined. So I think that that's probably a good thing for them to use the one person who can reassure people. And I think he's done a pretty good job of saying a couple of things. This is going to be a long war. The American public needs to be patient, and I think hearing that over and over has made the American public cognizant of the fact it's going to be a long time. Last week, we started to see the word "quagmire" creeping back into stories about Afghanistan. This week strategic cities are falling all over Afghanistan. So patience is a good message. The president is often the right and only messenger.

Mike McCurry: Credibility counts most. Telling the truth counts most. I think that is true of those in government who speak on behalf of government and  certainly true on behalf of those who report the news . . . [A]nything that erodes the credibility of either a news organization or a government spokesman in a time in which there is a bewildering chaos of information available is quite dangerous to the quality of our civil discourse.

The adversarial relationship is critical to this seeking of truth in our system of public information, where the press must be skeptical of the government and be circumspect when analyzing public information. That skepticism cannot erode into cynicism. I think part of the problem is . . . that the sneering reporter who seems to have utter disdain for the government official [and] the government official who is so cynical [as] to believe that [the government] can stage manage the news and withhold truth are both poison in the system of public information, and we have to eradicate it from that system.

I think that this war reminds us of the importance of public information and civil discourse as we try to run a great country that has the awesome responsibility of world leadership we now have, and we have to seize this moment.

4

National Security Decisionmakers

Gather three former senior government officials around a table to discuss matters of national security. Listen. Then let your mind wander back to Thomas Jefferson, especially on the issue of a free press, and you'll understand. For it was Jefferson who set the example for almost every other official who has held great power in governing this country and in the process has had to contend with a rambunctious press. In office, Jefferson extolled the virtues and values of a free press; once out of office, he rarely wasted an opportunity to criticize it, saying on more than one occasion that the press routinely operated in the gutter and never gave him a fair break.

The three former officials we gathered on December 12, 2001, followed the Jeffersonian example, except that they tried to convey the impression that their criticism was offered reluctantly, as a way of improving future interaction between the media and the government. The officials were

—**Jeane J. Kirkpatrick**, who served in the Reagan administration as U.S. representative to the United Nations from 1981 to 1985

—**James R. Schlesinger**, who played numerous roles in both Republican and Democratic administrations, as director of central intelligence for President Nixon from February 1973 to July 1973; as secretary of defense for presidents Nixon and Ford from July 1973 to November 1975; and finally as secretary of energy from August 1977 to August 1979 for President Carter

—**R. James Woolsey**, who was director of central intelligence for President Clinton from 1993 to 1995.

Kirkpatrick battled against a sophisticated program of disinformation operated by the Soviet Union during the cold war. Shortly after Soviet aircraft shot down a Korean airliner, KAL-007, killing hundreds of passengers, the Kremlin denied any knowledge of the tragedy. Indian newspapers peddled the notion that Kirkpatrick was intent on dismembering their country, another example of "pure disinformation," she said. When the U.S. invaded Grenada, a small island in the Caribbean run by Marxists who supposedly threatened hundreds of American medical students, President Reagan ordered a blackout on news of American military action. There were to be no leaks. Reagan did not even inform his closest ally, Prime Minister Margaret Thatcher of Great Britain. Kirkpatrick said, "I don't think I personally lied," but she described the episode as "one of the absolute low points" in her dealings with the press.

Schlesinger had a more difficult problem. He ran the Pentagon during the final period of the Vietnam War, when the United States was pulling out of Vietnam but hoping to avoid a blanket betrayal of its anticommunist allies in the south. The American press, in his view, had "a totally hostile" attitude toward the U.S. engagement in the war. "There was a conviction in the press," he said, that "we were on the wrong side." When the North Vietnamese attacked in the spring of 1975, "there was very little that anybody could do to persuade the press that the U.S. should intervene."

It was almost as though Schlesinger was blaming the press for the stunning American collapse in Vietnam. "No," he explained when asked, but "it was a major contributor."

Woolsey's biggest headache, it seemed, was not the spread of terrorism marked by the founding of Osama bin Laden's network; it was handling the embarrassing case of CIA spy Aldrich H. Ames. No matter what he did, he said, "the press story was Woolsey fails to fire anybody," compounding the deeper question raised in one news story after another: "How could you be head of such a rotten institution that [it] would have a spy in it?" Woolsey's disenchantment with the press was deep and unshakable.

So sustained was their criticism that Hess, surprised, raised the performance of Defense Secretary Donald Rumsfeld and his frequent Pentagon briefings and asked, "Surely you had opportunities from your position to influence positively the press coverage in the way you wanted, the leaks, plants, flattery, whatever it might be." Yes, Woolsey replied, but "most of the press that was covering us . . . was not objective about the CIA's importance or what it did." Schlesinger later added, "The press cannot only turn hostile, the press is engaged in a game of criticism."

And yet Kirkpatrick, Schlesinger, and Woolsey, now years separated from their distinguished government service, all recognized the inescapably crucial role played by the press in all matters of national security, and they argued, if possible, for a cooperative relationship with the press and against a national secrets act, such as the one that exists in Great Britain. They believed that the press has become so important, so central to the decisionmaking process in government, that coexistence between these two powerful institutions—press and government—is the only reasonable option. Look back at the Gulf war in 1991, at Mogadishu, they said, and you see the impact that the media now has on government decisions. Look at the Iraq war of 2003, too.

Marvin Kalb: *Jim Woolsey, what was the most compelling national security issue that you faced in office, and how did you think the press handled that issue, and how did you handle the press?*

R. James Woolsey: I think the most attention the press paid to anything during my two years as DCI [director of central intelligence] was the Ames case

[Aldrich Ames, a CIA counterintelligence officer, spied for Russia for nine years]. Part of the problem was lack of cooperation with the FBI. In late 1991, the CIA appointed a remarkable man, Paul Redman, to be the head of the counterintelligence office, and Paul essentially solved the Ames case with very thorough cooperation with the FBI for two years. We knew who Ames was by early '93, worked closely with the FBI, and at the time of his arrest in February '94, I was all set up, I thought, to hold a joint press conference with [FBI director] Louis Freeh, and we were going to announce this common success in catching this traitor.

It didn't go that way. The FBI decided at the last minute they wanted to do the press conference alone. The press went off on the story of how God-awful the CIA must be to have had somebody like this as a spy. I made a number of decisions about restructuring counterintelligence and security at the CIA, which were barely reported. And by late summer of '94, I determined that there were eleven people, four of whom had made serious errors of judgment but were already retired [and] seven people [who] had made some modest mistakes of one kind or another, a few of whom were still in the agency. I wrote letters to each one, and [to] the four that were retired, I wrote very strong letters. But that's all you can do. You can't take away somebody's retirement unless he's committed a crime.

The press story was, Woolsey fails to fire anybody as a result of the Ames case. And no matter how many times I said, Look, there were four people who deserved to be fired but they're already retired and I'm not going to fire somebody just to fire somebody, it never got reported, essentially.

Kalb: *When the FBI had its press conference, did you have yours?*

Woolsey: I had one, but by that time the issue basically for the press was solely, How could you be head of such a rotten institution that [it] would have a spy in it?

One very distinguished senator who has since left the Senate but is a friend of mine called me over the phone and shouted, "Just fire the first three people through the door." I said, "Damnit, what if the first three people are the three people who caught Ames?" So the blood was up. Everybody wanted somebody fired. I still think I made the right decisions in the case. Clearly, I suppose I could have managed the spin better, but I'm comfortable with the decisions that I made and that the agency made back then.

Kalb: *Jeane Kirkpatrick. The major problem, how did you handle it, how do you think the press handled it?*

Jeane Kirkpatrick: I was in government from January '81 through July '85. That's the first Reagan administration, plus a few months. The cold war was

the greatest problem. There's not much doubt about it. Our relationship with the Soviet Union, the Soviet Union's relationship with us, was our greatest problem. And it was a chronic problem. It was the underlying problem on top of which all manner of small incidents developed. And certainly it affected our dealings with the press. For one thing, it was a really serious problem in international security, and both parties in the Congress and most people in the press, most Americans took the cold war very seriously. They understood that it was a serious problem because the Soviet Union was a very militarily strong power. And that meant a lot of things. It meant there was a lot of classified material which was relevant to a good many issues that the press was dealing with.

It also meant that the Soviet Union was engaging in a good deal of disinformation. Disinformation creates a very special kind of problem, but the Soviet practice with regard to disinformation was frequently a UN issue. For example, . . . take the shooting down of the Korean airliner, KAL-007, in which some 260 people or so were killed, maybe 300. It was tragic. The Soviets denied that they had had any role in this whatsoever; they denied that they knew the plane was in the air. The United States had a tape which it was my obligation to play at the United Nations in the Security Council. The tape was of the Soviet pilot, the pilot of the Soviet plane which shot down the Korean airliner, talking to his commanding officer in the Soviet Union and the commanding officer telling him that he should shoot it down. It was very simple. And the pilot telling the commanding officer, the general, that he had shot it down.

The most extraordinary kinds of disinformation were developed even around this fairly straightforward episode because there were Soviet bureaus who claimed that the whole thing was an American fiction. Not only had we made up the story, but we had made up their role in it, and we made up the tape and the tape was a conspiracy. There was an Englishman, a professor, and there was an American in California who actually claimed not only that the tape was doctored, but that I had played it in a way that further distorted it. This was a family joke, because I am the least technically skilled person. I could barely turn off and on a tape recorder.

There were a number of such things that were just total disinformation. It was once asserted, for example, when I was in the government at the UN that I personally had written a forty-page paper on the dismantling of India deliberately timed to be released at the time that the nonaligned congress [of nations theoretically not aligned with the United States or the USSR] was meeting in New Delhi. This was peddled around a number of Indian newspapers. We knew it was coming. It was just pure disinformation.

Eventually the person who wrote the paper—the Soviet who wrote this paper, which was released under my name—eventually talked about it on the record in Moscow.

There was one occasion in which a story was released suggesting we were trying to involve NATO in Central America and that there were maneuvers off the coast in Honduras which were just designed to involve NATO and Central America. The fact was, of course, that the Reagan administration didn't want NATO in Central America. I don't think that kind of disinformation was probably much [of]—I hope it's not—a continuing issue in press-government relations.

Woolsey: There's a story that's believed by a number of people in the Middle East still, that the Mossad [the Israeli intelligence agency] did September 11. There are hundreds of thousands, maybe millions of people in the Middle East, as a result of very biased press coverage in carrying this idiocy, who believe that sort of nonsense.

Kalb: *There may be a distinction between sloppy biased coverage in the press and a deliberate government program to disinform the world.*

James R. Schlesinger: When I became secretary of defense in 1973, the press was totally hostile to our engagement in Southeast Asia. Now it's a rule of thumb, never argue with anybody who buys ink by the barrel, and that is the press. But that was an uphill fight.

After 1968 and the Tet offensive the press had turned totally against our involvement in Southeast Asia, and the improvements that came after that with regard to the security of South Vietnam were simply ignored. The Tet offensive had basically destroyed the Viet Cong, and after General Abrams

took over, the North Vietnamese were neutralized. The Christmas bombings [in 1972] had chilled Hanoi just as the successful bombings in Kosovo and Afghanistan had shown the might of American power. Yet by that time there was a conviction in the press that probably we were on the wrong side, and when the North Vietnamese started their offensive in late '74 and early '75, there was very little that anybody could do to persuade the press that the United States should intervene.

We had made commitments at the time of the Paris Accords to bring air power in the event of such an invasion, but during the latter phases of the Watergate affair the Congress had imposed upon the president an appropriations bill [stipulating] that no military forces of the United States could be used in, off-shore, or over former French Indochina. As a result, all we could do was to watch the collapse in Southeast Asia. It was frustrating.

Kalb: *But Jim, you're not ascribing the total collapse of the American position in Vietnam to the press?*

Schlesinger: No. It was a major contributor, but there were lots of major contributors. There [were] the defects of our initial strategic doctrine. There was the evolution of the congressional attitude. There was the weariness of the American people. . . . All of these things came together, and as a result there was little we could do in '75 when the North Vietnamese unleashed ultimately eighteen divisions to invade South Vietnam.

Stephen Hess: *The Jims on the panel were not happy in their dealings with the press. But did you ever call the editors, the publishers? Did you file complaints? Did you have any satisfaction? What was the interaction with the journalists who you felt abused by?*

Woolsey: Yes, I would make occasional phone calls, two or three probably of that sort in the course of the two years I was there, but it never did any good. In the press's behalf, let me say that on a couple of occasions we had the classic situation in which we knew a story was going to run because of the questions the reporter had been asking, and we knew that if it ran it would betray a source and method. In one case it would have betrayed a very important source who would almost certainly have been killed. I called on the senior executive of a media organization that's well known for its investigative and excellent journalism, and I disclosed everything privately one-on-one about the case, the source, the circumstance. The executive said, Thanks, we understand; we can run it without that paragraph in the story.

And it seems to me that's the way you have to operate as a DCI and that's the way a senior executive of a media organization ought to respond. It ought to be voluntary. There ought not to be any kind of national secrets act, unless the government imposed legally a prior restraint, but in that case and one other I got good cooperation from the press on what I would call matters of life and death.

Kalb: *And did any of you ever go to the press, present evidence, say, Please, in the interest of national security, don't run this, and the press said, Nuts to you, we're going to run it anyway?*

Schlesinger: Indeed. Indeed. In fact I am the most recent person and perhaps the last person to get out an order of prior restraint against the press. I think that that earns me a hanging in effigy by many defenders of First Amendment rights. This was when *Progressive* magazine decided to print the details of how to build a hydrogen bomb and to have diagrams. Under the Atomic Energy Act, which, of course, is constitutional until decided otherwise, the secretary of energy has the responsibility of seeing to it that such designs remain secret. So I got the attorney general to take to the courts a request for prior restraint. I was ultimately defeated. The reason I was ultimately defeated was that the *Progressive* magazine sent these prints up to Canada where my prior restraint order did not operate. It was subsequently published in Canada. Now the interesting part is it reflects the fact that you cannot confine news to a single nation. On the international scene, things will develop that under national law should not be released.

Hess: *We have three panelists, members of former presidents' cabinets, who were not exactly hapless giants, as they present themselves, in relation to the press. The morning paper talks about one of your successors, Donald Rumsfeld, as being brilliant at calculated leaks. Surely you had opportunities from your position to influence positively the press coverage in the way you wanted, the leaks, plants, flattery, whatever it might be.*

Kirkpatrick: We had a very good press bureau at the U.S. Mission to the United Nations when I was there. We had a top-flight seasoned journalist who had been for quite a period the head of the *Washington Post* bureau in Saigon. Joel Blocher, who handled our relations with the press. Of course there was another difference. At the UN we were dealing with the world press. I don't mean every country who is a member of the United Nations has a journalist in New York, but many countries, more than simply the major powers, have a significant journalist corps in New York. We really dealt as much with the foreign press as with the American press. I was personally rarely involved in trying to influence in any way the press, because that was somebody else's job, not mine. I was so busy at the UN.

I think our most dramatic relationship with the press and our biggest unpleasant relationship came at the time of our landing in Grenada. That was one of the absolute low points through eight years of the Reagan administration's relations with the press, and it posed an interesting problem. It's one time I thought absolute suppression of news was appropriate because what we knew would have endangered the lives of hundreds and hundreds of people had we released it, and there were 670 or so American medical students in Grenada at that time. There were also 400 or 500 other Americans in Grenada at that time.

We knew several things about the men who had conducted the coup in Grenada. I'm sure nobody in the room has as vivid a memory of the Grenada events as I do. The man who governed Grenada was a Marxist Leninist. He'd been governing Grenada for a number of years, four or five years. We had perfectly civil relations with him. This was Maurice Bishop. He was shot and four members of his cabinet were shot dead by generals Austin and Coard, who were conducting this coup. At the same time they announced a . . . twenty-four-hour-a-day, shoot-on-sight curfew. Because they had just shot the whole Bishop cabinet we knew they were prepared to shoot. They arrested the American students. They took them and divided them in two groups, one up high on a hill, one down in the valley, and kept them lying face down in buildings in which they had located them, and they were under heavily armed guard at all times.

The governor general of NATO was in continuous radio contact saying don't wait any longer, this is a desperate situation. Ronald Reagan was so concerned about saving those lives, particularly of the students, that the whole administration, the whole cabinet went to real extremes to make certain there were no leaks. He did not even inform Margaret Thatcher, his very good friend, the prime minister of Great Britain and his closest associate probably.

Kalb: *Did you find the need to lie if a reporter came to you with information?*

Kirkpatrick: I don't think I personally lied. I certainly avoided the press. I personally carefully avoided the press. I didn't talk to anyone who had ever even had a relationship with the press in their lives. But it was only a matter of about forty-eight hours. And it was over.

Mrs. Thatcher was quite unhappy with Ronald Reagan, quite unhappy, which was a most unusual situation. He tried to explain to her that . . . he had [no] question . . . whatsoever [about her], but he did have some concern about the leaks in the British bureaucracy, as he had concern about leaks in the American bureaucracy. There was no leak, and the students were all rescued, and everybody lived happily ever after.

Schlesinger: You were invading a member of the Commonwealth.

Kirkpatrick: That's right. That was her point.

Schlesinger: And the Queen was rather distressed by that as well.

Let me point out how difficult it is in this democracy to carry out the kind of covert and deception operations that were standard, let us say, in World War II. When the airlifts started in 1973, the airlift to Israel [during the Yom Kippur War], I had been told by the White House to get . . . the Israeli military attache and that he would make a commitment to me to unload those planes—which would land under cover of darkness—and have them out before dawn so that the American hand in resupply could be hidden. Well, fate worked against us, to say the least. There were cross-winds in the Azores; the aircraft began to pile up at Dover Air Force Base. So even though the first planes got in under cover of darkness and were unloaded, because of the delays caused by the cross-winds, out of the skies come C-5As, which were the largest planes anyone had ever seen in Israel, and half of the population of Tel Aviv goes out to the airport to cheer.

Now those were circumstances in which a covert and deception operation was not entirely successful.

Kalb: *Mother Nature conspires. Jim Woolsey with the CIA and Jim Schlesinger with the CIA. You don't normally have press briefings. So when you want to get information out on those rare occasions, how did you do that? Were you engaged in selective leaks? Would that be the general way in which information was out? Testimony that you would give on the Hill?*

Woolsey: By '93, '94, we were doing a certain amount of public testimony to give an assessment, sort of a state of the world and where things are in proliferation and the like, and I testified publicly a number of times in the two years that I was there. So most of any clarification, which is really what you're involved in, would be done by the CIA press office, usually on background. If there was some added factor that could be released that would augment something that had been said publicly, we'd do that.

But the CIA—at least in my tenure, and this was true most of the time although not always—is not a policy player in the sense of the DCI offering policy advice. That has occasionally happened; I'm sure it happened with Bill Casey [CIA director under Reagan], who was a friend of the president. It has happened from time to time but certainly not during my tenure. I had a hard enough time getting in to see the president with intelligence, much less policy advice. But we're not really a policy player. Everybody has had polygraphs, everybody every five years is asked whether or not they have released classified information without authorization. It's really a fairly disciplined operation. So people don't have the incentive as they do in, say, the State Department or sometimes Defense or other agencies to help win the policy argument for their boss by releasing or leaking some information.

Kalb: *Does the director ever have a news conference?*

Woolsey: Occasionally. I had one on Ames. I had one on the procedural reforms that I had proposed to change a lot of the aspects of the way security and counterintelligence were handled. I probably had three or four press conferences in the two years I was there. I did meet with the press for interviews occasionally. In the midst of all of this mess about Ames and then later [about] a very distorted version, propagated principally by the chairman of the Senate Intelligence Committee at the time, Senator DeConcini, of a nonscandal involving a National Reconnaissance Office building out near Dulles airport. Material had been fully disclosed to the Congress, which the House Committee acknowledged, but Senator DeConcini wanted to make a big deal out of this, so we had a very angry hearing. [In 1994 the CIA came under fire for excesses in the construction of a proposed $300 million headquarters of the agency's spy satellite division. Senator Dennis DeConcini accused the NRO of burying the "excessive" expenditures in the agency's operations budget and misleading the Intelligence Committee about the size and cost of the facility.]

In the midst of all this, for some reason, David Broder called me from the *Washington Post* and wanted an interview. I said sure. He came out and interviewed about a bunch of things and ran a story the next day, and there wasn't anything really remarkable in it. I called David and I said, David, listen, all I want to say is thanks. This is the first time in months I've been able to say this. Thanks for just writing a straight story. He laughed and said, I appreciate it.

Kalb: *That's a very sad commentary. Do you all believe that the press generally does not write straight stories?*

Woolsey: My experience is this. In the aftermath of the cold war, during a time in which a lot of people believed the CIA only existed for the cold war and indeed had done a lot of things wrong in the cold war by helping support dictators in some circumstances and covert actions and the like—and when even as respected an individual as Senator Daniel Patrick Moynihan is calling for the abolition of the CIA—from the point of view of, I would say, a generally liberal press in the United States, the CIA was basically the enemy. Government secrecy was the enemy. The CIA was not an institution, with rare exception, that I think was treated fairly or in a balanced way by the press. Some of this may have been my fault in not being good at handling the press; some of it was the circumstances of the time, such as the Ames affair; some of it was intentional distortion, such as, I think, the DeConcini hearings on the NRO building. But I would say that although we did the best we could, my general impression was that with rare and important exceptions like David Broder, most of the press that was covering us, including for the national dailies and the like, was not objective about either the CIA's importance or what it did.

Kalb: *Jim, was that your judgment as well?*

Schlesinger: Sometimes yes, sometimes no. It all depended on the circumstances . . . [I]f the story was friendly it was regarded as a good story, and if it was unfriendly it was not regarded as a good story. Let me make a point about this. First, when Dick Helms became director of central intelligence in 1966, and he saw John Stennis, who was chairman of the Oversight Committee, Stennis said to him, "Mr. Director, you are doing a great job. I don't believe I've seen your name in the press in the course of the last six months." That was the notion in those days, at least behind the CIA.

Kalb: *What changed it?*

Schlesinger: What changed it I think was Watergate. The allegations about the CIA, the attempt in some quarters to make the CIA the culprit behind the Watergate affair because some ex-CIA people had been caught in the Watergate. They were being run by the plumber's unit in the Executive Office rather than by the CIA, but that led to an attempt to put the blame on the agency, and it was some extended period before it could escape from that. From that point on I think the press felt that it had the obligation as well as the right to look very hard at the agency and at all of our intelligence agencies.

Hess: *Marvin, I'm going to direct a question to you. Our panel didn't quite understand calculated leaks; it's something they never had dealt with apparently. [Laughter] You were the chief diplomatic correspondent of CBS and NBC. Was there no secretary of state who perhaps leaked a little something to you, flattered you more than you should have been flattered, manipulated you* *in any way that you felt manipulated? Surely these folks have some tools to use against the poor souls like you.*

Kalb: *I've always felt that the word "leak" is one of the most misused words in Washington jargon. A leak is a calculated effort by the government to transmit information to a certain reporter, going way out of channels to do so, with an understanding between the government and the reporter that we're both play-ing this game, we both understand it, and let's move on and nobody talks. That to me has always been a leak.*

The good reporter reads the press diligently, goes to all of the briefings, reads the speeches, watches the nuances change. I remember Dean Rusk once telling me, you know 95 percent of what I do. What you don't know is the timing, the source, somebody passing on a little bit of information, that sort of thing. But you know the overall policy, and I think a good reporter does. And people who say, It was leaked, I think quite often are misusing the term and misunder-standing the process of the transmission of information.

Woolsey: One thing that's done a good deal in government—which I would-n't really classify as a leak although if the government agency is run right it's done as an intentional decision by the head of the agency—is that one may tell one's press office, look, don't give any fresh information, but it's in the coun-try's and the public's interest for things that are dead wrong not to be out there, and if a reporter comes up with a story and tries to check facts with you, don't give them any fresh facts, but you can off the record confirm or deny that a particular path of inquiry . . . is accurate or inaccurate.

That lets the reporter have two sources for something when they need two sources; it doesn't put the agency on the record; and [it] keeps a press story that otherwise might have some accuracy in it but [also] some wildly crazy thing that [the reporter has] been lied to [about] by somebody that is not [in] anybody's interest . . . to run . . . [It] lets the government agency essentially say, That's a completely wild tangent. The rest of the story I'm not going to say any-thing about, but I won't argue with you about it. That sort of thing happens in Washington all the time.

Kalb: *There was a great State Department spokesman named Bob McCloskey many years ago, and you'd go to him with a tale, something that you'd heard and you wanted to check it. McCloskey would often say, Hmm, if I began to talk about that I would get a little bit pregnant . . . I don't think I want to be a little bit pregnant, so I'm not going to talk to you. Which is a way of saying, You're onto something buddy, but I can't deal with it. Or he would provide a bit of* *information and say . . . [T]he rest of what you're telling me I'd be careful about. That kind of help—genuine, serious help—is valued by a good reporter.*

I want your judgment about what's going on today with respect to not just how the war is being managed but the way the war is being covered. Are the American people getting enough information? Your view of how the secretary of defense is doing? Is he wasting his time on daily briefings, or is this a good spending of his time?

Kirkpatrick: I think he's doing very well. I think he's doing well with the war, but he's also doing well with the press. He's a man seasoned in Washington. He's not only had experience, but he's had time to think about his experience. And it seems to me that he's being reported in friendly and what I'm prepared to take as an accurate fashion.

I feel that the war is being well reported and well covered. I've been pleased, personally, by the amount of background information that's been provided by the *New York Times* and the *Washington Post* and so forth on the war.

Kalb: *Jim Schlesinger. Running a war from the Department of Defense. You've got so many other things to do. Why spend that much time with the press?*

Schlesinger: Because the press not only can turn hostile, the press is engaged in a game of criticism.

Now I go back . . . [before] the successes that have occurred since the collapse of Mazar-e-Sharif [a city in Afghanistan] and the subsequent collapse of the Taliban. Remember way back when, two months ago, the press was filled with stories [questioning Bush's conduct of] this war . . . ? Why is it so slow? Why are the B-52 strikes being delayed? "Give war a chance"—that was the slogan in the press.

Now nobody, not even the press, will argue with success. What we have seen is success. But before then the press stories were along the lines of why everybody in the world hates the United States, even our allies. I remember a story in the *Los Angeles Times* that said, Yes, we are dropping humanitarian food packages for . . . starving Afghans, but one of those packages damaged a house in Kabul. So you had, prior to the collapse of Mazar-e-Sharif and the collapse of the Taliban, stories that were very questioning.

If the war turns badly, I think that the press will turn again. If you go back to Vietnam, people forget that in 1965 the press was cheering our entry into Vietnam. There was the vote on the Tonkin Gulf Resolution, total congressional support, and General Westmoreland was brought back from Saigon to address a joint session of Congress, with a standing ovation. When you are successful or you expect to be successful you have the public and the press with you. When there is [a] question about success, the critics become dominant.

Kalb: *Is that necessarily a bad thing? This country was deliberately set up so that the press would have an independent position, would be able to be outside of the government looking in and saying, You guys are right, you guys may be wrong. Shouldn't the press be a questioning organization? That's what it gets paid to do.*

Schlesinger: Rely on the press. It is there, and it is questioning. If you look at the question of military tribunals, read the editorial page of the *New York Times*—this is a violation of the Constitution, of American tradition, and the like. Nobody is going to, perhaps regrettably, quiet the press. They will be there; they will criticize.

Woolsey: Telling the press they ought to be sure to be questioning enough is sort of like telling high school students that they ought to be interested in sex. No matter what you do, they're going to be.

Question (from the audience): *My question is about technology and diplomacy. In the early 1970s within the communications circuit there was a view that the medium was the message. That was before the cable news network. In the particular context of the conduct of war since the introduction of cable television, could you comment on whether that has had an impact on diplomacy?*

Schlesinger: It was, I believe, the images on television and the discussion of the "highway of death" during the Gulf war in 1991 that led the administration to decide [that] we've got to terminate this thing or allow this to be terminated. The impact of television images as opposed to the written word has just been immense.

Woolsey: Absolutely. George Will once said that if television had existed at the time of Antietam, which was the single bloodiest day in American military history—the second day of Antietam—we would be two countries today. And there, I think, is something to that.

We lose the two helicopters in Mogadishu and we leave. The marine barracks are blown up in '82 in Lebanon and we leave. I think that in the administration I served in, the lack of willingness to see casualties coming back in body bags on the evening news fundamentally influenced policy decisions. It's why we sat off at a distance and shot cruise missiles into empty buildings in the middle of the night in order to retaliate for Saddam's effort to kill former President Bush in the spring of 1993. I'm not sure why President Clinton thought that going after Iraqi night watchmen and maids in the empty intelligence service building was going to be an effective deterrent. But it showed something blowing up on television, so you looked like you were doing something anyway, and it didn't risk any body bags.

Kirkpatrick: I think the CNN effect is also felt in foreign policy decisions. Such, for example, as the American involvement in Bosnia. There was a long period when the first George Bush was resisting American involvement in Bosnia at the time that our allies were becoming involved in Bosnia. I think one of the very most important factors was the large presence on our television of the outrageous bombing and beating and starving and burning of Bosnian civilians, helpless civilians. I think it changed our policy.

Question (from the audience): *My question has to do with U.S. agencies that were responsible for a long period of time with communications and presenting the U.S. message abroad. The U.S. Information Agency, which was essentially dissolved or absorbed into State Department two years ago, was responsible for the U.S. message and presentation of our position information to foreign markets. And with the end of the cold war I believe there was a lot of thinking that there was no longer a need for that, and that hastened its demise or absorption into State Department, with the vision that CNN can do it. What would you say to the fact that maybe we're reaping the negative aspect of letting someone else "do our advertising for us"? I don't think Procter & Gamble would let General Foods do its message.*

Schlesinger: I think that's right on the mark. The most significant aspect of developments not only since September 11 but prior to it was the poor American image in the Middle East for a variety of reasons, and we have failed dismally either to worry about it or to have effective public diplomacy. It's going to require getting people from the Middle East to speak favorably about America's response to the actions taken on September 11, [who] have not been notably forthcoming. But we are limited in public diplomacy because we are dealing with an entirely different culture and mindset.

Woolsey: There are two aspects to this. One is presenting a message of the United States in an attractive and interesting and available way, that's Voice of America. The other is doing the job that a free local media would do if it existed in places where freedom doesn't exist. One of my favorite questions of audiences is, What was the CIA covert action that was said by both Lech Walesa and Vaclav Havel to have been the single most important thing the United States did during the cold war? The answer is, of course, Radio Free Europe, because for the first two-thirds of its existence, RFE and Radio Liberty were CIA covert actions. And the reason they were so successful is that they were not propaganda. What they were was setting up Eastern Europeans and Russians to run a radio station in Munich or wherever to broadcast into the East in the way they would be free to do . . . if that country were free. So they would report critically on things, Little Rock and race riots in the United States or whatever. They reported objectively, and it's one of the reasons they had such a wide following. So one of the things we need to do in working on this is we have to have two sets of institutions, one for a country like Iraq or Iran or Syria or North Korea. What we need to be able to do is create a sort of a shadow free institution that is what their media would be like if it were free. Not just something to present the American view.

5

The CNN Effect

t's called "the CNN effect." And for a time, during and immediately after the Gulf war in 1991, it was associated only with
CNN—the effect of live and continuous television coverage of
foreign affairs on the conduct of diplomacy and the waging of war. CNN covered the war, beaming its signal into foreign and defense ministries all over the
world. Dick Cheney, then secretary of defense in the first Bush administration,
often acknowledged that he got more timely, relevant information from CNN
than he did from U.S. diplomats. Soon, with the explosion of violence in
Mogadishu, mass starvation in Ethiopia, and the ethnic wars in former
Yugoslavia, old and new networks, spawned in the age of new technology, followed CNN's example of providing continuous coverage of dramatic events, at
home and abroad. Though it was still called the CNN effect, it included more
than just CNN coverage—it meant that the world was now wired, open to
instantaneous coverage, and that the coverage affected everyone and everything, including world leaders and their tactics and strategy.

In 1992, President George H. W. Bush saw television images of starving
children in Somalia, and he felt obliged to send U.S. troops there to distribute
food and establish security. Less than a year later, President Bill Clinton saw
television images of Somali fighters dragging the desecrated body of an American soldier through the streets of Mogadishu, and he felt obliged to withdraw
the troops. Was it policy, or the power of television to influence policy? Was it,
in other words, a graphic example of the CNN effect at work?

CNN's Judy Woodruff put special emphasis on the power of a picture, even
if shown for only a brief time. CNN's editors had a half-hour mini-documentary
on the soldier's body, but, after lengthy deliberation, they decided to show only

two and a half seconds of the footage. The impact, she said, was "magnified" and magnetic.

On January 23, 2002, we invited a former U.S. diplomat, a German journalist, a scholar, and a TV anchor to discuss this extraordinary phenomenon in the context of a war against terrorism. They were

—**Lawrence S. Eagleburger**, who served President Bush as secretary of state from August 1992 to the end of his administration

—**Claus Kleber**, who was finishing a long stint as Washington bureau chief for the German TV network ARD

—**Steven Livingston**, a distinguished scholar at the George Washington University who has written on the CNN effect

—**Judy Woodruff**, one of CNN's principal anchors and a senior correspondent based in Washington, D.C.

For Eagleburger, there was "no question" that television affected U.S. policy in Somalia, no question either that CNN in particular made a "big difference" in the Gulf war. "We sat with our television sets tuned to CNN throughout that whole time," Eagleburger recalled. "CNN has an impact at least on decisionmakers, because it's there all the time." Diplomats, if they work in a democracy, have to respect public opinion, and CNN helped shape it. So it has been since Vietnam, which ended with an American defeat. But even with an American victory, Kleber reminded us, Washington had to be mindful of the impact TV images had on public opinion. When television disclosed the full dimensions of the U.S. victory on the "highway of death" running from Kuwait northwest into Iraq, with bloodied bodies scattered everywhere and military equipment left in smoking ruins, the American people felt that enough was enough—the war should end. Livingston stressed the importance of the new technology in allowing instantaneous coverage. While television equipment once was costly and heavy, now much of it is light and portable, opening even faraway places to live coverage.

Woodruff added another dimension to the panel's deliberations. When an administration fails to construct and articulate a clear policy, television talk and images tend to fill the vacuum. "Here come these dramatic pictures of one form or another, either troops or human suffering," she explained, "and, oh, now we have at least the outline of what a policy could be, might be, until government catches up and says, Here's what we should be doing based on these rational reasons."

Everyone recognized that coverage of the war against terrorism would be very costly. The question was whether the networks and the newspapers would pay the extra cost of covering it. Would the public interest be satisfied? Or would newspapers continue to insist on 20 to 30 percent profit margins and local television on 40 to 50 percent profit margins? Woodruff boldly and bravely stated what everyone knew to be the case: "You cannot ignore what management tells you," she said. "If they're only going to spend so much money on international news coverage, what are you going to do? You can continue to work for that news organization, and they say, We're going to devote this amount of money to covering stories outside the U.S. Here are the ratings, and we expect this, that, and the other. You cannot ignore that if you're the executive producer of a program or the anchor or whatever." No, you cannot.

Marvin Kalb: *I think our first responsibility is to define what . . . the CNN effect [is] . . . [D]oes it work in all cases or in some cases? With reference to Somalia, there are a couple of quotes that I'd like to read. One is from Secretary Eagleburger: "I will tell you quite frankly, television had a great deal to do with President Bush's decision to go in in the first place; and I will tell you equally frankly, I was one of those two or three that [were] strongly recommending he do it. And it was very much because of the television pictures of the starving kids, substantial pressures from the Congress that came from the same source, and my honest belief that we could do this, do something good at not too great a cost. Certainly without any great danger of body bags coming home." The second quote is from President Clinton: "This past weekend, we all reacted with anger and horror as an armed Somali gang desecrated the bodies of American soldiers." So, Mr. Secretary, help us understand the impact with respect to Somalia.*

Lawrence S. Eagleburger: Somalia, yes—television made a big difference because of the daily drumbeat of pictures of starving children. No question

about that. But that was television across the board, that wasn't just CNN by any means. I'll try to describe it as best I can now. Remember, this was also the time that there was a lot of pressure on the Bush administration to go into Yugoslavia, or into Serbia.

So [we] had two cases running at us at the same time and a lot of television on both. Let me start by saying there's no question that television made a big difference. But I remember thinking at the time that we had two cases where we were being pressured to get involved, and I was convinced that if we got involved at that stage in the Yugoslav mess we'd be there for a very long time and it would hurt a lot. Here was the Somali case, where there was clearly a humanitarian need but there was also a way for the administration to make its point on that subject and at the same time, to be blunt with you, take some of the pressure off [because we were] not doing anything in Bosnia.

I went to the president—I wasn't going to do anything, if I could avoid it, on the Yugoslav case at the time. The Somali case was a much easier case and permitted us at the same time to do something right and to make it clear we were doing it. I went to the president, and to my great surprise nobody, including the chairman of the joint chiefs, nobody raised any objection—on the understanding, and on this Bush was very clear, that we went in, fed, and got out. And indeed, he called then President-elect Clinton—my understanding from President Bush was that Clinton in effect said, Yes, go ahead. It's certainly clear that he didn't say don't do it.

I've got to say, from the beginning in President Bush's mind and clearly in mine, it was feed and get out. Let me just make one other point. After we had left, the administration had changed, that objective changed. There's no question, I think—I wasn't around at the time but I think there's no question—that TV pictures of the dead GI had a lot to do with our leaving. I think that's always a serious mistake if, when somebody's killed, you pack up and leave. But my point is yes, it made a big difference, but it wasn't CNN as such. CNN as such made a tremendous difference in the Gulf war.

Stephen Hess: *What is so fascinating about the story you just told is [that] "the CNN effect" is usually [understood to mean that] "television made us do it." And you're saying that at least one type of CNN effect, television effect, was that you used television in order to do what you wanted to do, which is very interesting.*

Kalb: *You said before that television was very important and you don't want to skip over that. How is it important? You're secretary of state. Something goes on television. So what? Why does that influence you?*

Eagleburger: The fact of the matter is we live in a democracy. American foreign policy—more often than I think should be the case—is affected by not just the news media and television, but by ethnic politics. Some of the things we ended up doing or not doing in Cyprus, for example, were purely and simply because of the Greek lobby. I could go through any number of these. My point is, when you try to manage foreign policy in a democracy you forget at your peril that there are a bunch of people out there that may vote your president out of office, and in my case they did. Not for those reasons, I think. But you can't ignore it. You may not always accept it, but you can't ignore it.

Judy Woodruff: If I can jump in, the pictures coming in from Bosnia were just as compelling, weren't they?

Eagleburger: Oh, sure.

Woodruff: And yet you made a different choice.

Eagleburger: A different choice: here were two cases where there was a humanitarian need. In one of them the consequences of becoming directly involved were at best totally unpredictable and probably could lead to serious consequences. In the Somali case, [there was] a much clearer opportunity to do something right and get the hell out. The mistake that was made was we didn't get out. But you make choices, and in this case, the television gave us an opportunity to make a choice, which to some degree took pressure off the constant drumbeat that the Bush administration didn't give a damn about human rights.

Claus Kleber: It sounds almost like there is something bad about the fact that American policy reacted to television pictures. I don't think they reacted to television pictures. They reacted to the facts on the ground that became visible. You couldn't hide them any more. This is why it's not a CNN effect, it's a television modern communications world effect that you cannot close your eyes to something that happens in Mogadishu.

Eagleburger: It's true. But at the same time I can cite you any number of examples where we have shut our eyes. The whole Yugoslav issue for a long time; move on to Burundi, where the pictures [of genocide] were pretty awful. But again, at some point it gets . . . back to the policymaker having to say, What are the issues we can affect and how much will it cost? If there hadn't been television and the reporting on the mess in Somalia, we would never have done it, absolutely correct.

Steven Livingston: I think a good way of thinking about the CNN effect is to think about the relationship between government officials and the media as  sort of a dance, and the claim of the CNN effect is that at various points in time it's the media who are leading in this dance. Government is responding to the initiatives of news media and journalists, whereas most of the time, scholarship suggests news agendas are established by the State Department.

I find it very interesting what the secretary said. We need to think about Somalia actually not as a single decision point but as two decision points. When we think about Somalia as the secretary is, he's thinking about [President Bush's] decision on November 27 [1992] to send in a large contingent of U.S. security forces. What we forget about are the various efforts before that in the summer of 1992 to do anything possible to get CNN and other news organizations to pay attention to Somalia.

My point here is that CNN needs to be thought of very carefully, because it was the effort of government officials to get the news media to pay attention to the situation in the first place [the first decision] that then led to those pictures that the secretary says the president saw and others saw that led to that second decision to inject the troops.

Hess: *Then what you're saying is that there [were] some people in government who [were] using the media to try to pressure the government. After all, that decision [had] to be made by the president of the United States, who [was] not necessarily inclined to make it. For one thing, he was running for office; he was rather busy.*

Livingston: Right. We see that the CNN effect isn't the idea of the media leading in the dance, but rather you have a circumstance in which some government officials are using the news media to move their agenda items further up the pay scale, to get it to the secretary's desk.

Eagleburger: As long as you don't exclude the other point, which is there are times when it is the media . . . [N]ot because . . . some government bureaucrat is talking to them but because events have captured the imagination of the media and that then translates into pressure on the administration.

Livingston: At that point you run into the two other manifestations [of the CNN effect]. Rather than working through the offices of the State Department and the National Security Council, the president ends up talking with other world leaders. There's an acceleration of decisionmaking processes. This isn't new to global real-time media.

Finally, there's this possibility that we saw in the case of the young Ranger's body being dragged through the streets. . . . That's the impediment effect— where you've got a mature policy . . . and then something like the body will simply derail the policy at that point. That's entirely different than suggesting that the media can on their own set the agenda of the State Department or of an administration.

Kalb: *Judy, you're the anchor, are you aware of all of these pressures inside the network decisionmaking process? Do you care at all that it's going to have an effect on somebody?*

Woodruff: Sure we care. If you're going to be smart about covering what's going on and telling people what's going on, you want to talk about as many factors as you know about.

Just to give you a little anecdote about what happened in Somalia: We didn't have anyone on the ground who was working for CNN when the heli-copter went down in Mogadishu. In fact, we didn't have any access to what happened. What we did have was a stringer who was there. Within twenty-four hours after this happened, he made known through channels to CNN that he had these remarkable pictures of what had happened. The scenes of this devastation in the city and some very grizzly scenes of the Americans, what had happened to them, the torture, and then the dragging of the bodies.

We got access to that as quickly as we could. I was just joining CNN at the time and was barely aware of what was going on. I've learned about it since then. But they spent some time in an editing booth looking at these pictures very carefully. They ended up with something like twenty or thirty minutes. We ended up airing only about two and a half seconds of the soldier's body being dragged through the streets. But it's been so magnified since then to be those dreadful images. But a lot of care went into that. We ended up editing down the whole thing to something like thirty seconds, and [we showed only] two and a half seconds of that. . . . And [despite the brevity] it had this very understandable remarkable effect.

We asked the White House and the State Department, I am told, before we aired it; we gave them several hours' notice and said, We're going to air these pictures, this is exactly what they look like, so be prepared. The Clinton administration chose not to say anything either at the White House or at the State Department. And as soon as we put it on the air, we immediately shared it with the networks and with others. It was made widely available.

Hess: *Reflecting how powerful an image can be on television.*

Livingston: At the same time it should be kept in mind too that the image of the Ranger in particular was replicated in the media all over. And there was a lot of debate at the time amongst editors and newspapers whether it should be run in color, in black and white, how large, all of that. So there was a cumulative effect. We shouldn't just talk about CNN.

Eagleburger: [Y]ou're sitting there thinking, now if it goes bad, what are we going to see and what are the consequences going to be? So even when you decide to do something, in the background with all of us—and I think it's still true—there's Vietnam sitting there, and it may have given us a lot of wrong lessons, but it's there in the back of your mind all the time.

Livingston: About six months after Somalia, . . . Rwanda occurred, April/May of 1994. [Ethnic violence erupted following the assassination of Rwanda's president in April of 1994.] The Clinton administration had been so burned by its mishandling of Somalia that it stood back and watched close to a million people be systematically exterminated in Rwanda and did not become involved in Rwanda until July/August of 1994, in the role of a humanitarian response, not in an effort to stop the genocide that had occurred months before.

Kleber: What was said about the pictures cuts both ways. If I'm not totally mistaken I think the pictures at the end of the Gulf war of the so-called highway of death, where devastation rained on the Iraqi forces, had a lot to do with the fact that America decided to let go. So it is not always America defeated which makes an event, it can be also gloriously victorious, speaking from a battlefield perspective, which changes the attitude.

But since you are asking for a European perspective, in my memory the icon of media coverage of Somalia was the American forces landing on the beach. And cameras lighting Special Forces trying to make a sneak attack, which was, of course, ridiculous. It shows that both sides were not ready for this kind of situation. It showed one more thing. The American forces brought the correspondents along. They landed on the same beach in the same minutes, and they were equally clueless about what they got themselves into. This is, I think, the shortcoming of American coverage of the continent of Africa or . . . [of] almost every other continent where there is no current war with American troops involved. CNN has a very specific role, but it also has a very small market share; it's extremely powerful but it doesn't address the audience at large. The audience at large in the country still gets the bulk of their international information from the big—declining but still big—television network news. They have decided for purely commercial reasons that having bureaus in Africa with constant staffs, with constant reporting, is not economically feasible. As far as I know, neither NBC nor ABC nor CBS had a full-fledged office with people with local knowledge—real correspondents, the rank of a Cronkite or Tom Fenton, let's say—in Africa. So not only were the American policymakers unprepared about Somalia, in fact the American public had no clue of what was going on.

A little anecdote from a couple of years later, when Clinton finally made an effort and visited Africa to put the continent on the map: my foreign network reported more . . . , I think fifteen times more, about this trip through Africa by an American president and the on-the-ground perspective—and the local reception and the problems he was addressing and all this stuff—than any American network.

Kalb: *Why?*

Kleber: Because I'm doing public television, and we felt there is an obligation to tell people about Africa, and Clinton's visit was a great angle to bring it into the main evening news. And we did that. Our commercial competition . . . unlike [in] America, we are leading the market in Germany, so they had to follow. Their correspondents had to offer a little bit of that stuff to their audiences too in order to be taken seriously. There is an information culture which still exists—otherwise I would be out of work—in Europe which has fallen victim in the United States to the bottom line of GE [owner of NBC] and the Mickey Mouse network [ABC] and so on, who calculate the news in a very different way.

Kalb: *But Claus, do you find in Germany that . . . your coverage, let's say the Clinton visit to Africa, has [an] impact on government policy?*

Kleber: It has the impact that when things went wrong in Somalia, the Germans were much less shocked and unprepared, and I'm not talking policymakers, I'm talking the public that supports the policymakers, than the Americans were. They thought they'd go in, everything's fine, the kids get fed, America is even more liked than before, and [they] get out. It is not that easy. It was a story that wasn't told until [Somali militia leader General Mohamed Farah] Aideed became prominent and Americans got captured, and these television pictures.

Hess: *Can I get back to Judy for a moment? Her intervention showed that in a particular situation, CNN is very, very careful in its selection of material. So Judy, you're sitting there, and you must know that you're being watched in every foreign ministry in the world. Mort Abramowitz, who was ambassador to Turkey during the Persian Gulf war, talked about going in to see the president of Turkey, who barely had time because he was so busy watching the monitor of CNN. How does this affect you?*

Woodruff: Well, you will remember that Ted Turner's famous admonition to all of us was that that word "foreign" was banned on CNN. We had to speak of international affairs, not foreign affairs. There's a distinction between CNN programming in the United States, what we call the domestic channel, and CNN programming outside the United States. After September 11, we were in a situation where we knew at that time the U.S. channel was being seen overseas everywhere for large chunks of time. Many times, I would say "we": "What should we do?" Meaning we in the United States. And yet we are the journalists, and they are the government. Now we're Americans. I know we who were on the air wrestled with this question of how [to] refer to ourselves. We are U.S. citizens. We are just as outraged and just as hurt by what happened as everyone else in this country. At the same time, we are supposed to be somewhat removed from it as journalists. So we did wrestle with that. I had to be careful not to keep saying "we." We put out all sorts of internal directives saying, Don't refer to the U.S. government as "we."

Livingston: I want to refer to Judy's first point, that is when we talk about CNN it's important to keep two things in mind. Not only is it true that there are different CNNs, and if you've spent any time overseas, you can see how much programming one sees in Europe is different than the programming you see here. In part there [are] considerably more international affairs program[s] on CNNI than there [are] on CNN, which is unfortunate. But the other thing too that I think is important is that the CNN that we were talking about earlier, the CNN of 1992, is . . . very different [from] CNN [in] 2002. Not just in the corporate relationships, but the technology has changed radically.

To cover Mogadishu in 1992, you used a satellite phone that was huge and required a generator. You most recently have seen satellite phone technology—the TH-1, Talking Head 1, the video phone—that is essentially self-contained in a laptop computer with a small camera, and that makes for a very mobile reporter who isn't anchored to the Al Rashid Hotel or . . . to a spot where there is juice and a transmitter. You've got a correspondent who can go to the scene of action. That makes for a different kind, at least the potential for a different kind, of news coverage of breaking crises than what you had ten years ago or even five years ago.

Kalb: *But might it not have the effect of intensifying the CNN effect?*

Livingston: It has the possibility of actually intensifying parachute journalism, which is not necessarily good. In 1995, let's say, the CNN bureau chief in London decides to cover something in Africa. He has to decide [whether] it [is] worth sending the KU fly-away unit [a broadcast satellite] that is going to cost him $50,000 just to get it in place. Now that decision can be made much easier: We'll put it in overhead luggage, and we'll send this correspondent there. But it has the potential for creating a more fragmented, disjointed international coverage, which is not necessarily something that the U.S. audience needs.

Kalb: *But couldn't one see it the other way, that if the technology makes it that much easier to cover a story and to get it on the air, doesn't that really have the effect of intensifying what it is that we're talking about? Because it's there, it's more easily available, you've got the technology, it happens.*

Hess: *It also means that broadcast networks—ABC, CBS, NBC, as opposed to CNN—are more likely to cover an international story.*

Kleber: What do they cover then? They send people only where action is happening. Rwanda—they didn't go there four months ago to see what has happened on the ground. Let's analyze. Let's talk to the people. Let's send a team there for two weeks and put together a decent story that gives a background and framework.

Woodruff: When there's a vacuum of policy, when policy hasn't been made, it seems to me media coverage is then more likely to fill that vacuum. We don't know anything, we don't have a policy about it. Here come these dramatic pictures of one form or another, either troops or human suffering, and oh, now we have at least the outline of what a policy could be, might be, until government catches up and says, Here's what we should be doing based on these rational reasons.

Hess: *One aspect of policy that we haven't really touched and is rather important or has been in terms of Afghanistan is the question of security. What do all these pictures mean when there are American troops on the ground? One question which CNN and the other networks had to deal with was the bin Laden tapes.*

Woodruff: Those tapes were made available—we have the man, the face of evil, and we can't get it out there fast enough. Then, of course, it became clear that it was much more complicated. It's not that a lot of thought didn't go into it, but in the beginning we knew what we had was something that was of great value in terms of informing the American people. They knew bits and pieces about it. But here he was talking, apparently before the events of September 11.

Kalb: *But Judy, wasn't that at least in part because the White House asked the networks to please not cover, not to give a great deal of—*

Woodruff: That was after. It was put on, and then the White House said to exercise restraint.

Eagleburger: I've never understood why the White House wanted to do that. One of the things, if I have learned nothing else in too many years in the government, is almost never should the administration and certainly not the White House get into the business of asking the media not to do something. Not only is it unwise because most of the time the media are going to do it anyway, but beyond that why should—[unless] we're talking about a troop ship going somewhere, of course—why did the White House not want those tapes shown? I still don't understand it.

Woodruff: I think that's a very good question. I think the judgment they exercised was questionable. I don't know what the value was of limiting his exposure. The American people are smart enough to look at this and judge it for what it is.

Eagleburger: And government ought to stay out of that sort of thing as much as it can. I really think that's wrong to do that. You can go all the way back to the Pentagon papers. My dear friend Henry [Kissinger] would have been a hell of a lot better off if he'd never said one word about it. That's the other point. You tend to hype precisely the thing you don't want to hype when you do that.

Kleber: Obviously nobody believes the official reasoning, that hidden messages might be there. Just for the record.

Kalb: *[T]he American government ask[ed] American networks not to run something, and for the most part the networks obliged the government. What about your network in Germany? Does it in any way become affected by a White House appeal of that sort?*

Kleber: No, certainly not.

Kalb: *Mr. Secretary, what about the pictures of the prisoners in Guantanamo and the way in which those pictures have affected at least the British tabloids.*

Eagleburger: And human rights groups here and there. You should never have asked me the question because my answer would be if they're going to show these pictures they should be followed immediately by pictures of planes flying into the two towers. Of course we shouldn't be vicious, nasty; we shouldn't torture; but I don't have the least problem with having them hobbled, being escorted around. Beyond which I'm prepared to take the word of the government, if you will, that you have to be very careful of them because if you're not careful they may end up slitting your throat. You've asked the wrong person. I have absolutely no sympathy for it.

Kalb: *But you're the right person. Why do you think Secretary Rumsfeld seemed to be so upset by the pictures and the criticism that he devoted almost all of his news conference yesterday to that one issue?*

Eagleburger: I can't get my head into his, but I will tell you I suppose it is because he sees this as the beginning of a major problem for the administration because we will be perceived to be vicious, nasty, and unfeeling. I'm serious. I can't have a hell of a lot of sympathy, and I'm simply saying you're asking the wrong guy. If I were Rumsfeld I would be just as upset about this.

Kleber: There is a European aspect to this. I'm a little surprised that the criticism arose in Europe. Maybe I've been in this country too long. It's just a knee-jerk reaction. Of course they are prisoners of war—they were combatants; they tried to kill American soldiers. They are living in relative comfort, from all I know, in Guantanamo, if you compare it to Kandahar, where they are kept in cages stacked one upon the other. In my reporting I used the sound bite of a young military police officer in Guantanamo who rightfully said, They are basically living like I'm living here. I don't have good protection against mosquitoes. What you hear from Europe, from my editors actually, who ordered the report and then said, Well, we think you too prominently displayed the young attractive soldier. I said, No, I did it just right.

The attitude in Germany is we are concerned about the American image in the world because they have the moral superiority in this war and they are now squandering it by not treating these people humanely. What really is worrying is after the war is over—of course it's not over, it will be going on for another twenty years, I guess—they think, Now let's everybody go home, nobody gets hurt, let's celebrate Easter or something and be nice and quiet and civilized. And the American attitude, which I share in this particular case, is, No, we are not at that point yet. [I]f I were the marine commander in Guantanamo, I personally would probably decide exactly like he did. But I would allow media there, allow them to film everything, [and drop] the fake argument [about] the Geneva Convention—which, by the way, doesn't apply, but it specifically rules out filming prisoners of war. So this one clause we enforce, all the others we don't care for. But this ridiculous irrelevant clause we enforce, putting a screen of secrecy over the whole thing, making it obscure and suspicious and causing some of the European reactions, which really mean more trouble than they are worth.

Kalb: *Is it a broad-based European reaction? You called it knee-jerk a moment ago. Is it quick and apt to end within a matter of a day or two or five? Or is this something that reflects a more deep set of problems regarding the European view of American policy in Afghanistan, or more broadly the war against terrorism?*

Kleber: Europeans have this urge that somehow if we all talk and have enough conferences and publish enough papers and send in enough relief workers all problems can be solved peacefully, including the war on terrorism. The American reaction is totally opposite. It's a problem, let's deal with it and do whatever it takes. These two attitudes, especially towards third world countries, collide again and again. It took the shock of September 11 to overcome these cultural differences, and apparently that was good only for a couple of weeks. . . . I got called to do a story on the use of terrible cluster bombs. Rumsfeld said, They are part of our arsenal, and we use them when we deem it necessary. Yeah, I think so. There's a war going on, and I don't think that the other side was terribly selective in their choice of weapons. But again, I may have been in this country too long. The use of cluster bombs was deemed to be somewhat against international law, and one should conduct the war a little more nicely.

Hess: *Is there still a war going on? Or have we gone back to business as usual? Katie Couric said off hand that maybe some of the loss of listenership for the Today Show was that maybe they stayed on the war too long. Aren't you all sort of interested in having the war over?*

Woodruff: We covered the war fairly well as long as there [was] a lot of activity—when there was bombing, when there was daily activity, we were covering it. But now we're down to a very small mopping-up operation. We're looking for Osama, we're looking for [Mullah] Omar.

Eagleburger: You've touched on something I want to mention anyway. You talked about the CNN effect, and here again I need to come to the Gulf war. We sat with our television sets tuned to CNN throughout that whole time. [A]nd this is a point that . . . unfortunately the Katie Courics of this world at least don't understand, which is CNN has an impact at least on decisionmakers, some at least, because it's there all the time. During the Gulf war you could always figure out by turning on the television where things were going in Iraq and a hell of a lot better than I could tell from any telegram. It's a very important point in terms of a particular crisis that CNN—not the networks, who are always worried about their money making, but CNN—was able to stay with these things when others were not, and I found that very, very important in the Gulf war.

The second point I would make gets back to this secrecy thing. And I think maybe it is also a CNN effect. That is, you get decisionmakers who resent the fact that they're driven by CNN, and so . . . when it comes to issues like [whether] we [should] let CNN or the television into Guantanamo, aha, this is a chance not to do it. It is always wrong; it always leads to suspicions . . . [If] the suspicions are correct, then I understand why they won't let you in. But if they're not correct, all they do is make the suspicions look real. Particularly in cases like the Guantanamo thing, [government officials] are stupid not to let them in.

Woodruff: We need you back in the administration making these arguments.

Eagleburger: It's so dumb. That's the basic point.

Kalb: *One of Steve's earlier points is that CNN today is not the CNN that the secretary just described. It's quite different. The management of CNN is different, the money structure of CNN is different.*

Livingston: One of the concerns I have about the contemporary version of CNN is that it's news as mini-series. You have Chandra Levy. You have these periods of intense concentration on a story, and then somebody wakes up one morning and says, The war is over and we can go on to the next bang-bang, the next action. You're defining news as a dramatic event rather than as a process. It leads people to not be able to understand the underlying conditions, the processes, that led to the war and that will lead to a war, perhaps, in Somalia or the Philippines or an invasion of Iraq. That's where the next phase of the story goes, and it's left to CNN to decide whether it's important enough to continue to cover it.

Kleber: There is a commercial interest, of course, in blowing up one story as big as you can get it. That may be Chandra Levy, it may be the Gulf war, it may be O. J. Simpson, it may be Somalia, it may be Afghanistan. You need one story because this is what the market responds to. Nothing complex—[that] is not how you make ratings. You want the nation focused on one story. This is a vicious cycle. One network feeds the other . . . and a lot of other stories don't get the coverage they deserve. They blow up tomorrow.

Hess: *Are we all convinced that it's back to business as usual? Is there anyone here who will take the position that Americans—because of Afghanistan, terrorism, because of the proposition that it's a long war—have become more interested in the rest of the world, at least as it affects them?*

Woodruff: My evidence is only anecdotal, but I have to believe that the American people are newly awakened to terror as a result of 9/11. Does that mean that everyone will now go out of their way to read those long pieces in the *New York Times* or in the *Wall Street Journal* or in the *Washington Post* about what's going on in, name a country, Latin America. I don't know. But I do think there is at least a heightened awareness, which does mean the news media have to respond to that. How much greater is it? I don't think we're going to go back to where we were pre-September 11, but have we done a dramatic change? Probably not.

Livingston: The concern is that after September 11, if CNN and other news media see international affairs news solely through the lens of the American war on terrorism, we are actually going to have less rich international news coverage that's not as varied, but rather it's going to continue to be seen through the lens of what the United States is interested in at a given point in time, and that's not [going] to prepare us well for understanding the world.

Kalb: *Two points. One, immediately after September 11 and for about two or three months thereafter there was not a prominent person in the media who did not say that the media had changed forever, September 11 has changed the media forever. I think that is a statement that is going to have to be reexamined. Point number two, it's a question of whether the people running networks and newspapers today can make decisions consistent with two points. One, what might broadly be called a national interest; and two, what more narrowly might be called the public interest. The question is can editors, can executive produc-ers, can the anchors see their responsibility in that light or see their responsibil-ity more narrowly as producing, in newspaper terms, a 22 to 27 percent increase in profit each year? That is an extraordinary pressure that operates now on newspapers, and I imagine in a slightly different way on networks. Judy, you're shaking your head.*

Woodruff: You cannot ignore what management tells you. . . . If they're only going to spend so much money on international news coverage, what are you going to do? You can continue to work for that news organization, and they say, We're going to devote this amount of money to covering stories outside the U.S., and here are the ratings, and we expect this, that, and the other. You cannot ignore that if you're the executive producer of a program or the anchor or whatever.

Eagleburger: I hate to say this, but if you all think you really make that much difference on a day-to-day basis, you're wrong. In and around Charlottesville, Virginia, where I live, the flags are still up that weren't there on the 10th. They fly them on their cars, they have them in their windows, they have them on the lawns, and the whole place is different. It's going to stay that way, I think, for a fairly long time. And what that, I guess, is telling me is as we all sit here and talk about this whole question of the CNN syndrome or whatever—and, as I'm the first to concede to you, if you're in government you worry about it a lot—

we may all be exaggerating the influence when you get out and around in the middle of the countryside.

Woodruff: They shouldn't accept what everybody says on television.

Kleber: Let me say something about the country as a whole. The European perspective on September 12 was, Now America has awakened and in the usual American way they will trample the world brutally, do something powerfully but stupidly, and [it takes] European civilization to steer the giant in the right direction. That was the common denominator in Europe.

So I made an effort, and I've covered the United States for twelve years, and . . . I [can] say I know people in all fifty states. So I just took my Rolodex, called the painter in Iowa or the rafting guide in Utah and people like that and said, What do you think now? I was surprised. I was struck by the differentiated tones I heard. I didn't talk to one ordinary American who said, Let's nuke them back to the Stone Age, or something like that. They said, Let's think about it. We made mistake. We had disassociated ourselves from the world. They did not always choose these words, but that was the message. Let's do this thing right. There is no hate. The problem has been around for twenty years. We can stand back and think for a moment before we act. So this totally unscientific telephone polling influenced my reporting on the future American actions to no end, and I'm glad. In the end it turned out to be right. So it was good to go to Charlottesville, even by telephone and talk to the real people.

Question (from the audience): *I think that's fascinating about the thirty minutes of tape CNN had that got edited down on the Mogadishu thing, down to thirty seconds and finally the two-and-a-half-second clip that we all saw. Who made the decision on the two and a half seconds and the thirty seconds? Was it producers? Were you involved, Judy, as an anchor? Is it executive producers? Exactly who [is] making those decisions on what clips we're going to see?*

Woodruff: In that instance, because CNN's headquarters is Atlanta, it was the executive of CNN there. It was Tom Johnson, who was then the chairman of the CNN news group. It was Bob Fornaud, who was then the executive vice president for programming. It was Ed Turner, who was then the senior vice president for news gathering. And one or two others. It was the executives. I don't believe that any anchors at that time— I was still new to CNN, here in Washington. My colleague Bernie Shaw was here in Washington. So it was a logistical thing in part, but also the executives thought, This is a very important decision, we've got to look at this, we want to make the right decision. And they collectively made the decision. They knew that running all twenty, thirty minutes was the wrong thing to do. They knew that running all five or six minutes of the most gruesome, grizzly pictures was a wrong decision. The tough call was, Do you run any of the worst pictures, and if you do, how much? And they chose to run very, very little, but just enough to give you a sense of how brutalized this—

Livingston: That decisionmaking process, too, I think is different in different circumstances. I've been in an editing booth at Chesterhouse [a press center] in Nairobi, where the decision was made [about] what to even offer the networks by AP Television, Reuters Television, of scenes coming out of Rwanda at the time because some of the scenes were really quite frankly extraordinarily grizzly, finding the bodies. And there were decisions being made in the editing booth [about] what to even put up on the satellite that would then be subsequently treated by the client at the other end, CNN or the networks. So it's different processes in different circumstances.

Woodruff: I'd just add one other quick thing. You didn't ask about this, but on September 11 we had the option of showing many pictures of people jumping out of the buildings, and we chose with two very narrow exceptions not to do that. We very carefully led into it; it was brief. Not every other news organization agreed with our judgment. You may not agree with it. I've talked to people since then who violently disagreed with it and said, The American people should know exactly what this event caused people to do.

Eagleburger: Just yesterday I talked to somebody who had been in an office building right near the event, and he said, and it shocked me, The worst thing in watching this was the people jumping out of the building. I said, Well, I've seen two or three pictures. He said there were at least 100. At least 100 people jumped. And he said it was the worst part of the whole event. I had no sense of it at all.

Livingston: BBC that was shown in the United States showed that repeatedly . . . if you watched the BBC America broadcast, they showed it repeatedly.

Kleber: European networks in general used more of this. I still wonder why.

Question (from the audience): Is there a sufficient check and balance between media, the government, and the public? Or does one or another have more power or influence at any one time?

Livingston: A good way of thinking about "the CNN effect" is . . . to think of it as coming into play at different stages. Sometimes, perhaps, as an agenda-setting agent where—particularly in a policy vacuum if you don't have a clear policy thought through—maybe media content will push new priorities on an agenda and you'll pay attention to Somalia where before you may not have. In other instances, it has the potential for impeding . . . operational security. If you disclose a special operation that's about to take place, chances are it's not going to take place in the absence of secrecy. And you're going to put people's lives at risk. The danger is that media today . . . have access not only to cameras but to satellite imagery. We haven't talked here at all about the fact that you've got . . . satellites that are offering high-resolution satellite imagery to news media. The administration ducked that issue during this war by buying all the rights to the satellite imagery. But you're going to have an international satellite market that's going to offer intelligence-grade satellite imagery. In that instance you're talking about impeding operational security. So in different circumstances you have different manifestations of potential media effect.

Kalb: *Judy, are you using this satellite photography at CNN?*

Woodruff: Yes. I would just say though that I'm not aware of a news organization right now that wouldn't bend over backwards not to get in the way of something operational in the works. If the Pentagon comes to CNN and says, Wait a minute, if you show this you're putting the lives of our young men and women at risk, we would back off. That's not what we're about. So that would be taken very, very, very seriously.

Maria Mann (from the audience): I'm the director of photography for Agence France Presse; it's an international wire service. I just wanted to add something because there was a woman involved in the Somalia decision, and that was me, on moving those pictures, and also on Rwanda, and also on September 11. I just think that the public needs to know that we, as the press, do understand the responsibility and the impact of those decisions that we make.

When I saw that picture of the Ranger being dragged, I really went through an emotional roller coaster, and my first reaction was shock, but my second reaction was anger. And I knew that that had to be shown, and I also knew the terrible consequence of showing that. It's not just three seconds. That's frozen in time as a still image in newspapers, like Professor Livingston said. But we understand those things, a good true journalist understands those things and the effects, and I don't think that we can back away from that. As an international news agency, we're there all the time, we understand that, and we know what the consequences are going to be. So anyone from the general public here, just so you understand that it is a heavy responsibility, nothing we take lightly, and we do feel that responsibility and we hopefully act accordingly.

PART TWO

War in Afghanistan

The Early Stages

6

The Pentagon and the Press

A ccording to one highly experienced Washington bureau chief, the Pentagon and the press are "two great institutions . . . that have totally contradictory objectives and purposes." The Pentagon must protect the safety of the troops and the security of the operation, says Tom DeFrank, of the *New York Daily News*, and "basically doesn't want us around." But the press has the responsibility of covering the conflict, so it must be "around." The result, in DeFrank's view, is an "insoluble problem," likely to last as long as the war—any war—lasts.

And yet, in this war against terrorism, these "two great institutions" have made an effort to understand each other's needs and basic requirements. Under the leadership of the assistant secretary of defense for public affairs, Victoria (Torie) Clarke, the Pentagon invited Washington bureau chiefs to regular sessions designed to air differences and seek compromises every week or two during the war in Afghanistan, while changes for the better still can be attempted. On other occasions, such as after the Vietnam and Persian Gulf wars, similar efforts also were undertaken—but too late to effect a possible improvement in actual coverage.

To support this effort, as the war against the Taliban regime began, Clarke proposed bringing her staff of top Pentagon public information officers to the Brookings Institution, which would invite Washington bureau chiefs. The on-the-record meeting took place on November 8, 2001, with James B. Steinberg, vice president and director of foreign policy studies at Brookings, presiding; but just as the meeting was starting, we got word of a bomb threat, forcing everyone to evacuate the building. Arrangements were quickly made to move the meeting across Massachusetts Avenue to the National Cable and Telecommunications Association, for which Clarke had once worked.

From the very beginning, it was clear that both sides wanted their joint effort to succeed, but both sides also realized that the gap between them might be unbridgeable. Clarke opened the meeting by acknowledging that neither her staff nor the bureau chiefs were going to "reinvent the wheel." There were differences between them, but she focused on one, which she thought was the key to the whole problem and which, if settled, could go a long way toward establishing better relations between the Pentagon and press—namely, access to the activities of special operations troops.

Clarke was to be quickly disabused of this notion. One after another bureau chief rose to raise other problems, which to them were equally if not more crucial to settling the mutual problem.

—Access to U.S. troops in countries such as Uzbekistan. No, an admiral said, that was not possible. Why? "Host country sensitivity," he answered. Political leaders there did not want any publicity, and he admitted that it was more important for the United States to satisfy Uzbekistan's political needs than to satisfy press needs.

—Casualties in combat. Was the Pentagon truly leveling with the press and the public about U.S. casualties? Yes, Clarke insisted.

—Embedding reporters with U.S. forces. An admiral okayed embedding reporters with aircraft carriers, so long as they didn't convey any information about delicate operations or tasks. A colonel flatly denied access to the Rangers—too sensitive, he insisted.

When the meeting ended, DeFrank's judgment seemed vindicated: two worlds in an odd form of cooperative collision. Clarke promised to provide as much information as possible, without jeopardizing the lives of troops and the security of missions. The reporters countered that they did not want to jeopardize lives or missions either but that there was a war to cover and they had a job to do. Everyone shook hands and agreed to meet again.

Victoria Clarke: We all say it is an unconventional war, and we're going to have to have an unconventional approach, which I firmly believe. But nobody is  reinventing the wheel here. I went back and looked at [former Pentagon spokesman] Pete Williams's first meeting with the bureau chiefs in 1991. It was the start of the Persian Gulf war, and he spent the first five minutes saying, "The first thing I want to do is talk about how different this war is, and it's unlike anything we've ever been through before." So I guess we all say it and we believe it. I know there is one important piece that everybody cares deeply about, which is the special operations activity, which will be a challenge for quite some time. There are different kinds of special operations activity: some highly secret—we don't even acknowledge [that] the people or the resources exist; some that are much more open. And what we're looking hard at is, How can we provide access to some of that activity? How can we provide access to some of those people?

I actually think things have been going well. I know some people in this room violently disagree with me, but I think most of it is going pretty well. I think the particular challenges center mostly around the special ops activity.

Chuck Lewis (Hearst News): I've been involved in this dialogue for almost twenty years, and I want to start out by emphasizing some of the positive parts

of the dialogue that we've been having. Secretary Clarke has certainly been an open, available spokesman for the department, and we appreciate her accessibility and the fact that we do have these ongoing meetings with her and her colleagues at the Pentagon. It means that small problems don't become big problems, hopefully, and if there are big problems, we get to talk about them. We have a big problem other than special ops, and that is access to American ground units in Central Asia. And in my mind, that is more of a problem than the special ops issue is for the simple reason that I don't know that anybody is stopping us from going into Afghanistan and trying to cover a special operations operation when it is underway.

The question of ground troops, for example, in Uzbekistan, reluctantly confirmed by the Pentagon. Now that it is out there in the open, we are not allowed to have access to the 10th Mountain units in Uzbekistan. The old story of host-country sensitivities is paraded. That is an old story for those of us who went through Desert Storm, because the Saudi royal family was so touchy, allegedly, about our presence that at one point American press in Saudi Arabia were urged not to cover Christian religious services underway for American GIs in Saudi Arabia. I think we eventually got around that ban, but that kind of represents the high point of host-country sensitivities in my experience.

We're seeing that same rationale used to keep us from American units in Uzbekistan, and I would put that at the top of the list of unsolved issues, ahead of the special operations issue. Is it a secret that American troops are in Uzbekistan? Of course it's not. Why can't we go ahead and gain access to these units?

Now I'd like to just point out one other problem, the problem of the relationship between what we decide with Secretary Clarke and her colleagues, on the one hand, and how it is translated into the field. This is a serious problem from Desert Storm, where the assistant secretary for public affairs invariably would help give a friendly hearing to our problems, would promise that steps would be taken to rectify whatever was going on in Desert Storm, and invariably nothing ever got done because Central Command ran the show.

Clarke: I'm going to ask Admiral Quigley to jump in on this, but let me just say a couple of things. At a recent bureau chiefs meeting . . . we were talking about the 10th Mountain, and bureau chiefs said, Well, if you can't get us physically to them, could we at least do interviews with some of them over the phone, and we did that.

You talked about the old saw about host-nation sensitivities. Maybe it is old, but it's new to me, and I just got back from Uzbekistan, Tajikistan, India, Pakistan, and Russia, and Italy, and it is a sensitivity. I'm not going to name particular countries or particular people, but on their own, unilaterally, it was raised to us again and again—we want to do whatever we can, as much as we can in the war on terrorism. You just need to understand how sensitive this is for us. We're trying to work through it, we're continuing to push on different people in different countries, but it's there, it's real, and as you all have heard the secretary say many times, he understands how difficult participation can be for countries. We are very welcome and appreciative of the support we can get. We want to leave it up to them to characterize what they're doing. There is not an inclination to cram too much else down their throats, to be perfectly honest.

Admiral Craig R. Quigley: I think of it as a math equation analogy. You have two variables. You have a variable of operational security, and you have a variable of host-nation sensitivity. And to solve your equation, you must have both variables solved. . . . So if we do not have an operational security issue, but the host nation has its own—for its own internal political reasons [it] does not feel that it can support access—you have not solved your equation. Or if the opposite is true—if a host nation says, Sure, no problem, but we feel that the operational security . . . obstacle cannot be overcome—you still haven't solved the equation.

On the one hand, you have the example of the British or the Australians who, [through] their prime ministers, have been very open and overt in a public way, saying, This is what we're going to contribute in the form of political support, in the form of military forces, what have you. On the other hand, you have a lot of nations who, for their own reasons, just do not feel they can do that but want to help. And if that's the price of poker, then that's what we'll pay in order to get their cooperation and continue the war on terrorism in their part of the world.

The second issue is the operational security part. I've just been to a lot of the places that have been discussed here this morning so far, and I went with an eye toward seeing how can we do this. That was my motivation when I was accompanying General Franks [commander in chief, U.S. Central Command]. And on a couple of occasions, for the life of me, I can't figure out a way to get there from here. There is no question you could ask, there's no description you could provide in your text that does not run smack-dab into operational security considerations from the first paragraph or the first image, and I don't know how to do it.

James Steinberg: There are lots of different aspects of operational security. There's the aspect of surprise; there's the aspect of technique. Maybe it would be useful just to try to explore what the dimensions are.

Quigley: Sure. Let me give you the easy example. I have a large number of news organizations on board an aircraft carrier, like we [have] today and have had for weeks. It's very overt, the world knows we have aircraft carriers, and if it's [the USS] Enterprise or [the USS] Carl Vinson or something else, the only thing I'm really looking for in the sensitivity area and ground rules there is the exact timing of the reporting from the carrier itself. When I have launched strikes, I don't want to have a radio beeper coming back that says, The strike has just been launched. Pretty obvious, it's just never an issue. I've never run into the news organization yet who is looking to put American forces at risk, so that's easy.

Otto Kreisher (Copley News): I'd like to raise the particularly sensitive issue of casualties. There's been this evolving story on the casualties on the Kandahar  Ranger and special ops mission. It went from nobody got hurt, to bumps and bruises on the parachute drop, to the secretary seeming to say that we had at least five frag wounds, which they now are attributing to guys hurting themselves trying to pop a door. I find it hard to believe that special ops guys, who practice it on a regular basis, hurt themselves with their own door charges. I think the one thing that will get in trouble the fastest is if there is any suspicion that we are hiding casualties counts. I don't think that anybody is going to try to hide somebody who is killed, but if we've got people who are being injured in combat and it is not being told, that's going to raise sensitivity very quickly.

Clarke: I agree completely. We've tried to be very, very straight about everything. We have stood up at the podium and acknowledged errant bombs when nobody asked. When General Myers briefed Saturday morning after the first round of special ops activity, he said, "Two people were hurt. One was a broken leg. The other, I think, was a leg injury that resulted from jumping out of the plane and a hard landing. Those were the most serious injuries." We were very forthcoming with exactly what happened to a pretty extraordinary level of detail. Now clearly, not enough level of detail. And I'm the one—I'll take the rap on this one. We started hearing about this Sy Hersh (of the *New Yorker*) article. A couple of people walked into the office and said, "Sy Hersh says there were twelve casualties in the special ops activity." I said, "Crazy, but I'll ask." I went and asked a few people, and I said, "Other than the two guys we talked about who got hurt jumping out of the plane, was anybody injured?" "No." "Okay." Over the weekend, I was with a couple of people on the plane from Central Command, and I said, "Help me out, why is this persisting?" They make a couple of calls and said, "Some of the guys got some scratches and they got some bumps in the course of it." I don't understand what happens when you blow out a door, but I wouldn't be surprised that you would get some splinters and something else that might flash back at you in some fashion. In their mind, those injuries—they didn't even think of them as injuries— were so inconsequential. Injuries to these guys, from what I know, is it keeps you from working. They were not kept from working—completely inconsequential. So, I think we were pretty forthcoming.

Maria Mann (Agence France Presse): Regarding the embedded pools, it's been our experience and the experience of other wire services that unfortunately the rotations are not really equal. I understand, because of the chaos and everybody wanting to jump on, especially on the carriers, that sometimes the person that screams the loudest is the one that gets on.

Admiral Stephen Pietropaoli: When we initially put nearly forty journalists on two carriers before the start of the strikes, we originally intended for that to be a pool because we weren't sure how many people we could round up in Bahrain on short notice and get them out to the carriers.

It turned out that there was such broad representation already in Bahrain that we had certainly every U.S. network and international wires. And they allowed them to go unilateral, and then they did pools of opportunity—or pools of convenience, really—with the electronic product, TV and still photography, just so that if one was on a Tomahawk shooter, not all cameras had to go there, and they shared that material. Since then it's been unilateral; it has not been pool.

What happened is, predictably, after about a week, you had six TV cameras aimed at the same person loading a bomb, and twelve still shooters, and six pencils. [T]hey all decided that they didn't need to all be there and [that] there were other stories out there to cover, and [they] allowed the wires, Reuters and

AP—not AFP. I don't know whether AFP volunteered or not [but] I know Reuters and AP stepped up and said, we'll be happy to stay out here 24/7 and provide product. We're happy to have AP and Reuters out there. Frankly, I think we'd be happy to have AFP out there 24/7 too.

Kirk Spitzer (USA Today): I know the Rangers are part of the special operations forces, but they're a little bit different; they're a little bit more conventional. Any reason that we could not, in some fashion, cover the Rangers a little more closely than we have been?

Colonel Bill Darley: If I understand the question, Kirk, the question is, Can you embed with the Rangers? The short answer, under current circumstances: No.

Spitzer: Is that a host-nation sensitivity, or is it an OP SEC [operational security] issue?

Darley: It's an OP SEC issue. Let me just bluntly say this: There are two types, really, of Ranger operations. One is what you would call a conventional white operation; then there's black. It has to do with the particular tactics, techniques, and procedures you're using to employ them. At the present time, embedding is out of the question. That's the bottom line.

Stephen Hess: *Torie, one of the things that interests me has been the use, if you will, of the secretary of defense. It strikes me from past wars the secretary of defense has an interview with Jim Lehrer and that sort of thing, but the idea of using him consistently as the briefer strikes me as interesting if not novel.*

Clarke: I think the secretary would object to being "used." And speaking of Jim Lehrer, I don't know if anybody happened to see the *Jim Lehrer NewsHour* last night—we went over there last night for what was to be about a fifteen-to-twenty-minute interview. You have two very intelligent, very experienced people; you've got a cast of thousands back in the control room; and the interview goes to about fifteen. It was really interesting, it was very thoughtful, and the two of them were just having a great time impressing one another. It goes to about twenty minutes, and then it goes to about twenty-five minutes. I think it went on for about forty minutes. So we like Jim Lehrer.

We like to play to our strengths. Secretary Rumsfeld—and I'm totally in the tank for him—is an amazing person who is very, very smart. He also has this incredible inner gyroscope, as I call it. He knows what is the best use of his time at any given time. He understands and appreciates the value of words. Words can have real meaning; words can have real impact. He is very, very sensitive to that. He cares deeply about what we're talking about here in this room. He understands how important it is; he understands his role in it. So he commits the time to it. He commits a lot of time to it. The briefings, by virtue of twenty-four-hour news cycles now and the incredible number of outlets that are covering this war, [are] a relatively easy way to get at what you want to say in pretty quick order. It's actually a remarkably efficient use of his time. So, he understands it's important; he wants to do it. In terms of going forward, I don't know. We'll use him as much as we think is appropriate and as much as he thinks he's adding value to the equation.

Tom DeFrank (New York Daily News): Torie, I've got to say to you, with the utmost affection, I think we're all talking past the core issue here. I think there is a crazy uncle in the basement, and neither side here is willing to deal with that, so let me deal with it. I've been going to these meeting since I was a second lieutenant in your office thirty-three years ago. I don't think the situation has gotten much better. I don't think it's going to get any better. I think the core issue here is insoluble, and it's insoluble, really, from an obvious institutional standpoint. There are two great institutions of our society and government that have totally contradictory objectives and purposes here. Some say that is not the case, but I don't believe that. Basically, it's what I call the genetic wiring of the military, and I say that as somebody who wore a green suit for twenty-two years, and I say that as somebody who, thirty years after he got his military ID, still carries it in his pocket. The military basically doesn't want us around, when you get right down to it. There are days that I say to myself, "I don't blame them one bit."

But I've got a very close friend who is a four-star general. He says it's as simple as this: You get in the way; you get in the way of operational security. And God knows there are valid operational security factors here, and there are lots of reporters in this room who have not printed stuff. I let my paper write something last Friday that was wrong because to correct it would have put an American soldier in harm's way, so we ate that. And I'm glad I did; I'm glad we did. So reporters understand that, and you've recognized that. But basically, I think the military sees the media as a pitfall to be avoided rather than an opportunity to be exploited.

And the other factor is, as my four-star general friend says, if my job is to do my mission and I get somewhat conflicting advice—one [piece] from an assistant secretary of public affairs saying, Let's have as much access as we can, and [another from] a three-star general saying, I don't want those people around here—who do you think I'm going to listen to? The ASDPA [assistant secretary of defense for public affairs] or somebody who writes my next efficiency report? I don't ascribe ill motives to this. I think there's a lot of good faith and a lot of goodwill on both sides here, but I do think there is this fundamental issue, and I don't think it is going to get fixed.

And I would just predict—and I hope I'm wrong—that however long this war lasts, there will be no access to Special Forces, special operations, or Rangers, and if I'm wrong about that, I think it will be extremely sanitized. Maybe that's the way it ought to be. The core issue here is essentially insoluble, and I hope we all keep working on it, and I hope I get proved wrong.

Pietropaoli: I think his insight about military officers, on one level, is exactly right. Most military officers, individually, if you asked them if they thought that an interaction with the press was going to be, in their wildest dreams, good for their career, they'd say, "Not a chance. If I screw up, it's deadly." And that is true, and that is at the back of their mind all the time: that performing perfectly in front of a press conference will get them no great acclaim in their military career and making a faux pas will be potentially damaging to them. That's just the way it is for regular Americans, too, not just military folks.

So that's there, Tom. You're exactly right. And I think at the core, if it comes down to operational security or press access, you're exactly right: military officers will always choose operational security.

That said, I think there has been a significant change in the mindset of most senior officers, and those vary some depending upon their experience. But the navy's experience—from a decade ago when we were very resistant to press on board our carriers in order to retain tactical surprise—the navy came out of Desert Storm with not many people in America actually understanding how much the six carriers contributed to the fight. That produced a sea change in the thinking of the mid-grade officers at the time, who are now the senior officers running the navy. So it has not been difficult for us to convince commanders. There's a morning network television show that is broadcasting live pictures from the bridge of the U.S.S. Enterprise and the flight deck of the U.S.S. Enterprise as she returns to her home port—live from the middle of the Atlantic. You know, a few years ago this couldn't be done. Now the commanding officer of that ship is extremely pleased to have this kind of coverage for his sailors and their families waiting for them to come home.

So while you are right, if it comes down to absolutely an operational security versus press access issue, military people will put the mission first, but they very much think that maintaining public support through the intercession and reporting of the media is essential to the long-term success.

Patrice Jarreau (Le Monde): I have the feeling that the official information you are giving about this war is a very conventional one and that your briefings are very conventional briefings about conventional war—or the conventional part of the war. I mean, what you claim to be unusual and new about this war is not in your briefings.

Clarke: We are very careful in what we talk about publicly. We do not want to paint a picture for the bad guys. So we don't talk very much at all about what we're going to do going forward. And we are also very careful about the kinds of information about what we did, because, again, sometimes giving a lot of information about what you've done can help them connect the dots and make it more difficult for your next operation.

So I'll fully grant you, we are very careful about what we talk about in that briefing room. It's always a balance. Now look, my job is to get out as much news and information as possible because my job is to keep the American people and the public at large and the world engaged and supportive of this effort. The more information I can give them the better. But the balance is doing it without putting peoples' lives at risk, without threatening future operational security.

Postscript

In her meetings with bureau chiefs, reporters, and media scholars, which continued for months, Assistant Secretary Clarke became increasingly sensitized to the journalistic complaint about lack of access and to the need to do something about it. But, during the war in Afghanistan, she couldn't do much about it. When Iraq loomed on the near horizon, she persuaded Secretary of Defense Rumsfeld to embark on a new, risky strategy of press management: not only to provide access, which reporters felt they were being deliberately denied, but also to embed hundreds of American and foreign reporters with U.S. military units. The reporters would be able to cover the war, with only two conditions—never to jeopardize the troops or the mission. The strategy worked. The Pentagon was happy, the press was satisfied, and the American people got coverage that was more up-close, personal, and immediate than they had ever gotten. If Clarke and Rumsfeld had not taken the risk, the embedding of journalists never would have been attempted.

For many years after Vietnam, the tension between the press and the Pentagon was oppressive, stifling debate between the two institutions. To the degree that the tension rotated around the denial of access, the problem seemed "insoluble," as DeFrank of the *New York Daily News* said. But by embedding the reporters, Rumsfeld not only provided access, he also provided total immersion, thereby doing much to change the relationship between the press corps and the officials in the five-sided building across the Potomac.

7

Three Months Later

I t was time for another check on relations between the Pentagon and the press. On November 8, 2001, the assistant secretary of defense for public affairs, Victoria Clarke, and a group of her aides had met with Washington news bureau chiefs to discuss ways of improving coverage of the war against terrorism, focusing at the time on Afghanistan. Now it was January 9, 2002, two months later. On this occasion she met with three veteran journalists who offered rich and relevant assessments of the Pentagon's wartime "management" of the media, a concept Clarke repeatedly rejected as an accurate description of her daily chores. This troika of press supporters included

—**Michael Getler**, ombudsman for the *Washington Post* and a former editor of the *International Herald-Tribune*

—**Bernard Kalb**, a former media critic for CNN's *Reliable Sources* who served briefly as State Department spokesman after a long career covering international affairs for NBC, CBS, and the *New York Times*

—**Sanford J. Ungar**, president of Goucher College and former director of the Voice of America who had been a journalist for National Public Radio and the *Washington Post*.

Hess opened the discussion by noting that only three months had passed since the United States first began bombing Afghanistan. Then the media were totally absorbed with the war. But in time other issues, such as the election of a new mayor in New York, had begun to crowd the front page of many newspapers, and the *New York Times* dropped its special section called "A Nation Challenged." Had the war in Afghanistan gone so well that it lost its fascination for American journalism? Had the media gone beyond their budget for this war? Was it time for a review of press performance?

Looking back, Clarke gave high marks to media coverage of the war in Afghanistan, praising the courage, imagination, and resourcefulness of many reporters. "Good, fair, and balanced" was the way she judged the coverage. She drew special attention to the fact that the Pentagon had allowed reporters to embed with Special Forces, which two months earlier had been the principal demand of the Washington bureau chiefs and which had been flatly denied. Access, she seemed to be saying, had been provided.

Clarke's interlocutors pocketed her concession but still expressed unhappiness about the degree of access, wanting more. They also complained that Defense Secretary Rumsfeld, who assumed the responsibility of conducting almost daily briefings at the Pentagon, had imposed an odd kind of stranglehold on the normal flow of information from other officials, placing reporters in the awkward position of having to depend solely on him. Clarke candidly acknowledged that this was Rumsfeld's intention, his way of cutting back on leaks, and for a time, clearly, the strategy worked.

Getler deplored both the intention and the strategy. Not pejoratively but descriptively, Bernard Kalb considered it a form of media management, normal for any large government bureaucracy but particularly appropriate for the Pentagon in a state of war. Nevertheless, Clarke found that concept offensive, and she linked it to one of her predecessors, Arthur Sylvester, who once delivered a speech defending the government's right to lie under certain circumstances. Strongly disagreeing with Sylvester, she stated, "I think it is absolutely inappropriate for anyone, particularly in the U.S. government, particularly anyone in my position, to ever lie or even come close to it." No one could argue with a spokesperson's dedication to telling the truth.

Stephen Hess: *This is January 9. The first bomb dropped in Afghanistan on October 7, almost exactly three months ago. The months have passed fast; events have passed fast. On the last day of the year you might have noticed that the* New York Times *said it was ending its stand-alone section called "A Nation Challenged," a moment that should have told us something. Then if you turned to the* New York Times *three days later, January 3, and looked at the front page, you would have noticed that the lead story was about the euro; the second lead was about the new mayor of New York; there were other stories that dealt with electrical deregulation in Texas, a murder in Norway, and a piece of legislation that Senator Daschle had something to do with. That was the first day since October 7 when there were no datelines from Afghanistan, India, Pakistan, or the Middle East. So this is a good time to have our initial assessment of the government's role in information and journalism in covering this war.*

Bernard Kalb: Three months into the process, how has the Pentagon done in telling its story?

Victoria Clarke: I think we've done very well. As we said more than three months ago, this is a very unconventional war. We're going against people who don't have armies and navies and air forces. We're going against people who hide in caves and tunnel complexes. So the military aspect of the war would also be very unconventional, as it has been.

There have been some aspects of it you can see, some aspects of it that you can't see; but we said we would make our best effort. Those things that could be appropriately covered, we would make our best effort to facilitate that coverage. And if you look at what has gone on since right before October 7 and right up until yesterday, the amount of coverage and the diversity of coverage has been pretty extraordinary. From carriers to bombers to being embedded with troops, to the highly unusual and highly rare instance of embedding media with Special Forces.

Special Forces are playing a part in this war, as everyone knows, unlike they have ever played before. Very unique nature, very unique things that they do. Secrecy is a very big piece of it. But the media—and several of us made the case—it's an important part of this war, we should try to facilitate coverage.

If you took a look at *Newsweek* this week, there is one story by Donatella Lorch, who was also embedded with one of the special forces teams. Several AP stories that have run as a result of an AP reporter, the widest reach possible, embedded with a special forces team. [Other stories ran on] the front page of the *New York Times*, the front page of *USA Today*, this week. Highly unusual, but media were embedded with special forces teams to cover that aspect of the war. People who have covered wars far longer than I have and been in this business far longer than I have said this is an extraordinary accomplishment. So obviously a subjective answer, and I have a bias, but I think the coverage has been pretty good.

If you want to look at some of the benchmarks along the way, prior to any U.S. boot being on the ground in Afghanistan, there [were] literally dozens and dozens of reporters embedded on carriers, interviewing bomber pilots, those sorts of things. And any of the conventional aspects of the war that could be covered, we facilitated that.

The very first time any significant number, more than a dozen, of conventional forces were on the ground in Afghanistan—it was the marines outside Kandahar, the place that [came to be] called Forward Operating Base Rhino— the media were with them in the very first wave. The media went in with the commandos.

Hess: *Torie, would you say a few words about how well you think the press did? What are the strong points and weak points?*

Clarke: In general, I think the press has done an extraordinarily good job of covering a very difficult, very unconventional war. I try not to generalize too much about the media. The Pentagon press corps in particular [who] tend to be people who really understand the issues, really understand what goes on with the military, have done the best job. And they've been most sensitive to the special concerns and considerations.

We have had challenges. We've had some problems, most specifically with what I call the newcomers—people who just came flooding into the building because it happened to be the hottest story for several weeks. But in general I think the media has done a very good job.

What I found interesting is nothing stopped reporters from going into Afghanistan. As a matter of fact, the most intrepid and the most entrepreneurial and the ones who were most committed to getting the story did exactly that. For quite some time, there were more media on the ground in Afghanistan than there were U.S. forces. I'll give you one specific example there.

Dan Rather himself and his people for about two weeks straight were calling day in, day out, calling me, calling several other people, saying, We want to go here, we want to go there; and we gave them the same answer we were giving everyone else, which [was], "We only have a handful of people on the ground, it's not appropriate at this time, we're not going to do it." God bless Dan Rather, he gave up on us and got himself into Kabul, and they rented a little space right there in town, and he started reporting from Kabul. So I actually have been impressed. One, the overall coverage, I think, has been quite good and quite fair and quite balanced. They take shots at us when we deserve it. Then I think there have been some in particular that have been extraordinarily intrepid in how they've gone about covering it.

Michael Getler: I think what Torie said about the reporters there is correct. Reporters in country, in Afghanistan and in the border areas of Pakistan, have  done a remarkable job, [an] extremely courageous job. They're not all Dan Rather. They don't operate with TV networks and with large support systems. Most of them are individuals who are extremely vulnerable, who have no protection, who have no support networks, who are loaded down with batteries and generators—and loaded down with cash in a very dangerous situation where they're sort of virtually walking ATM machines, very vulnerable to robbery, extortion, or worse. So the reporters who have gone in there on their own in a total no-man's land, I think we all are in their debt for excellent, excellent reporting. Very different from any other situation we've had.

A large [issue] is [that] we don't know what we don't know. We really don't know. This is a very, very closely held war in terms of information and secrecy. There are obviously some reasons that make that legitimate. My concern as an observer is that it goes well beyond that. I think what we're seeing now is a situation where the United States has been attacked; the public wants the enemy defeated, as they should be; and they really are not concerned about press concerns or access concerns or secrecy concerns. They want the job done, and you can't blame them. I think aside from a couple of hundred reporters and editors and press junkies, there's very little concern about the kinds of things that Ms. Clarke gets criticized for—not personally, but that the Pentagon and the administration get criticized for. I don't think there's any real constituency out there that cares much about the press's complaints in this area, and I think that's a problem.

My feeling is that now the Defense Department and the White House can basically do whatever they want to do. There is no penalty. There's no real cost to pay with the public as far as the imposition of any kind of secrecy, whatever level of secrecy, whatever kind of restriction they wish to impose. There's no embarrassment factor, either. I think this is an ongoing battle. My own view is that . . . the whole sequence from almost the Falkland Islands to Grenada to Panama to the Gulf to now is a further and further distancing between what American forces do on a battlefield and what the press is able to see.

B. Kalb: To what degree does the fact that the United States is winning the war shape a positive assessment of both the Pentagon and the press?

Sanford J. Ungar: I think it does. I think the coverage since October 7 has to be compared to two things. First, [compared with] the last major conflict within

our [more recent] memory, the Gulf war, the access is so much greater this time. As Mike says, there's probably a lot we don't know, but I think that in general the public is much more honestly familiar with what's happening now than it was during the Gulf war.

The other thing—some very, very unfortunate remarks made by people in the administration, the White House press secretary saying, "You have to be careful what you say," and then demonstrating how careful you have to be with what you say, erasing that from the transcript of his own briefing the next day so that nobody could document that he had said "You have to be careful what you say." And some very unfortunate and again perhaps understandable moments. There is an element of reporting on the home football team, the hometown fans and hometown football team headed for the Super Bowl, and that's perhaps understandable. You don't want—nobody, I think, wants—to splash cold water on this sort of mood.

Torie and other people have been very careful to say [that] this is going to be a very long war; it's going to be very complicated. The secretary of defense certainly has said this over and over again, but I don't think the American people really believe it. I think we are accustomed to short-term results and answers in this era, and I think we ask—even while saying, Yes, yes, yes, we understand it's going to be a long war: Have we won? Is it over yet? There's the sense that we haven't won completely but it's going rather well so we can relax, and the *New York Times* can go back to reporting other things, and life will resume, and there will be this unfortunate episode that lasted perhaps six months or so.

Getler: I would offer a correction of one point that Sandy made. The access now, in my opinion, is much less than in the Gulf war. During the Gulf war there were reporters with every major unit. They didn't take reporters on B-52s, but there were reporters with all the major army and marine corps units. The problem in the Gulf was that you couldn't file. The military took control of the dispatches, and they sent them when they got ready to send them, when the war was over for most of them.

When people wanted access was two months ago. Everybody understands that you can't take twenty-five reporters on a commando raid. But I would argue that early on there could have been an effort to put a small [group]—one or two reporters—embedded with a special forces headquarters unit. [N]obody [has] ever been on the [aircraft carrier USS] Kitty Hawk where they operate from. There [was] nobody really early on with the 10th Mountain Division. And you need to stay with troops to get to understand and know what they do and what their life is like and what's going on. You can be told, Look, we'll let you see this, [but] you can't report it until Thursday or next week because it's an ongoing operation. Meanwhile, nobody has seen it.

Clarke: I think both of my friends here greatly underestimate and undervalue the American people. They confront us, they challenge us, they question us every single day. There have been instances where they said, We want more information. Why aren't you telling us more about why this JDAM [a bomb that uses a global positioning system for increased accuracy] went awry? Why aren't you telling us more about the special forces guy who was killed? Why aren't you giving us those sorts of information?

They equally take us to task when they think we've been giving out too much information. I don't see polls and research the way I used to in my private sector life, but there is poll after poll evidently in which the American people say [that] we're giving out too much information.

In October the media said, We want to see what's going on with the special forces. In the first raid—it was a covert raid in the middle of the night in Afghanistan—we brought back footage, combat camera footage from that raid, and we showed it on live national television the next morning. Many, many Americans took us to task and said, You're giving out too much information. I think you greatly undervalue and estimate their thoughts, their interests, their understanding. I for one don't think they have a short attention span, particularly on this conflict. Their level of understanding of how difficult it is going to be, how unusual it is, is pretty extraordinary. That's one thing.

Two, on many more occasions, we have stood at that podium before we have been asked and we have acknowledged bombs that have gone awry. When we have solid information about civilian casualties, we talk about it and we explain what happened. We had a B-1 that went down into the water off India, off Diego Garcia [a small island in the Indian Ocean that houses a British air force base]. And before they were even back on board the ship that was involved in the rescue, we were briefing it from the podium. So time after time we've gone out there.

Something else you hear, particularly from Michael Getler, is [that] people have a frame of reference and it tends to be whatever happened last time. They do not look at reality and understand how incredibly different this conflict is and view it in that sense. They keep saying, Boy, in the Persian Gulf war, in Kosovo, in Vietnam. This is none of those conflicts. It's very different. And we constantly challenge ourselves, and the bureau chiefs and the people who come to my bureau chiefs meetings know this. They hear me say repeatedly, It's very different; it's very unconventional. In terms of how the media and the military work together, we too need to think unconventionally.

B. Kalb: Tell us a little about the management of the news conference, because in fact that seems to be the way that most people are getting most of their news about this war. What decisions you've made there and so forth.

Clarke: It's very little management, quite honestly. It's dealing with reality. If you have a team of eight or ten special forces doing an extraordinarily dangerous operation in the middle of the night, it's a bit much to expect them to stop and do a briefing. That is very different than the Persian Gulf war, in which you had thousands and thousands and thousands of people on the ground and you [had] operating bases that were there for months and months. It's a completely different situation. So we do what we think is appropriate at any given time.

You'll hear me say it a hundred times, it's a very unconventional war. It is not just about the military operations, it's also about what goes on economically, politically, financially, those sorts of things, and I for one believe that the American people need and deserve to hear from their leaders what is it you're trying to accomplish, how . . . you plan to go about doing that. That's one of the reasons you see Secretary Rumsfeld out there, in addition to the fact that he's one of the most effective spokesmen of the effort. So we deal with the circumstances as they come along, but for anybody to think that [we're] going to do the same thing that happened in the Persian Gulf war is just ludicrous.

I'd make one more point. There are any number of . . . people who can and will give background briefings to reporters. And the amount of leakage and the amount of inappropriate backgrounding and leaking of classified information and information that should never have gone out has dropped considerably. That is because Secretary Rumsfeld has made it a personal campaign [to] reduce the amount of leaking of classified information by people in government and [to] reduce the amount of inappropriate backgrounding of classified information. So you have a fair number of people, not a lot, but you have a fair number of people who are going through a bit of a culture shock. There is not quite the flood of information that there has been in the past, and I will fully tell you that I believe a lot of that information was inappropriate.

B. Kalb: I want to talk about the adversarial relationship between the media and the Pentagon, and inevitably I've got to go back to the Vietnam War. The  Vietnam War drove that credibility gap wide open. And you come to that question about the residual resonance of the relationship between the media and the military. In Vietnam the arithmetic done after the war was that many in the military felt that the media had stabbed them in the back and was responsible for the collapse of the U.S. position. It seems to me that we cannot let that go in defining the nature of the relationship today. You resisted the word "managed," but management of the media from your point of view would be an ideal world, wouldn't it?

Clarke: No, not at all. Not at all. And again, I won't generalize to the extent you will about the relationship between the media and the military. There is as much diversity in those two constituencies as you have in this room, so I won't generalize. There are some who I'm sure carry with them from Vietnam and other places hard feelings on both sides. But what I've found is that you talk about the core constituency, so, for instance, the Pentagon press corps or . . . the people who are running this war from the military's perspective, they're making extraordinary efforts to work on this relationship.

At the end of the day, I think it's a very healthy tension. I think it exists for a reason. The preamble of the Constitution calls for a common defense. The First Amendment, freedom for Michael's colleagues. I think that's a very good thing. If we agreed on everything it would not be a healthy world, and we'd probably be living in [a place like] the Soviet Union. I think it's very appropriate that there is this healthy tension.

And as I said before, we actually have some pretty common objectives. It is in my interest for the American people to get as much appropriate news and information about this war as possible. If we keep them informed, if we keep them educated, they will stay with us. They won't leave us if bad things happen or more people get killed. They will leave us if we're not completely straight with them. And that's one of the other things we hear from them, they appreciate that we're very straight with them.

The news media, it's your business. It's your obligation to get out as much news and information as possible. So we have common objectives. There is a healthy tension. What's the level, what's the appropriate information? There are probably mistakes and variations on each side, but I happen to think it's a very healthy tension.

Hess: *If we go back to October and think about what we were being told by analysts, columnists, editorial writers, and so forth, let's sort of tick it off: "Quagmire" was the favorite word. "Just look at the Soviet Union, how they were trapped in Afghanistan. Is this going to happen to us?" " Air power. Look at the geography of this. How can this possibly work?" "The Arab street, this is going to be a revolution that we're creating." On and on and on. It strikes me that the people who were opinionating through the media were incredibly wrong. Partly [because] when you get right down to it, and now some of them admit it: "Hey, I've never been to Afghanistan."*

Ungar: The area was so little known, and not just by the American public but by the American media, and when you look back and think about the regime that was in power in Afghanistan, in part in power because of American weapons that were fed to people to fight the Soviet-sponsored regime in Afghanistan, it is a shocking thing.

The organization that I used to lead, the Voice of America, was one of the few media institutions that was doing any reporting about what was happening in Afghanistan. The Taliban was a uniquely horrifying regime in many respects, and we knew very little about it. Very little done, unlike now, about what was happening to women in Afghanistan, which was extraordinary and almost unequaled on the face of the earth in the last couple of decades. I think that it is therefore understandable . . . how little was understood about the country and the region.

Getler: I disagree with you, Sandy. We didn't understand anything about Vietnam either. There was understanding of Afghanistan in different places. There was a whole group of reporters. I spent time on the Afghan-Pakistan border as a foreign editor in '87. There were a whole bunch of people who had covered the mujahadin and the war against the Soviets in the '80s. And the *Post* defense correspondent grew up in Afghanistan, Tom Ricks. There were one or two other reporters there that spent a lot of time there.

But the most important thing is I want to separate what you're saying. There clearly were people—analysts, thumb suckers, editorial writers—who would, I'm sure, like to have some of their columns back or some of their talking head performances back about now, but that's not a press issue. That's not the kind of issue that I think about and that reporters think about. That's opinion, analysis, sound bites on television. What my concern is and what news editors' concerns are and reporters' concerns are [is] news reporting, access to news. Not whether somebody calls this a quagmire on the editorial page or something else. That is true. It's conveyed in newspapers and on all twenty-four-hour-a-day cable channels. That is not news. That's thumb sucking. There's a difference.

B. Kalb: But let me interrupt, Mike. It colors the perception of what the media is reporting. Right or wrong, a pundit on television must never be hesitant. We have seen a great deal of that, as Steve is suggesting, in the profile of the ludicrous estimates at the very outset. So . . . while you may draw a distinction between opinion and news columns, the fact is [that] so much of opinion, particularly television opinion, has a way of shaping the perception of what . . . the media is saying, and that is inevitable.

Getler: But that's not what the press is important for. The press is important for establishing an independent historical record of what the United States did here, here, there, and there. What our forces did. And that is what is absolutely central to this argument.

B. Kalb: No argument there. But let's pick up the point about whether or not the press was indeed helping the American public understand the issues at work in Afghanistan prior to September 11. You talked about people who indeed were raised in Afghanistan, who wrote about Afghanistan and so forth.

But after the Soviet Union collapsed, the end of the cold war, the anxiety at the end, this country—the press in this country—went into some sort of sand pit in terms of foreign coverage.

Suddenly we are [now] reinvited to join the world against our will. Columnist Charles Krauthammer had a lovely phrase, "The United States has been on a holiday from history." So the question is, the responsibility of the media. Yes, the public during the '90s may have been disinterested in foreign news, but if you do the arithmetic on coverage [scandal got this, domestic got that, and foreign news was a distant third]. That seems to me to be an accurate, emerging portrait of what the media collectively was in the '90s.

Ungar: And further, Bernie, I think it has to be said that the sort of excuse that's very often given by the media—that the public is not interested—is frequently a self-fulfilling prophecy. The lack of coverage creates a disinterest because how is the public to express its interest? How is the public to demand greater coverage of South Asia? It's not going to happen.

B. Kalb: At CBS, Dick Salant [former president of the news division] used to say, We give them what they need to know or what they want to know, and you have to strike a balance between the two. But the need to know is critical, and to a large degree the media abandoned that in the '90s.

Getler: I think the danger here, Bernie, is talking about "the media." The point is the *New York Times*, the *Washington Post*, the *Wall Street Journal*, the *Los Angeles Times*, a bunch of other newspapers did not stop covering the world. There are just as many foreign correspondents on those newspapers now as there were then, and so the material was there. It dropped off in a lot of other parts of the media. American television totally abdicated, with the exception of CNN.

Hess: *Torie, you've got to sort out who you want to give your exclusives to, who you want to give your interviews to, and so forth. You want to be on the* Today Show *first?*

Clarke: Again, it depends on the circumstances. It depends on what's going on in the war, what we think is important to communicate. It's a situation in which more than size matters. We believe we have a responsibility to reach beyond just the American people in terms of communicating. We think international audiences are important. So, for instance, we make a special case for AFP and Reuters, much to the dismay of some of the domestic news organizations. I think if you had to put one watchword to it, it's diversity.

Getler: Good management.

Clarke: No. Other people can decide what management means. In this town that tends to have an evil connotation. But we make judgments every single day. What is the best way to get out as much news and information about the various aspects of this war? You'll go to different news organizations.

B. Kalb: Who are your favorite Pentagon journalists, and I don't mean to destroy their careers if you mention their names?

Clarke: For me to say anything complimentary about an individual will cause the person undue harm so I won't do it. I'll say something bad about a few, and they'll get a pay raise. I will talk about the Pentagon press corps as a group. I have never found a group as dedicated, as committed to their jobs. These people, in general, come in at 5:00 or 6:00 in the morning. I will say this, . . . Here's where my bias comes in terms of deciding where . . . we grant interviews and those sorts of things. If I have a bias, it is towards long-term Pentagon correspondents and organizations—people and organizations that made a commitment to the [Pentagon] and to covering [the] U.S. military well before September 11.

Hess: *Torie, remind us, in 1992 after the Gulf war, the Pentagon got together with the major bureaus, and they worked out a set of protocols on how the next war would be covered. What's happened to that?*

Clarke: Well, the operative phrase [is], "nearly a decade ago." It's just one of the many conversations we've had with bureau chiefs. Many of the people who I know spent extraordinary amounts of time and hard work on those principles nearly a decade ago, felt very committed to them. We felt very committed, we are very committed to the general press principles and essence of them. We suggested, queried, challenged people: "Gosh, more than a decade's gone by; maybe we should take a look at these." There was no inclination on the part of any bureau chief that I can remember to change anything. We said, Okay, we'll endorse them. The secretary himself met with the bureau chiefs and endorsed those principles.

More importantly, we meet just about every two weeks with the bureau chiefs as a group. I talk to individuals regularly. I talk to the network bureau chiefs on a regular basis as a group. So for us it's more of a living organism, if you will, and we're constantly working on it.

B. Kalb: This session cannot end with some discussion about the role of the secretary of defense himself. The new cover boy.

Clarke: What you see is what you get. He answers questions as directly and forthrightly and openly as he can. If you've ever read Rumsfeld Rules [a published list of "rules" that Rumsfeld has accumulated over time], one of them that he's had for a long time [is], "I know and I can tell you, I know and I can't tell you, or I don't know and I can't tell you." He just says, "I just tell them what I know and what I think I can tell." One of the reasons you often see him pause and think about what he's going to say [—] you think about the reams of information that come into him every single day, on paper, in person, on secure calls, in meetings—[is that] some of it is highly classified, some of it is classified, some of it isn't. He is mentally going through what's appropriate here to reveal and what's not. Again, those who know him very well will say, If you understand him and you watch him closely, he puts out an awful lot of information.

May I ask a question? I'll tell a little story to ask the question of Michael Getler, who has written a column about this. When I was trying to get ready for this job months ago, I was doing tons of reading and talking to every live predecessor I could find, reading all of those transcripts of the commissions, the media, and the military. People would say to me, "Whatever you do, look up what happened to Arthur Sylvester," who was one of my predecessors.

So I go to look up what Arthur Sylvester had done, and I haven't seen the speech myself but according to all the reporting he gave a speech in New York in which he said he thinks it's okay for the government to lie. And if you go back to the transcripts of the confirmation hearings of every one of my predecessors, every time there was a senator on the Armed Services Committee who'd ask, What do you think about that, and do you think it's appropriate for someone in your position to lie? You'd say absolutely not. And I think it is absolutely inappropriate for anyone, particularly anyone in the U.S. government, particularly anyone in my position, to ever lie or even come close to it.

Michael did write a piece once in which he took the Pentagon to task for not doing what he thought was a good enough job, and he said he thought it was unfortunate that the journalists don't have the kind of advocate in the Pentagon like Arthur Sylvester. So I would ask you, Do you want someone in the Pentagon who will lie?

Getler: No, of course not. Of course not. I think the point was, Torie, which you well know, the point was that in the military-press relationship, there's built-in tensions as you said, absolutely, sure. But [they] can come together so that reporters can have more access and do their job in a democracy in an area where sometimes they need the military to let them see things or even to protect them. So my point was that one way this will happen is if there are strong advocates within administrations who will fight for that access. That wasn't really meant as an attack on you.

Clarke: Since the hallmark of Arthur Sylvester's career was saying [that] it's appropriate for U.S. government officials to lie, I would suggest . . .

Getler: There were four or five people mentioned.

Clarke: . . . you should be careful not to generalize about groups of people.

Getler: First of all, he lied about the Cuban missile crisis. Secondly, there was Tom Ross and several other assistant secretaries of defense who all came out of a strong journalistic background who were in that column. That was the point.

B. Kalb: Let me just pick up that point, if I may, because in a personal way I had that experience at the State Department when I had about eighteen months or so as an assistant secretary of state and spokesman and was in the State Department because of the experience you're suggesting, Michael. It is possible to push the doors open as wide as you can. You keep pushing. They might not open as wide as you'd like. On the very simple theory that the press is out there to convey the point of view of the State Department to the American public, because without U.S. public support, policy is foredoomed to failure. By the same token, as you fight for greater opening with the State Department, there may be a time when it comes to resign, which is what I did at a certain point on the question of disinformation as reported in your newspaper and the *Washington Post*.

Question (from the audience): *I'm John Martin with ABC News. There's no Ernie Pyle in this war. Many of you may not know who Ernie Pyle was, but he was probably the most beloved correspondent of the Second World War because he spent weeks at a time living with the troops, writing about the troops, using their real names and their real home towns, and it brought the war to people here—what the sacrifices were and what everyone was going through. I wondered, if Ernie Pyle were alive today, could he report from Afghanistan? Could he live with the troops?*

Clarke: Sure. The short answer is sure. The long answer is it depends on the circumstances and . . . where. Steve Vogel of the *Washington Post* lived on a carrier for weeks, and day in, day out there was incredible reporting, putting faces and names, not always what the home town was, but putting faces and names and a life to these men and women who serve day in and day out. I think we have the Ernie Pyles of the twenty-first century, and I put Steve Vogel right up there, who gave an extraordinarily real image of what these people are going through.

Getler: The question is, Could they do it on the ground where it is so dangerous? Not very many journalists want to do this.

Clarke: They are doing it on the ground. A fellow from a news organization I will not name came into my office yesterday to thank me because he had spent two or three weeks with the marines near Kandahar. Two or three weeks sleeping on the ground with the bugs, the cold, everything else, and he said it was extraordinary. And to the extent [that] you can facilitate more of this, do it. So six or seven months, I don't know. But weeks yes, and it is going on. And to that point, the more we can show people what the men and women in uniform are like and what they are doing and the conditions under which they operate, the better off we are, and we are doing this to the greatest extent because they are incredible people.

A few weeks ago, when we flew with the secretary into Afghanistan and we took thirteen, fourteen media with us, it was only four or five hours [but] the impact on all of us, and the impact on the media—they've told me this themselves—was extraordinary. These people are so dedicated, they are so committed, they are so responsible. This was just a week or so before the holidays. I'd be talking to them around the edges, and I'd say, "What's it like? You're going to be here over the holidays, are you sad about that, are you missing your family?" And to a person, . . . to a person they would say, "This is my family, this is where I should be," and this is so important. It's just incredible.

Ungar: Unfortunately I think, though, the Ernie Pyles of this era would not have the audience that Ernie Pyle had in the Second World War because of the great multiplication of sources, of information that people have. They're just not going to depend on a newspaper column for that kind of insight.

Question (from the audience): *Bill Hammond, the Army Center of Military History. I've seen references to the enormous expense of covering this war. I looked at the Vietnam War and saw the average age of reporters declines by almost ten years from the beginning of the war to the end because [younger reporters] were cheaper. Are we going to evolve into a kind of cut-rate coverage?*

Ungar: We're all haunted by Vietnam. I think in some ways there are probably still people in the Pentagon who believe that the press lost the war for the United States, and they're going to avoid those mistakes again, still, even if they don't fully understand them. But I think the ability of the media—and again it's using too broad a term, I suppose—to stay with it is a really important question. Who's going to go, this rotation issue, will there be a large enough group of people who really understand what needs to be done? I think that is a very important long-term issue.

B. Kalb: Bill Hammond wrote possibly the definitive book on the relations between the media and the military, financed by the army, and Bill's ultimate conclusion was, on Vietnam, the media got it right.

Getler: I would agree with that. I think 58,000 dead GIs is what lost the Vietnam War and not the press. But I don't think there's going to be cut-rate coverage. I think the major news organizations will do what they have to [to] finance this coverage. Hopefully they take their role seriously. If you do, this is an investment in what you do. This is an investment in how people perceive your newspaper or your television network and how they count on it in a crunch. I think people are seriously committed as publishers and owners; they're not going to pull back on it.

PART THREE

The Journalist's Dilemma

Three Stories

8

The Hart-Rudman Commission Report

On January 31, 2001, an eye-opening report described as "the first comprehensive rethinking of national security since 1947" was released, warning that foreign terrorists would attack and kill many Americans—in the United States—and soon. However, there was nothing eye-opening about the coverage of the warning. Most Americans never heard of the report until after the 9/11 attacks. The media were asleep. How come?

The U.S. Commission on National Security/21st Century, which produced the report, was co-chaired by two former senators, a Republican from New Hampshire, Warren Rudman, and a Democrat from Colorado, Gary Hart. On February 6, 2002, a little more than a year later, **Senator Warren B. Rudman** was joined by three journalists for a panel discussion aimed at explaining how the American media, arguably the best in the world, could have blown the story. The three journalists were

—**Thomas Kunkel**, a former reporter who had recently become dean of the college of journalism at the University of Maryland

—**Susan Page**, White House correspondent and Washington bureau chief for *USA Today*

—**Bob Schieffer**, an anchor and chief Washington correspondent for CBS News.

Rudman stressed that the commission had hired a public relations firm to ensure widespread coverage, visited news bureaus in New York and Washington, briefed key senators and representatives, and finally unveiled its results at a highly publicized news conference on Capitol Hill. And yet, except for a smattering of coverage here and there, the story was largely ignored. Most bitter for Rudman was the decision of the *New York Times*, the most respected newspaper in the country, to publish not one word about the report.

Both Page and Schieffer expressed regret that their news organizations had essentially ignored the story too. Page ascribed it to a small staff, timing, and the commission's failure to mobilize the White House. Schieffer added another dimension—that "terrorism was not on anybody's front burner in those days." He said that terrorism, like arms control in earlier years, was not a subject designed to attract attention until it was too late.

Most important to Kunkel was that networks and newspapers had reduced their budgets for foreign coverage, leaving the American people "ill-informed" about terrorist threats from abroad. "There's no excuse," Kunkel declared. Schieffer agreed. "Incredible financial pressures on all the networks," he said, had caused "the scale-back in overseas coverage."

Page concluded on this sobering note: "It's probably unrealistic to think," she said, that the "huge" increase in media spending on news coverage of terrorism after 9/11 is "going to go on forever, because newspapers that pay no attention to the bottom line are no longer published."

Stephen Hess: *One year ago this week the final report of the United States Commission on National Security was released, a report that has become quite famous in retrospect. One of its recommendations was that the government create a National Homeland Security Agency. Look at that evening's news on ABC, CBS, NBC, CNN,* Nightline, *or the next morning's* New York Times—*there wasn't anything there.*

Marvin Kalb: *Senator Rudman, you had what you considered to be a big story in the report, had it ready for the press on January 31 last year. In anticipation of the actual release, what did you do to sell it to the press, to alert them to the fact that this was something special?*

Warren Rudman: Knowing that this was a difficult story to understand and [that] it covered all of national security, not just terrorism, we set out with some good advice from professionals to go out and tell that story mainly to the print media.

Kalb: *When you say professionals, do you mean professional PR people?*

Rudman: We hired a professional PR firm in the second year. We went to editorial board meetings with all the major media that I can recall.

Kalb: *The* Times?

Rudman: Oh, yes. The *Post*. We did talk to the television media as well. So we thought we had done everything that we should have done. I've often felt in  dealing with the media, unless you can create an aura of immediacy, [you're] going to have a hard time getting off the classified page. The most striking thing to me was [that] we did advance briefings of major players in the Congress—Senate and the House. And when we had our roll-out in the Mansfield Room, room 207 of the Senate, not only was all of the commission there but we had uniquely a number of major players in armed services and intelligence and foreign policy from both the Senate and the House who stood, if you will, shoulder to shoulder, and we proceeded to do this briefing.

I've been around the town a little while, and I've never seen a better presentation than that one. Anyone who was listening said, Hey, these people have come up with a number of incredible recommendations, and we ought to pay some attention to them. *The New York Times* is called the newspaper of record, and I guess that's probably true. They had a reporter there. I won't name him. It's not important. The reporter walked out about ten minutes before the end of this briefing, and one of our people caught up with him and said, "What's the problem?" He said, "There's no story here." They said, "What do you mean there's no story here?" He said, "There's no story here." In terms of immediacy I suppose there wasn't. The thing that shocked me more than anything else—the *Post* did a story, it was a good story—but the first time anybody knew of the Hart-Rudman Commission was on the morning of September 12 when a very good *New York Times* reporter wrote an expansive story on what we had done.

Let me just add one thing. The wire services did a good job. I read about it in my New Hampshire paper. All the other papers in the heartland of America ran something about it, but not the major media outlets.

Kalb: *We're trying to understand what it is that makes the press work as it does. Just going through Nexis/Lexis, what I came upon that day: There was a CNN report, Chris Matthews did a story that night on* Hardball, *Charles Osgood on CBS Radio did a piece the following morning, Norm Kempster of the* LA Times *did a substantial piece, and Steve Mufson of the* Washington Post *did a substantial piece. Other than that in the major news organizations, I didn't find anything anywhere. How is one to account for that?*

Susan Page: Well, what *USA Today* did that next day is a "brief," and I'd like to thank Paul Leavitt, the editor who does the briefs, so we had at least that in the paper the next day. I make no excuses for what we should have done. I wish we had done more on this report in particular and covering terrorism and

homeland security in general before September 11. In hindsight we certainly should have.

[One] of the reasons that we didn't [is] the size of the staff we have. We have to make decisions about who would cover what on that particular day. I talked yesterday to a reporter who was in some ways the obvious reporter to have covered this, who recalled talking to her editor about homeland security. He didn't know what that was, he hadn't heard of that, didn't sound compelling to him. The timing of the report was also a factor. It was ten or eleven days after the inauguration: so there was a lot of attention being paid to other places, including the White House. I think a third factor is that while the press can set the agenda on a big story—and ought to often—the press also covers the things that other people do. So if President Bush had had a news conference about it—or had Senator Hart and Senator Rudman to the White House to highlight this report and say it was important to his administration—that would have generated more coverage because we would be covering the president. Or if Congress had immediately scheduled a hearing saying, This has got to be a top priority for the year, we would have covered that.

Kalb: *So there were two things. One of them is that the major press didn't do it, and the other is that the major players in the administration, very new [in] the administration, also did not pick it up and highlight it.*

Page: And reflecting also what we know now, the public until September 11 didn't see this as a driving concern in their life. They certainly do now, but the press had the same short-sightedness at the point that your report came out.

Bob Schieffer: We should have done it, we didn't do it, I wish we had. . . . One thing that defines what is news is not just how important it is to the public, but

on what day . . . it happened. I learned that during my long tenure as the anchor of the CBS weekend news, when there sometimes is not as much news as there is during the weekdays. I'll never forget many years ago I was anchoring the 11:00 p.m. newscast on Sunday nights. I remember the lead story. I came on the air one night, and I said, "Good evening, the largest brushfire in the history of Orange County swept through—" I don't think you would have gotten that on the weekday news. But the fact of the matter is there just wasn't anything else going on that day, so we gave news coverage to a grass fire.

This story was competing with a lot of other stories. The new administration had just come in. There was an electricity crisis in California; interest rates had just been cut. The day this came out, we did two stories on that. The Lockerbie verdict had just come in that night. So the fact of the matter was there [were] a lot of other stories competing for attention that night.

Still, having said that, we should have covered this story. Here's one of the reasons we didn't. There is another part of what determines news, and I'm not sure how you overcome this: sometimes there's just no appetite for a particular story. Terrorism was not on anybody's front burner in those days. I remember after that gas attack, the terrorist attack in Japan, [former senator] Sam Nunn had done quite an extensive report. He saw terrorism [as] just as serious as you did. And I remember we did a piece on it; we did the whole *Face the Nation* one Sunday on that piece. And Sam made a lot of sense on that program, and we must have gotten one of the lowest ratings we've ever had on CBS on *Face the Nation* in the eleven years that I've done it. For some reason, you just couldn't get their attention on terrorism in those days.

When I used to cover the Pentagon, I became interested in arms control. I really got into it, . . . and I couldn't figure out why I couldn't get other people interested in it. One of the reasons, I finally concluded, was [that] nuclear war is so horrible to contemplate that people really can't envision what it is. This terrorism until September 11 was so beyond all of our imaginations that you really had a hard time getting people interested in it. So I think that is probably one of the reasons that we didn't give it more attention, why the editors in New York didn't order up the piece. It was on the wire service. We all knew about it. But I think that's part of the reason that it didn't get attention.

Thomas Kunkel: I think one thing you need to remember is it is human nature to want to push off the outside world. I was going back through some of these  clips and came across a quote from Senator Rudman shortly after September 11 in which he said, "We Americans have the ability to procrastinate until we get hit over the head with a two-by-four." It's true. Maybe that's a shame, but I think we shouldn't forget that there was a strong isolationist tendency in this country until Pearl Harbor. Churchill spent years trying to warn England about the buildup of Nazi Germany, largely ignored.

There had been several reports and hearings for several years leading up to this. There wasn't an appetite for it. And there wasn't really an appetite for it in the media. Senator Rudman alluded to it earlier—the notion of "What's the hook?" "What's the peg?" It used to drive me crazy as a reporter. You wanted to write a story, and the first thing your editor would say is, "What's the hook?" You prayed there was an anniversary or something so that there was some bogus hook to hang it on. I think the media is in a trap that way sometimes. So all these things came together in this instance to give us [a] conclusion that was unsatisfactory on every level.

Hess: *It strikes me that there are two players here. One [is] journalists who need a story and want a story; the other [is] newsmakers who want a story and need a story too. And somebody—the newsmaker—if he's wise, figures out that this doesn't have a hook or that people are scared of nuclear explosions or all of these things. You or the public relations firm, Warren, were aware of those things. What I'm curious about is didn't someone say, Hey, why don't you break this story on Friday because there's no news on Saturday? Or the opinion leaders that you really want are the ones who read* Foreign Affairs, *and you really should brief those people.*

Rudman: We did all of those things. We not only briefed the media, we briefed a lot of opinion makers and academics and editors and government officials and congressional people and think tanks. We did all of that.

I would take exception with one thing that was said here from a factual point of view. I think we did have a hook, but of course if you weren't there, you couldn't grab the hook. We said, Look, the evidence is in front of us. It already started. It started in the early '80s with killing American servicemen in bars and discotheques in Germany. It moved on to Beirut with killing our ambassador, our CIA station chief, and then 243 marines. This was Islamic fundamentalist terrorism—it was ethno-terrorism from the beginning. Number three, they went after the ambassador in Islamabad, killed him and part of his staff. Then they blew up the two embassies. Then they blew up the USS Cole. We told everybody that we met with, Look, it's moving here and it's going to happen here. Listen to us. It is going to happen. So there was a hook.

Kalb: *You seem to be particularly obsessed, Senator, about the* Times.

Rudman: Oh, very. I told them that. I have a lot of friends there. It's a great newspaper; they do great work, but they sure blew this one. There should have been on the page between the sports page and the classifieds, I don't care where it was, something there that said this commission—which spent $10 million of taxpayers' money, which traveled all over the world, which was the brainchild of Newt Gingrich and Bill Clinton, which was mandated by Congress, which had an incredible group of people, a wonderful staff—worked for three and a half years [and] produced this report. It deserved that much in the *New York Times.*

Schieffer: Let me just say one thing. We didn't cover this because we made the wrong decision. It was a bad mistake. These are human enterprises, and mistakes happen. There was no agenda for it not getting on the news.

Page: I don't think we have to have a president focusing our attention on an issue to cover it. There are lots of cases where the press makes something an issue even though no one in the government is talking about it. But it is one of the great powers of the presidency to focus attention, to force people to pay attention to an issue he or she cares about. So it's something that would have catapulted this report to a different level if he had done that.

Kunkel: It's very interesting and instructive to talk about why this particular story got dropped, but to me what's really worrisome about it is that I think it's symptomatic of larger issues about the media and Washington that ought to be very concerning. Unless it's happening at the White House and unless it's happening at Congress, increasingly whatever happens in the rest of Washington, this big huge factory, pretty much goes unnoticed. We have whole agencies, the Interior Department, where one or two or maybe no reporters are working full-time anymore. And that's troubling because there's a lot of important regulatory action that's going on, important policy that happens. We have these blue-ribbon committees that are occurring largely under the public radar. Combine that with the extent to which the media are pulling away from covering international news and you have a recipe for disaster in terms of an informed public.

I'm not going to tell you that if they had written more about this report and we had done more stories about Afghanistan that September 11 wouldn't have happened. But I think there's no excuse for the fact that the American nation is so ill informed about some of this, and that cannot help the situation. And I think we all have to bear a fair amount of responsibility.

Kalb: *Why do you think that's happening?*

Kunkel: It's happening for two reasons, in my estimation. One is frankly financial. It's been documented that the networks had major reduction in overseas bureaus since the end of the cold war as part of cost-cutting measures, and no one is more frustrated about it than the people at the news divisions. At the same time, and more on the print side, you have a situation where you have a finite amount of reporters out there and you have editors saying, Well, nobody cares about Afghanistan; nobody cares about public policy. When you actually poll the public, it turns out that's not true. They care very much about it. But inside the newsrooms, increasingly we have let ourselves believe that people don't care about it, and it becomes a self-fulfilling prophecy. And if you get out of the Eastern or Western corridors and you read the papers in the Midwest, the South, it's rare to see much in the way of news from overseas. It's down to less than 2 percent of the average newshole in most American papers. So it's a problem.

Page: I certainly agree that there are huge areas of the government that we don't cover, and then you have this mob of people covering the White House. We cover whatever seems to be the sexy story. Actually, I think that's even happened now. Since September 11 the ball that everybody is chasing is terrorism, homeland security, at the expense of other issues that are also important and that we should be covering . . . [I]n a year or two maybe we'll be doing a story about why weren't we covering a global warming report that came out today or some other important issue. It's hard to have the kind of smart perspective, although I know that we try to, and I know that CBS tries too, and all serious news organizations do.

Rudman: I've always thought of the media since I came here twenty-some years ago as a gigantic fire department and all the engines are ready to go. As soon as there's a fire they all go to the same fire, no matter what else is going on in town. And if you're in the Senate and you've got a very important hearing the morning that some scandal breaks out and nobody's there, it's very disappointing.

Schieffer: I think, number one, there are these incredible financial pressures on all of the networks now, and I think that has been the main thing that has caused the scale-back of overseas coverage. But the second thing is that historically when there is not a foreign threat to this country, people turn inward. When the Soviet Union collapsed, people suddenly became more interested in what was going on in the United States than what was going on out there. I think we've seen that happen down through the years. We tend to turn inward when there is no threat out there. I would also say that just because people are not interested is no excuse for not covering the news. I am one of those who believes we have a certain obligation to educate and we should push that, but it is very easy when interest falls off in foreign affairs to not cover foreign affairs.

Hess: *Are we already getting to that point in this story? If you pick up the morning newspaper, I think there may have been one story on the front page of the* Post *this morning, but only one. And a certain sense that this is already passé.*

We won the war, more or less, in Afghanistan. The president tells us it's going to be a long war. But where's the shooting?

Schieffer: I'm not sure we have lost interest in it. I think what sets this situation apart from Vietnam, where people never understood why we were there—we'd gone off to this country that most of us had never heard of, and we were there to do something or other, I'm still not sure what—[is that] people know what this is about. Americans were killed. And Americans don't forget that. So I don't agree, Steve. I think people are very interested in this.

Kalb: *Is journalism capable of covering more than one major story at a time?*

Schieffer: With difficulty.

Page: On September 12 we took our Washington economic reporter and put him on the Pentagon because we needed an additional person there. And as of about January 1 he went back to doing Washington economics, because we had the budget coming up and important stories on that front. The economy's a good story too, the recession. So those are the kinds of decisions people make.

But I agree that terrorism and homeland security continue to be a very compelling story for readers and for news organizations. I don't think there's a sense that the war is over. I think that doesn't happen until we know where Osama bin Laden is and what's happened with him. I think there continues to be a lot of concern that there will be another terrorist incident—and that certainly will focus attention once again front and center on this issue.

Schieffer: This war will not be over for me until we can take down these barricades around the United States Capitol, until we can open up Pennsylvania Avenue, until a free people can walk among the symbols and monuments that represent their freedom. That's when this war will be over. We're only now beginning to understand when the war on terrorism began, and only now are we beginning to understand what a price it has already extracted.

Kunkel: There's no silver lining in this terrible tragedy that occurred, but I do think one thing that's happening is [that] the media are examining their responsibility, their obligations, where they put their resources, where their budget cutting went too far.

Rudman: We've got one important missing guest here this morning and that's the CEO of CBS or NBC or CNN. Ask them the tough questions. Why are they cutting the budgets of these news organizations? I looked at the number of bureaus that were cut overseas by the three networks in the last three years. We looked at that as part of our study. It's incredible the number of bureaus that were just closed. How in the world do you expect to get that kind of coverage, no matter how good you are, without people on the ground?

Kalb: *Is there any indication from the newspaper side that you know of, Tom, in your studies, where a news organization is increasing the budget in anticipation of a far more demanding news agenda?*

Kunkel: I think we're seeing a lot of evidence in the last couple of months that many major news companies have, even in a recession, thrown the budget out the window and put the resources they felt . . . they had to into this, and I think that's entirely commendable, and they're continuing to make that commitment. A little further down the road, we'll see. In the last year, I think for the first time, I'm starting to see a little bit of soul searching on the part of the CEOs. They typically don't come to these kinds of forums, because they don't like to get beat up any more than the rest of us do, but I think they maybe are finally starting to think that the pendulum maybe swung too far. After all, for these news divisions that is the product, and if you take too much flour out of the cake eventually you're not making a cake that anybody wants to eat. I try to be optimistic, and I see some hope, but I think the next six months or so will be very telling about that.

Schieffer: I don't know of any industry that does more soul searching, that does more second-guessing of itself, that does more reexamination, and we don't do it like any other business does. We do it out in public, and everybody knows about it. So I really have no apologies for that. But I think there is one point here that we haven't talked about. The news media, the television networks, we're there to explain, we're there to tell people what's going on, but it's the American people who decide what kind of a government they want, and it is the American people who decide whether they want to believe us or not. People decide when and where they want to make changes, and they are the ones who decide the direction this country goes. We have a very important part to play in that, but we are not the decisionmakers and we are not the people who decide the policy of the United States.

Page: The reason that we have the privilege of the airways and the pages of the newspaper is to show good judgment, to do stories even if the American people don't think it's the right story to do or the president doesn't hold an event. So that's clearly our goal and our purpose, even if we sometimes fall short. It's certainly true that newspapers and networks have thrown huge amounts of money at this story since September 11—even with the recession, ad revenues

. . . down—putting additional pages in the paper even though that's costing a lot. But it's probably unrealistic to think that's going to go on forever because newspapers that pay no attention to the bottom line are no longer published. So I'm certain there will be an accounting at some point about what you continue to fund and how you make sure that you're continuing to make a profit.

Hess: *Let me ask Warren a question. The president gave a remarkable State of the Union, at least the foreign policy part of it, which suggested a new doctrine, a new way America should be thinking about the rest of the world. You spent twelve years in Congress and understand the media. Isn't this a time that we should have a discussion the way that William Fulbright, for example, had a public discussion on Vietnam? And then, of course, the media would focus on that because as they say, they cover what you're doing as opinion makers?*

Rudman: Absolutely, if there are major debates in the Senate or in the House on what is really a new doctrine of foreign policy. President Bush has said something really remarkable. What he is essentially saying is no longer are we going to sit back and wait to have the first blow inflicted on us. We've identified some people out there, and unless they change their ways, we're going to get them. I'm putting it in my New England lexicon. That's what he said. But unless you get a lot of debating on the floor of the Senate and the House—I mean, the news media can't debate each other. There can be op-ed pieces. But to get some really meaty reporting on this, you've got to get people standing in the Senate making their points with emphasis and with a little colorful language, and now you have a story.

9

The Anthrax Attacks and Bioterrorism

L
ess than a month after 9/11, with the nation still in a state of shock over the terrorist attacks in New York and Washington, the American people suddenly faced the terrifying possibility of another form of terrorist attack—bioterrorism. First in Florida and soon after in Washington and New York, twenty-two Americans were hit by potentially deadly anthrax infections. Seven died, and approximately ten thousand people who might have been exposed to anthrax bacteria took antibiotics as a preventive measure.

Was this the work of a lone fanatic? Or was it the work of al Qaeda, a frightening follow-up to 9/11?

No one knew, but the story dominated the headlines and raised profound questions for journalists, scientists, and government spokespeople. For example, what is the proper balance between informing and needlessly alarming the public? In the absence of hard evidence, what if anything should be reported? How is a spokesperson to deal with scientific uncertainty? On December 9, 2001, we invited four experts to discuss these questions. They were

—**Ceci Connolly**, a *Washington Post* science and health care reporter who formerly covered politics for the *Post*

—**Susan Dentzer**, health correspondent for PBS's *NewsHour with Jim Lehrer* and a former economics correspondent for *U.S. News & World Report*

—**Kevin Keane**, assistant secretary for public affairs for the U.S. Department of Health and Human Services

—**Jonathan B. Tucker**, director of the chemical and biological weapons nonproliferation program at the Center for Nonproliferation Studies at the Monterey Institute of International Studies.

Throughout the discussion, the reporters, the government spokesman, and the scientist agreed on one thing—they all were operating in the dark. They knew very little about anthrax, except that it could be deadly and, in the context of the time, a harbinger of bioterrorism. The spokesman did not want to alarm the public; the reporters didn't either. As Keane put it, "This is new." As Connolly said, we are operating with "huge scientific uncertainties." And, in this "crazy cycle of uncertainty," Dentzer added, "we in the press have to come up with a better way of communicating" the story.

One sign of the problem was the choice of words of both a reporter and the spokesman. Dentzer at one point referred to the anthrax scare as "the first large-scale systematic bioterrorist attack . . . in U.S. history." "Five innocent people are dead," she pronounced glumly, "but it could have been millions." Keane's retort: "That's an example of hyperbole, because there's no way a million people could be infected."

They all accepted the criticism that the government could be better coordinated to handle such crises and the press better prepared to report them. What was on the horizon? Dentzer listed smallpox, reportedly a terrorist favorite; food safety, since so much of the food distribution system was now global; and the U.S. public health system, which was described as poorly prepared to manage the normal load of heart attack and cancer, much less a bioterrorist assault. Connolly underscored the vulnerability of the public health departments around the country, describing them as "decimated," lacking even e-mail access and reduced to handfuls of staffers unable to take care of infectious diseases.

Have news organizations awakened to this threat? Said Dentzer, "No, a lot of the press and news media are still fighting the cold war," meaning that they were still oriented toward issues ten or more years old. Connolly's concerns were "shrinking budgets and shrinking staff—there are only so many hours in a day [and] there are only so many inches in the paper."

Tucker concluded with sharp criticism of the *New York Times*, in particular, for publishing detailed stories about the "weaponization" of toxic agents such as anthrax. He worried that terrorists could learn potentially devastating information from such stories. Connolly pointed out that if the *Times* had the story, so did the Internet, and any terrorist could boot up his computer and learn the same thing.

Stephen Hess: *I was impressed when I read Jonathan Tucker's resume to find that he had been a biological weapons inspector in Iraq under the auspices of the United Nations. And we must mention his new book. If you have read* Germs, *now you must read* Scourge: The Once and Future Threat of Smallpox.

Marvin Kalb: *Here's the* Washington Post *with its lead story, and the* New York Times *putting it on the front page. "U.S. Will Offer Anthrax Shots for Thousands." This story jumps at me, because for the past month it has not been a front-page story. There does not appear to be an immediate direct threat to the American people. So why is it suddenly on the front page?*

Ceci Connolly: First of all, it's an unprecedented decision by the federal government to use unlicensed vaccine in a post-exposure treatment. Second, this

story has been building over some period of time. We at the *Post* started asking questions about this five weeks ago and did not initially get much in the way of answers. Last week we had inside the paper a little bit of a buildup that this was being considered. And finally, you have to keep in mind our readers. This is a very important local story for the Washington, D.C., area. You have the Capitol Hill workers and all of the postal workers in this area, who are the primary focus of this program.

Susan Dentzer: I think the main reason it's back on the front page is it's literally a timing issue. What happened is that people now are coming to the end

of the initial sixty-day cycle of antibiotics that they were initially instructed to take if they had been exposed to the anthrax spores, both in the case of Brentwood [postal facility where mail handlers were exposed] and the case of the workers on Capitol Hill. So the sixty days are now coming to an end.

In the interim, the federal health officials have gone back and looked at the literature. Literature in this case is a fancy word for two studies. Two studies that in fact were done on monkeys. One of them as recently as 1956, the other one 1993, where a small group of monkeys were given the anthrax vaccine and then challenged with bacteria, and those monkeys had spores in their lungs. Even after getting the vaccine and even after getting antibiotics, they continued to have small amounts of spores in their lungs for days afterwards. That number of days more or less coincides with the number of days that has now elapsed since people were exposed to anthrax.

So putting all of this together, government officials have said, if a bunch of monkeys could have a spore in their lungs sixty and seventy-five days out, even after having been treated with antibiotics and vaccine, maybe we'd better give people the option of protecting themselves beyond the sixty-day period. What happened yesterday is the government said, Not only is the vaccine going to be available, but we also want to encourage people to think about taking another forty days of antibiotics, or both [the vaccine and the antibiotics]. Or nothing. Because in the end, as they stressed yesterday, the scientific evidence of this is very, very thin. It's these two studies.

So all of us are groping our way through this uncertainty, but in fact that's what it was. It was the timing issue that drove this decision now on the vaccine being made available. The fact of the matter is we don't know how many people are going to take the vaccine. It could in fact be a very small number of people who elect this choice. It's just going to be made available to them.

Kalb: *Kevin, for our purposes, you're Mr. Government. You don't know a great deal about what is happening now with these spores that have been inhaled, whether after sixty days they will actually lead to an infection. We're operating on a "cover your backside" basis, aren't we?*

Kevin Keane: This is new. We haven't had this happen to our country before. We haven't had humans attacked by a release of anthrax, so there's not a text-book. The Centers for Disease Control (CDC) and the National Institutes of Health (NIH) and our best scientists are literally writing their textbooks as each day passes and they're learning more. This is kind of the evolution of dealing with the anthrax attack.

We focused first of all on treating the people who were exposed in the initial attack. Then you had some ancillary incidents flare up. So it's a natural evolution of, "Okay, what do you do after the sixty days of antibiotics are up?" Because the best science has at times told us, sixty days of antibiotics should be effective in treating the disease, and it has been. People who have been on antibiotics have been served well by those antibiotics, and they're doing well because of those antibiotics. But as the scientists went back and reviewed . . . the studies Susan referred to, which are slim and thus frustrating to our scientists because there haven't been more studies—and frankly, I expect there hasn't been a need to have more studies because we haven't had these types of attacks, not just in America, but in the world—what they came to realize is [that] there's a theoretical risk that once you go off the antibiotics, you could have a spore still in you and that spore could germinate. The question has been, How do you deal with it?

Kalb: *But you're dealing with it now. Has anything new developed?*

Keane: The newness that developed is we started with the initial protocol of the sixty days of antibiotics. What happens after that sixty days? There are some studies that have shown theoretically [that] you could have a spore in you after that sixty days. After 100 days it's unlikely.

So two options that scientists have decided to make available to folks [are], You can have another forty days of antibiotics, which takes you up to the 100 days, or you can get the shot, the vaccine. And again, you say it could be to cover your backside. We would say it's out of an abundance of caution, to make sure that people know that those options are out there, to make sure that people know they can have that extra protection if they choose to take it.

There's a decision that needs to be made. D. A. Henderson, who is probably one of the most respected scientists in the world, eradicated smallpox, and now he's working in our department as our lead scientist. And Jeff Koplan, who helped him eradicate smallpox, again, a brilliant man. And Tony Fauci, who is our lead guy on AIDS. I mean these are brilliant men, the best scientists we have in the country. And they just want to be safe. They just want to make sure all options that are available to them, as doctors, are then presented to the public.

Again, we're dealing with a very limited population of those who [may have been] exposed to anthrax. So you're talking about roughly 10,000 people.

Hess: *You described an important decision made by scientists. At what point are you or your colleagues, as the public information people, called in to discuss the ramifications of this with the public?*

Keane: As the scientists started, we became more involved. What you may do is add a little bit of pragmatism to make sure they're thinking through some of the pragmatic ramifications of this and how the public may see it. How do you communicate with the public, how do you educate them on their options? That was one of the big things we raised with them. We've got to make sure that when [we] go this route we let the people know the options and the risks.

If you say, I want the vaccine, you're going to have to sign an informed consent, because it is still an investigational drug for this post-exposure use. We're encouraging everybody to make sure you have a physician with you to help you make an educated choice and understand what the pros and cons are. I think Health and Human Services (HHS) and its scientists are very involved in that process too, and making sure they're available to physicians, to health leaders, to answer their questions and make sure they can make informed decisions.

Dentzer: What we were told yesterday was that the postal workers in particular are far from decisive on the subject of whether they're going to get the vaccine or not, and in fact they have asked for a week-long educational period where various experts are going to come before them and presumably be subject to a lot of serious questions and answers. Needless to say, the Brentwood postal workers above all have a very low level of confidence at the moment in what they're hearing from all aspects of government and particularly from the Postal Service.

Jonathan B. Tucker: This is one of the reasons why CDC and HHS are erring on the side of caution, because they came under such severe criticism for not  predicting that the postal workers would be at risk from the sealed envelopes. In 20/20 hindsight, perhaps they should have been aware of that eventuality. I think it's a little unfair to criticize them for [not] predicting something that had never occurred before. But in any event, they came under severe criticism. Having been chastened by that criticism, HHS is erring on the side of caution . . . to take every step to prevent people from developing anthrax down the road because of latent spores that are not killed by the antibiotics. So it's sort of an insurance policy, both medical and political, inoculating HHS from criticism as well as inoculating people from the disease.

Kalb: *Ceci, from a journalistic point of view, were there questions that you're aware of now that you feel you should have asked two months ago? You were all in this together, journalism as well as the government, and the scientists seemed to be exploring new terrain.*

Connolly: One of the questions that we have yet to get an answer to is why HHS and CDC began this effort on the vaccine in late October. It was October 24 that Secretary Thompson asked the Pentagon for the vaccine. It was on October 26 that CDC filed a 100-page document—it's referred to as an IND, investigational new drug—with FDA (U.S. Food and Drug Administration) asking for permission to use this in a new and different way, post exposure.

I remember having a conversation with David Flemming of the CDC on October 26 in which he said, We want enough vaccine for a thousand of our CDC workers. So we have persistently been asking what is this all about.

Dentzer: They were pretty straightforward about this yesterday. I mean nobody knew at the end of October whether we were on the cusp of 20,000 anthrax-contaminated letters being disseminated around the country, or whether it was going to stop. Unaccustomed as I am to defending the government officials, standing in their shoes, [I know that] they had to make sure that they had something out there, anything, other than doxycycline and Cipro and other antibiotics with which to potentially combat a much larger-scale outbreak than they had. So it was, just as is being done now with smallpox, stockpiling . . . vaccine—which frankly, if there were a smallpox scare tomorrow, that would also be administered on an investigational new drug stipulation because it hasn't been approved. Same thing. You had to get ready for the worst-case scenario.

I think all of us who were covering this were quickly made aware of the huge scientific uncertainties surrounding almost everything about anthrax, and in part it was because we haven't had to cope with this before so there was no reason to accumulate reams of information about it. Early on we were told certain things by government officials, which we took at face value. I think a lot of us doubted the underlying scientific basis of them, and I wish we had pushed them further to admit to complete uncertainty. Let me just give you an example.

When there were the initial deaths from inhalational anthrax, and then there were these cases that appeared to be unexplained, particularly the case of Kathy Nguyen, the woman in New York who was killed, there didn't appear to be an immediate smoking gun about why she was killed. A leading supposition was that there was cross-contamination of mail, that a letter that had a lot of spores in it bumped up in the postal process against other mail and somehow spores ended up on other mail and people like Kathy Nguyen opened that mail and got contaminated.

A major newspaper wrote in November that federal investigators said that one possibility was that Kathy Nguyen had crossed paths with the perpetrators of the bioterrorism. But federal investigators were kind of musing on what was the realm of the possible. It goes to a reporter, who writes it and puts it on the front page of a prominent newspaper, and all of a sudden that becomes the story. You've got this crazy cycle of uncertainty.

Keane: Not just the government was musing. The media was musing about that too, and asking the questions.

Dentzer: Here's what I guess I would hold us accountable for. Sure, that was a possibility. But there's a difference between saying, It's a possibility for which we have zero evidence and nothing that would lead us to think that this is true [rather than] other things [that may be] true. That's one way to report it. Another way is to say that and then put it on the front page of a major newspaper, which most people believe is the record of truth. Think about the psychological implications for New Yorkers, all of whom are already traumatized. And now they're being told that maybe the guy who's doing this is riding the subway. We in the press have to come up with a better way of communicating this.

Kalb: *There have been a couple of stories that it could have been developed inside different labs. Do you have enough time as someone who covers the story on a daily basis to be allowed to peel off and go on a political kind of detective hunt for evidence as to who did this? The government may not tell us anything until they actually have the person in hand.*

Connolly: Right, and you're getting at one of the extra complications in this as a story, which is that it's both a medical and science story with a law enforcement investigating piece to it. Just as we talk about law enforcement and . . . medical officials not always coordinating so well, you have a dynamic in the newsroom where you've got certain reporters that are talking to FBI sources, certain reporters [that] are talking to, say, Jeff Koplan, the head of the CDC, and hearing very different things. So we in our newsroom are day in and day out right on deadline saying, Wait, my expert is telling me X, your expert is telling you Y, how do we make sense of this? Usually what we do is kind of put both views into the story.

At the *Post* we're fortunate enough to have enough staff that some of our investigative reporters have been able to peel off and pursue more of that story line of which labs have this. But I would agree with Susan, that we in the media were probably slow to ask some of these tough questions about who in the United States has had this stuff, and where [it is].

I was at a session with science writers a while back, and Brian Kelly, managing editor at *U.S. News & World Report,* chastised them: "You folks are reporters first and scientists and medical people second, and you've got to put on your investigative reporter hat now and get to the bottom of this, not sit around and think deep lofty thoughts about studies conducted over years."

Tucker: I think this is both a medical mystery and a law enforcement whodunit. There are huge uncertainties—evidence pointing in different directions towards some kind of international involvement, toward a domestic perpetrator—and I think people are just speculating, which is a natural activity in the absence of hard data. I'm hoping, for example, that the forensic analysis of the Leahy letter [an anthrax-contaminated letter that was sent to Sen. Patrick Leahy but intercepted by authorities before it was opened], which was intact and contained a relatively large amount of material, will yield some hard evidence that will point in one direction or another, but until that information is available there is a kind of vacuum. And the news media abhor a vacuum, and they have to fill it with something, and it's usually with speculation.

It's important not to put too much weight on any different hypothesis. To say Kathy Nguyen was exposed by direct contact with the perpetrator, that was just one hypothesis and it should be just mentioned as one of many competing theories and not too much weight put on it. But I think it's understandable that everyone is speculating, including the media, and until we have hard evidence it's natural.

Kalb: *What you're saying is that even as a scientist you can't provide helpful hints to Susan and Ceci to look for ways of advancing the solution of this anthrax mystery.*

Tucker: I think as more is known about, for example, where the strain is available, what laboratories have the capability to process anthrax in the way this material was processed, we can limit the range of hypotheses to those consistent with the facts, but until we have more facts, it's perfectly natural for experts or the news media to speculate. It's just important not to put too much weight or credence in any one particular hypothesis until we know more.

Hess: *What's the responsibility of government to tamp down speculation in this regard?*

Keane: It's tricky for us, too. What if one of those speculative pieces turns out to be right? What we've really tried to do since October 4, and we learn more every day ourselves, is to stick to the science and what we do know. If you look at the secretary and some of the scientists who were doing daily teleconferences every day, if you look through those transcripts, the secretary says, We don't know a lot. We don't. He wants to have that out there, that we're still investigating a lot of these questions and a lot of these issues, and we don't have answers yet.

But conversely, if we know a reporter is going down the wrong path, really doing something that's unfair or unduly scaring people, we do get pretty aggressive and try to pull them back, especially with the TV folks. My biggest worry as a government communicator, when October 4 happened, I was worried about the cable folks and the sensationalism. And I have to say I think they did a pretty darn good job. And I think one of the reasons they did a good job is the CNN types and the FOX types have medical correspondents now, and they quickly turned it over to those doctors, and those doctors kept things in perspective. Certain types within those newsrooms wanted to get a little more sensational, a little more on the edge. The doctors pulled them back. I think that's been a wise move—not only for the cable networks to bring these medical experts on their teams, but to turn to them and to give them prominent roles because I think they've helped keep it in perspective.

Kalb: *The press was criticized very energetically about a month ago for having pushed the nation way beyond where the facts should have taken them. As you look back upon that now, Ceci, do you think the press overdid it?*

Connolly: No, I don't think we've gone overboard, and I certainly know in our newsroom that there were very serious heated conversations over the past several months about this concern of scaring people needlessly. Keep in mind, we're hearing from a lot of the "experts," some in government, but frankly many out of government who are more comfortable saying, Look, this is really serious, we've been trying to get people to pay attention to this for years.

On the other hand, these stories have to say, This is what we know about a possible imminent threat right now. Again, keep in mind we have to take some of our cues from people like Tom Ridge and the FBI. When they stand up and issue one of their mysterious alerts, what are we supposed to do with those things? I think that's one more piece of data that we as journalists are taking in in weighing what sort of stories we want to pursue and where we play them in our newspaper.

Kalb: *Susan, even on the* NewsHour, *and looking beyond just the* NewsHour *to television, do you think you put too much out at the beginning? Or was it just right?*

Dentzer: I think on balance it was about right for the following reasons. This has been the first large-scale systematic bioterrorist attack in history, and certainly in U.S. history. Tell me what the appropriate upper bound is of the coverage of that topic? I don't know what it is. We didn't know how widespread this is going to be, and it is true, as we've now established, that there were enough spores in one of those letters that went to Daschle to kill a million people. A million people could have been killed by that. And we now know, or think we know, that only a handful of spores could do the trick, because that appears to be what happened in the case of Kathy Nguyen and Ottilie Lundgren [the Connecticut woman who died of inhalation anthrax]. That they got a couple of spores on a letter. That is the leading speculation. It's bad enough that five people are dead, five innocent people are dead. But it could have been millions. And in that uncertainty I don't know where you draw the line and say too much coverage.

Keane: I think that's an example of hyperbole, because there's no way a million people could be infected by a few letters through the mail. That's a theoretical dose in terms of numbers of spores, but the key factor is delivery, how they're delivered. So one would have to take those 500 spores, or whatever, and individually infect a million people. But of course there's no way that would happen by cross-contamination.

Dentzer: But as I say, we didn't even know if that was the end of those letters. Nobody knew.

Hess: *The basic question, Jonathan, two and a half months later, looking back, did the press get it right? Were they unnecessarily frightening us?*

Tucker: I have no criticism with the responsible media, the *New York Times*, the *Washington Post*, but I do think the cable channels went way overboard. In fact, whenever I appeared on a show like the *Geraldo Rivera Show* or the *Larry King Show* and I tried to tamp down some of the hysteria I would be cut off because I was not saying what they wanted to hear. They wanted to hype the story because it was good for their ratings. I think that was very unfortunate and it created a kind of dynamic in which the various cable channels did create a very negative dynamic.

Kalb: *Jonathan, was this your impression, or did somebody actually say that you're not responding as we would like you to respond?*

Tucker: I would be on shows in which there would be an alarmist and I would be the one trying to tamp down some of the hysteria, and the alarmist would get 90 percent of the attention. So I assumed that it was because he was saying what they wanted to hear. They didn't say explicitly, We don't want to talk to you because you're not saying the right thing. But it was clear to me repeatedly on a number of interviews that when I said, "I think this is unlikely"— when talking about smallpox or large-scale attacks—[and] I would go into the technical hurdles involved with dissemination of large amounts of anthrax through the air, things like that, I would basically be cut off. And the person talking— for example, experts on the more alarmist side of the spectrum, who tend to, I think, exaggerate the threat—would get more attention. So there was a certain perverse incentive or dynamic going on, at least on the cable channels.

Kalb: *Kevin, it's not in your interest to attack the press, but how did they do?*

Keane: I think on balance they did a good job and they're doing a good job. The only thing I would continue to caution them to remember is, it is new. You always have to remember [that] it's new and that we're learning. You can't get into a situation where it's kind of like you would blame Jonas Salk if he didn't come up with the polio vaccine soon enough and people suffered because [of that]. The scientists are learning; they're adjusting. I have every confidence that our guys are going to come up with a good, solid, clear anthrax treatment some day. It may take them a while, but they're on that path; they're pursuing it. They're smart enough to figure it out one day.

Kalb: *Talk a little bit about smallpox. As one looks ahead, from a journalist's perspective, what is the story that you ought to be looking into?*

Connolly: That really is the next subject, or subtheme, of the bioterrorism coverage. Again, we take some of our cues from government. They made the decision very early on to stockpile this vaccine because of their concern about the threat of this. One of the real challenges and obligations of the press when it comes to the smallpox coverage is explaining the pros and cons of getting the vaccine. So far there's been a good deal of confusion about [the notion that] it's just like getting your measles vaccine when you're a kid, because decades ago that was a standard vaccine. But there are real risks.

Dentzer: I agree. The one clear lesson we all take away from this is that the press has a lot of trouble with scientific uncertainty. We just do. First of all, if you wrote a story like this, very truthfully, you would never get it on the front page because you would say, Well, there's a lot of gray areas here, there's a lot of ambiguity, some people say this, some people say that, we don't know this, we don't know that. Your editor would say, Why are we writing the story? There's no there there.

That's the problem we have going forward with all of these stories, particularly in a case like smallpox—even just writing about the possibilities of a smallpox attack, the kinds of caveats you have to build into any kind of description of what the likelihood is of that. The ability to walk the line between telling people what is really true and what is really possible.

Tucker: I think it's a real dilemma both for the press and for policymakers to deal with low probability/high consequence threats such as smallpox. Probably unlikely that terrorists would get their hands on it, but if they do, the consequences could be very severe. Policymakers generally have to err on the side of caution. They have to do a worst-case analysis, stockpile vaccine as . . . insurance, just in case, because they are responsible for the security of the United States. Journalists, on the other hand, have to err on the side of caution in terms of not panicking the public. So it's a different kind of calculation that a policymaker makes and a reporter makes.

Uncertainty is not news. On the other hand, you have to point out that this is a possible threat but not a likely threat, but the government needs to take certain precautions to reduce our vulnerability. I think it's been very difficult for the media, particularly television, because they have so little time to provide those qualifications and a depth of explanation to reassure the public.

I also think there is some blame to place on the side of the government because of the confusion, the panoply of voices coming from different government agencies with different messages: Tom Ridge providing one message, Tommy Thompson providing another, CDC providing another. I think at least initially there was a lot of confusion for the media because of this conflicting information coming out of the U.S. government. Even on factual issues, such as the quality of the anthrax, Senator Daschle [was] saying one thing, Tom Ridge [was] saying another, and that was confusing for analysts like myself. I couldn't really come to any conclusions until I knew [whether] this [was] weapons-grade anthrax [or] garden variety anthrax. And there was really no consensus in terms of the information being provided by the U.S. government.

So it is a dilemma for the press to deal with this issue because it is highly complex, it involves scientific uncertainties, and . . . the calculations made by officials are different from those made by reporters.

Hess: *Kevin, how do you coordinate within the government? What's the connection between Thompson and Ridge and the CDC in Atlanta?*

Keane: It's going to help a great deal to have Tom Ridge there, and frankly, I think he took some hits early on that were unfair to him because he was new. The man literally just got there and was expected to be the expert on all these issues. But since he's been there there's been a lot better coordination in terms of getting information and disseminating it, distilling it and then figuring out how you can disseminate it.

I know within HHS one of our biggest challenges is the fact that CDC is in Atlanta. It's not like the secretary can walk down the hall and sit down and talk with Jeff Koplan and his array of scientists. They're in Atlanta, and you do it by teleconference. That creates more problems than you might think. It's not as easy to communicate and talk. But I think we're doing a much stronger job coordinating and putting out a clear message and disseminating information that we have within HHS. It's only been a couple of months. I think we've adjusted very rapidly. If you go back and look at some of the other crises we've faced in this country, including health crises like AIDS, like Love Canal and those challenges, I think we're doing a heck of a lot better job.

Kalb: *How do you actually coordinate? Is there somebody on Ridge's staff who calls you every morning at 8:00 or 9:00?*

Keane: I did miss my call today because I came here. It's just old-fashioned talking to each other. And it's not as easy as it sounds because people are so busy. Jeff Koplan and his scientists—they're trying to figure out what's going on, they're trying to analyze the data, they're getting asked 100 questions by 100 different people. Same with us.

Kalb: *Who at the White House deals with this? Do you have a regular call at a certain time every day? Is there an agreement that these issues I will handle and those you will handle?*

Keane: We sort that on the conference call. Susan Neely, who is head of communications in Homeland Security, coordinates with myself and colleagues at the other agencies, and we decide what's going on, who should handle it, what's the message out of it. More importantly, at the higher level there's a homeland security meeting that the president chairs and holds twice a week that the secretary's at, Governor Ridge is at it. The secretary and Governor Ridge talk several times a week, and if things are up they'll talk several times daily. The relationship there is great, and I think a lot of that goes back to their prior relationship and that they know each other. So from our perspective at HHS, we think the system is working very well and [that there is] much better coordination of information, much better sharing of information.

Kalb: *Ceci, do you share Kevin's view that there is this better coordination, [that] you can turn to one or two people and at least get a good handle on what the data is?*

Connolly: I would say that certainly the communications have improved in the last couple of months—in particular, the conference calls that are arranged for reporters can be very useful. It still takes quite a long time to sometimes get answers and responses, and especially in this environment of daily news, 24/7. Hours really do matter. One of the real troubles with these conference calls is that they're usually at 4:00 or 5:00 p.m., and you're asking a lot of a news organization on deadline to make sense of this complicated uncertain material. Then you're following up with people at 6:00 p.m. with your follow-up calls. So I think there are still a lot of problems. It's still not clear to me who is in charge of the communication effort for the Bush administration.

Hess: *If they had this perfectly coordinated and there was one person who stood up there each day, would that be satisfactory to you? You all have your own sources at the National Institutes, in Atlanta, in the universities; you want to* *triangulate. Isn't this the nature of your work, to look for multiple sources that in fact are telling you somewhat different things?*

Dentzer: Yes. Things have gotten a lot better. These daily press briefings, and for those of you who don't know, essentially we went from an environment where you were desperately trying to call the CDC, calling up, getting some receptionist to take your question down, and maybe four or five days later someone would call you back. We've moved from that environment to the environment of these daily press calls. Yes, it would be better if they were earlier in the day. But it's much better. And frankly, the quality of the information and the honesty of the information has improved considerably because people now are saying, We don't know.

Hess: *Jonathan, you're the expert. Where do you get your information then?*

Tucker: Most of the information I get is actually from the media. So it's a bit of a vicious cycle. I have a few other sources, but because the government is not telling me things that it isn't telling the *New York Times*, I am quite dependent on that news cycle as well; so it is a bit of an incestuous process.

Connolly: It's not just a bunch of reporters sitting around whining, saying, Can't you give us a nice cut-and-dried story where you're going to say, Do X and do Y? It's medical personnel who are expressing the frustration. I can't tell you how many e-mails and phone calls I get from random doctors I've never met or heard of in my life saying, Please, please, please, I don't know what to tell my patients.

Keane: But you see where you two contradict each other. On the one hand you're saying you like the honesty when we say [that] we don't know, we don't have the knowledge base. On the other hand, you're saying how can we not give clear-cut recommendations. Well, we don't have the science and the 100 percent foolproof evidence to give a clear-cut recommendation. So you've got to go with the best of what you know and what you have and what your scientists are telling you.

Dentzer: To make it really dull and academic, [the] cross-jurisdictional issues that factor into all of these health issues are spectacular when you have local governments making decisions, and particularly [in] the D.C. area, where you have three. One whole issue in this coverage has been [trying to determine] what . . . people say in D.C. that really should pertain to people in Maryland but people forgot to tell the people in Maryland. You complicate that where you've got the district government, you've got the state and local governments, you've got public health officials sometimes, you've got the national government, then you've got the multiple agencies of the federal government—things get very confusing.

Kalb: *In my mind, just summarizing some of the large points here: You need better coordination, but there has been progress so far in that direction. This story touches people. It's not a theoretical exercise, and so a lot of those people will then turn to reporters for help. Even doctors will turn to reporters for help. And that's a very large point because the government is asking an individual who might be affected [to] turn to [his] doctor . . . when that doctor may not know what [to] do . . . [W]e're all in something that is very new, and we're all struggling together to come up with some common understanding and guidelines.*

Hess: *We did mention smallpox, but mostly we've been talking retroactively. Look ahead at what other things should we be planning for. Susan, you have a whole unit at the* NewsHour. *When you sit down with your unit and think about the stories for the next six months, what are you thinking about?*

Dentzer: Rather than going off onto the list of all the other things that we could be attacked with, we've at this point confined our efforts to smallpox. We haven't moved on to Ebola [a fatal hemorrhagic fever] . . . and plague and all the other things that we could do. All those could be done.

[There are] some obvious areas that don't get sufficient attention that we will be looking into; one is food safety. The administration in its request to Congress for assistance made very clear that that's one possible avenue that they take very seriously for potential future attacks. And it would in fact be because our food supply now is global; because we have a very paltry number of food inspectors. It would be rather easy to create havoc by contaminating food that was exported to the United States.

Then more broadly, this crisis has had the useful impact of exposing how weak our public health system is overall. Not just to respond to bioterrorism, but to respond to the things that really kill Americans consistently in large numbers, like heart disease in particular. And what a world it would be if . . . we had a public health system that [not only] was geared up to respond very quickly to the rare instances of bioterrorism, but also was far better equipped to deal with the things that are killing us in large numbers routinely and costing lots of money. I think we'll focus on that, too.

Connolly: I absolutely agree with that. We've been having discussions in our newsroom about [providing], if this threat quiets down to some extent, more coverage in terms of the preparedness issues. Looking at . . . how ready . . . hospitals [are] to respond if there would be some larger crisis, [looking at] the public health system. The one and only story I've gotten to do off the news was going to New York and writing about their health surveillance system, and it's phenomenal. It's so impressive, but it's also unfortunate in that it's one of the only ones in our country. If you go to other places in the United States, health departments have been decimated over the years. They don't have e-mail; they don't have Internet access. They have one and two staffers doing all sorts of things. That's the direction that we'd like the coverage to go, if in fact things quiet down.

Tucker: I would agree on the importance of stressing a public health system, not only [because] of bioterrorism, but also emerging infectious diseases. Because as the world grows smaller and people travel readily across borders, they can bring with them exotic infections that we normally haven't had to deal with in this country.

I think there's been an unfortunate tendency to respond either with panic or complacency. There's been a vacillation between being very concerned about these issues or being excessively unconcerned. Part of that is because of the nature of news coverage. It tends to be a spotlight that focuses on an issue for a while, and then it goes away. Whereas bioterrorism is a long-term emerging threat, as more and more countries acquire biological weapons. As biotechnology spreads around the world, more and more people have access to the materials and the know-how to use these infectious diseases for nefarious purposes, and we're going to have to deal with this threat in the future, perhaps on a much larger scale.

We've had this wake-up call, fortunately a small-scale incident. Now is the time to strengthen our public health system, to become more prepared, less vulnerable. But that effort has to be sustained, systematic, strategic over a period of years. And because of the nature of news coverage, my concern is that if there isn't another incident in the next six months or a year, the public will become complacent again and it will be difficult to sustain support for congressional action to spend real money on strengthening the state and local health departments.

So the next thing that the news media could think about with more analytical pieces is this emerging threat and the forms it's likely to take, not only terrorist use but also perhaps state use as an asymmetric weapon against either our troops or our population. Then [about] how should we respond as a nation in a reasoned, systematic way.

Hess: *Do you have any sense that the news organizations have awakened to this threat?*

Dentzer: No. Not as much as probably should be the case. I still think that a lot of the press and news media are still fighting the cold war, and a lot of the orientation still is toward subjects of ten years ago. And that it's taken a lot of people a lot of time to think in terms of health stories as being the critical stories for our time.

You can see this even now. The war has pulled lots of attention away to it because there are bombs and there are people dying, and in television terms it's much better coverage than public health epidemiology. So we're not quite there yet. I could put a lot of people at the *NewsHour* to sleep if I said, You really have to do a piece about emerging infectious disease trends. I could knock them out real fast. Because until people are actually dying from it, it's not real. And that's the dynamic that we're going to continue to have to fight.

Keane: Maybe if you framed it as the Ebola outbreak in Gabon and [asked what would happen] if someone from Gabon traveled to the United States. During the incubation period of the disease, they could spread it here.

Dentzer: And they [would say], That's really interesting, maybe six or seven months down the road we'll be able to get to a really good story on that. Look at how many people are dying of AIDS/HIV. How much press coverage is devoted on a day in/day out basis to that?

Connolly: This has been a cultural change in newsrooms in that when this started, there would be a national security meeting in the newsroom and none of the health reporters would be included. So it's even taken a little while to just kind of say, Hey guys, we need to change the way that we have been thinking about the issues and the way that we're going to cover them and the different kind of reporting partnerships that we're going to start forming [with] reporters that maybe didn't speak a common language in the past or have much need to. I do think that newsrooms have shifted their attention and their focus to a number of these issues. Certainly mine has, and I think many others.

My great concern is that most of these newsrooms [have] shrinking budgets and shrinking staff, so that, for instance, at our place we now have two people full-time on the homeland security beat—a beat that didn't exist three months ago. But one of those folks was pulled from court coverage, and one of them was pulled from environmental coverage. Again, the answer from editors is always, Well, you can do that too, in your spare time; you can keep up with the EPA. And you try as best as you can, but other things will get short shrift.

I know as a health reporter [that] I feel terrible the days that I can't be writing about the uninsured, AIDS, what's going on in the pharmaceutical industry, Medicare coverage. But there are only so many hours in a day; there are only so many inches in the paper.

Question (from the audience): *It seems to me that not only are we reading the papers but al Qaeda and their people are reading the papers and watching TV, and maybe some sick people that might have done this anthrax thing. And right after September 11, through the media, they were projecting [that] it could be anthrax next; it could be smallpox next. I'm not saying that it's wrong to do that; I'm just wondering can it be harmful?*

Connolly: I remember a week after September 11 . . . having a story conference session where we were debating [whether we should] move on to the potential of coverage of bioterrorism, and there were conflicting opinions on both sides of that question. We said, What if we had come in on August 11 and said, Let's do a story about people who hijack planes and drive them into the World Trade Center and kill thousands of people. Of course we would [have said], That's crazy. Please, it's time for a mental health break.

You had to be in that mindset the week after September 11. What's possible? Anything was possible, and we had extremely credible people telling us, look at the state efforts that are underway—that we know are underway—in bio weapons. And frankly, among the people we now consider our allies, like the Russians. You notice that the United States government is very careful not to . . . include Russia among the list of people that we think has an active bio weapons capability. Why? Because it's politically indelicate to say that right now. But we do believe that they have an ongoing bio weapons capability.

[I]f state-sponsored terrorism was a fact as of September 11, as clearly it was, it was a very small leap to say, Why couldn't it be bio weapons? Why couldn't it be chemical weapons? Why couldn't it be nuclear? It was the responsibility, I think, of news organizations, to begin to put that out there as a potential—again, subject to all the caveats we've [mentioned] about low probability/high risk. But we could not be relieved from the obligation to say that this was a possibility.

Tucker: I have concern about some of the coverage because of the level of technical detail that was provided that might potentially be of help to terrorists. There's a very fine line that the press has to walk between informing the public and not providing so much information as to assist terrorists. And some of the reporting in the *New York Times* in particular was so detailed and went into such scientific depth in terms of electrostatic charges and pumping of anthrax spores and the chemical additives that would have to be added to the spores to make them more readily airborne—sort of identifying all the steps that terrorists would have to overcome to actually achieve a super weapon—that this I thought was counter-productive.

Dentzer: But you could read all that on the Internet.

Connolly: Let's face it, if even the best reporter at the *New York Times* can make sense of the clumping and the chemical treating, you don't think that these terrorists are able to get that information? And not only that, but it's one thing to be able to read a document that lays information out. But [if] we're talking about something like an anthrax attack, [we're] also talking about a certain amount of skill in the laboratory, a certain amount of expertise. So we had very serious thoughtful conversations weighing [what to do]: do we want to aid and abet, do we want to steer people, do we want to give them a recipe and a map? And we certainly don't want to do any of those things. On the other hand, we have to be realistic about the information available on the Internet, in books, in government documents, and again, give people a little credit and treat them like adults. This information is out there, and it's available.

Tucker: But most of the information on the Internet is interspersed with misinformation or disinformation. When it appears in the *New York Times* as all of the dimensions of weaponization, it gives it a certain credibility and there is a kind of road map that is laid out. So I'm not saying [that] there shouldn't be detailed reporting on this issue, but there should be some kind of informed judgment about how much is too much. I do think the *New York Times* in particular went over the line in that area. These things were well known to experts, but we felt very uncomfortable for public discussion of some of those detailed technical parameters.

Postscript

Judging by media coverage a year later, in December 2002, one could easily conclude that everyone had exaggerated the impact of the anthrax attacks. Very rarely was there even mention in the press that seven Americans had been killed and thousands inoculated against an anthrax offensive. The U.S. government was supposedly conducting an extensive investigation, but the FBI and the Pentagon took a button-your-lip approach to the occasional journalistic inquiry about the investigation, and reporters did not follow up. No arrests had been made. The *Washington Post* reported, once, that the government no longer believed a "loner" was responsible for the anthrax letters; now it believed that a small group of five or six highly trained people seeded the letters with toxic spores. Perhaps these people were Americans; perhaps they were foreigners.

The shape of the story changed again in mid-2003 when the press reported that the FBI was draining a small pond near Frederick, Maryland, for clues that might lead to a "loner."

10

Dissent

I n wartime, dissent carries an additional nuance—it not only denotes a difference of opinion, it suggests the minority squaring off against the majority, righteously arguing its case. Like the Supreme Court justice who registers a dissenting opinion, the dissenter, even the lone dissenter, has the right in a free country to register his or her opposition to the majority opinion of society and to government policy. So it was during the Vietnam War, frequently enough that dissent in war came to be seen as a natural appendage of public opinion in recent American history. So the question arose, after the U.S. destroyed the Taliban regime in Afghanistan and prepared to fight Saddam Hussein in Iraq: Where was dissent in this ugly and unusual war against terrorism?

To discuss the question, on February 27, 2002, almost six months after 9/11, we assembled five specialists, all involved one way or another in this war:

—**Alex Arriaga**, director of government relations for the human rights organization Amnesty International USA

—**Peter D. Hart**, a leading public opinion analyst, often for Democratic Party candidates and causes, and head of the Washington firm of Peter D. Hart Research Associates

—**Mark Jurkowitz**, a *Boston Globe* reporter specializing in the media and a former ombudsman for the paper

—**Geneva Overholser**, a former editor of the *Des Moines Register* and a professor at the University of Missouri School of Journalism

—**Robert Siegel**, anchor for National Public Radio's *All Things Considered*.

It did not take long for consensus to emerge. Everyone seemed to agree that there had been no room or time for broad, vigorous dissent in a war so popular, so swift, and so successful. Hart tried to put things in historical perspective. He asked whether dissent weakens the defense of the nation or keeps us prepared. In 1985, Hart said, 57 percent of the American people felt that dissent kept the nation prepared. Now it was 49 percent—not, in Hart's view, a significant difference. He concluded on an optimistic note—that the American people, generally speaking, value dissent. But only generally speaking.

Jurkowitz pulled other statistics out of his attaché case to support a contrary view. Who should decide what should be published during wartime about military operations—the press or the Pentagon? By a two-to-one majority, Jurkowitz said, citing a Pew Center poll, the American people favored the Pentagon. He then produced anecdotal evidence to support his view that reporters were trimming their editorial sails out of concern that critical stories would kick up a patriotic backlash against the press. Overholser agreed with the Jurkowitz line of analysis. She believed that too few tough questions were being asked, too few dissident voices being heard. The result, according to Arriaga, was that our civil liberties were being jeopardized.

Siegel provided yet another perspective. Normally the journalist was the one who produced the "first draft of history," said the NPR anchor. Now, it was the Pentagon and its unorthodox spokesman, Defense Secretary Donald Rumsfeld. By briefing almost daily, he controlled the message. Even if reporters ran contradictory stories, Overholser said, the public tended to believe Rumsfeld—he commanded the PR field.

Patriotism was the administration's ally, building a protective wall around its policy. Americans were outraged by the terrorist assaults, and they overwhelmingly supported the president's response. The Taliban regime in Afghanistan collapsed so quickly that there was no time for dissent in the United States to emerge and grow. Siegel noted that there were few protests on campuses, fewer demonstrations in central squares. If there was real criticism or anger, he said, NPR would cover it, "but that's barely happening." This was a "fascinating moment" of "near unanimity" in American public opinion. If the war continued for years, he projected, there still might not be dissent of the type seen during the Vietnam War.

Interestingly, as the panelists ventured to judge the future, they noted that 75 percent of the American people were willing to commit ground troops to a war against Saddam Hussein in Iraq and that the reason for this support was the stunning U.S. military victory in Afghanistan. If Afghanistan had proved to be a more daunting challenge, coverage could have changed, public opinion could have soured, support could have weakened. Iraq was the next problem and the next test of dissent in war.

Marvin Kalb: *Peter Hart, do you know whether the American people are content with the amount of information about dissent they're now getting on this war against terrorism? Is there a feeling that there is something out there that they're not getting that they ought to know about?*

Peter D. Hart: [Americans] think the media's done a pretty good job. Our feelings about the media have risen about 20 points over the course of this war.

Given that, how do we feel about dissent? I don't think our view on dissent has changed all that much. Andy Kohut of the Pew [Research Center] has done some great work in this area. One of the questions he asked [was] "Some people think that by criticizing leaders news organizations keep political leaders from doing their jobs. Others think that such criticism is worthwhile and it keeps political leaders from doing things that should not be done." Even at this stage in the war, the November period, by a margin of 54 to 32 the American public says criticism keeps leaders from doing things that shouldn't be done. And if you go back to 1994, it was about 66 percent. So it's come down, but it's still support. And the second thing is, "Does dissent weaken the defense of the nation or keep us prepared?" While the numbers are not as robust as they were back in 1986 and 1985, when about 57 percent said it keeps the nation prepared, today it's 49 percent. So I don't think that we've moved away from our fundamentals, which [support] criticism and a full expose of what's going on. In terms of the vigorousness and the importance of that kind of a debate, it's still very much there and the public welcomes it.

Kalb: *Mark Jurkowitz, what is your feeling about the American public and journalism as an institution—the editors, the publishers—on this issue of dissent? Is it a frightening concept at a time of general patriotic feeling?*

Mark Jurkowitz: It is a frightening concept, I think, to a lot of people. I'm not quite as sanguine as Peter. I think there's one other interesting survey that the

Pew Research Center did early on, which asks the question, "Who should decide what news is fit to print? Should it be the Pentagon or should it be the press?" Now, a healthy, normal society would like to believe it would be the press that makes those decisions, [but] by almost a two-to-one margin at the beginning of this war the answer was, We want the Pentagon to control the flow of information. That's not atypical. That's very much what it was like in the beginning of the Gulf war and very much what happens at the beginning of military engagements unless and until things go wrong. But I think the sense is that it created tremendous pressure on American journalists who are cognizant, A, of public opinion and public support for this war; and B, worried about economic issues at their own institutions. I'll give you just a couple of pieces of anecdotal evidence. On September 28, *USA Today* broke a story about American troops already being on the ground in Afghanistan even before the bombing campaign started. We later learned that Knight Ridder, another news organization, actually had the story earlier but held it at the request of the Pentagon. I don't know how the story got out. I think anybody here would be hard pressed to suggest it changed the course of the war. But even as someone who wrote about that story and the ideology of that story, I got angry calls from people saying, "How dare you put our boys at risk? These people did a horrible thing by writing this story. You shouldn't even be writing about it."

Len Downie, the editor of the *Washington Post,* was up in Boston talking about what the patriotic pressures mean for journalists even now. And now that we are starting to see, for example, accountability stories, as he calls them—stories about civilian casualties in Afghanistan caused by the United States—he's saying, We're getting angry e-mails for doing that kind of reporting even months after the fact. So I think in an atmosphere in which it's clear that the public overwhelmingly supports the president, overwhelmingly supports the war effort, I think journalists and editors [are] keenly aware of that sentiment, and I think it manifested itself to some degree in what they covered. And also in some of the behavior.

There was a news cable channel in Long Island where the edict came down from management that on-air staff was not to wear an American flag lapel pin. They could have it at their desks, they could do whatever they want privately, but that their on-air personalities would not be able to wear them. There was so much anger vented at this station that they later issued a statement in which they basically said, We're good Americans, we swear to God.

David Westin, president of ABC News, perhaps awkwardly answering a question at Columbia University when asked whether or not the Pentagon might have been a legitimate military target, tried to make the point that "as a journalist I need to be so objective that I can't really answer that question. I have personal feelings about it, but as a journalist my job is to report what happened, not to allow my views to get in the way." Several days later there was a hasty, very contrite apology in which he said [that] under any circumstances that was a criminal act. So I think we're seeing a lot of behavior that we wouldn't have seen in normal times as a result of that pressure.

Kalb: *Let us say for a moment that 98 percent of the American people, according to the polls, believe that the government is doing exactly the right thing in pursuit of this war against terrorism. What is the responsibility of journalism in the way in which it handles the 2 percent? Does it get any play at all? Do you simply dismiss it? Or do you feel some sense of obligation that a distinctly minority view ought also to be heard?*

Geneva Overholser: Absolutely, you feel that sense of responsibility. We never edit newspapers by holding our finger to the wind and thinking . . . Okay, now what percentage of people are for this candidate? We ought to give 60 percent of the coverage to this candidate. It's more difficult in times of war, certainly, than it is on the political question. It's more difficult partly because journalists always struggle with being citizens and also being journalists. But in this time when we were attacked here at home and when journalists in fact were victims of anthrax, there has been even greater hesitation on the part of journalists.

But I think Peter Hart's most interesting statistic is the degree to which the popularity of the media has been unusually high, and I think that's precisely

because we have been uncustomarily unquestioning right from the start, with the U.S. Patriot Act [passed in the wake of 9/11, the legislation gave the United States more power to fight terrorism but raised questions about civil liberties]. I think the coverage of that act was way different than it would have been. It's obvious [that] if we had not been in a time of war we wouldn't have had the act, but you think about the kinds of things that that act did, with [its] restrictions on the FOI [Freedom of Information] Act and with wiretapping, with e-mail, tapping into private e-mails. There would have been far more questioning coverage. . . . And in fact I think perhaps we haven't done a great job of that.

But even more important, Do you ask the kinds of questions which you may know the public doesn't really want to see you asking and may be uncomfortable with, but which [you] owe it to the public to ask? So really, all the way from the Patriot Act to the detainment of people in this country, to the treatment of prisoners in Guantanamo, to the degree of civilian casualties in Afghanistan, to the biggest increase in the military budget proposed in a generation—are we asking as many questions in our coverage and allowing as many voices of dissent into the newspapers as we normally would? And it seems to me the answer is clear that we aren't.

It's changing now. And what strikes me—I guess I'm just inveterately a child of the '60s—[is that] it's always true, right? Everything has its season. Somehow we as humans inevitably respond this way when our nation is attacked, and somehow it takes a certain period of time before we can ask the questions. Now we're asking them.

Kalb: *Robert Siegel, supposing the statistics were a bit more problematic—55 to 45 [percent], rather than 98 to 2. How do you at NPR figure out the handling of dissent when it comes to the number of stories that you would do, the letters to the editor, the selection? Be as specific as you can.*

Robert Siegel: There are entirely different sets of decisions made about [whether] a reporter [should] do a story about rallies being held or about
 meetings being held or interview people, and next [whether] we [should] have a commentary from somebody who advocates that particular point of view, and lastly, which is I think the lowest threshold of all, [whether] we [should] read a letter from somebody who is complaining about our coverage and voicing that point of view. The answer to that is [that] letters are from everyone and the more vituperative the better.

I think the first number you threw out, 98 to 2—while I agree with you in spirit—[raises issues that are] actually tough. Because there are streams in American life—of white racists, of flat-earthers, of all sorts of people who might reach 2 percent—who we will routinely ignore.

On the other hand, there are very real issues that we've experienced, [for example] the interviews with the detainees describing their experiences, who probably account for the barest fraction of the American population, a very small group of predominantly Middle Eastern men. I can recall interviewing four of them and setting their stories out, getting remarkably angry e-mail in response. Some of it I thought extraordinary. Some, I felt, was a bit extreme. And I was struck by the impatience they might support [in rushing to judgment of the detainees]. What they support is their business, but I think we're entitled to present people with experiences and stories that might run contrary to the expectations of the majority.

Forty-five to 55 [percent], whatever that means, that's life. I think most things that we report the country is somewhat divided on.

Kalb: *Alex Arriaga, do you feel that the media has been in fact "responsible" in the way in which it has presented dissent? Do you feel, for example, that contrary points of view . . . are being presented in the media in some fair manner?*

Alex Arriaga: Does the media have a very difficult task? No question. In the immediate aftermath of the attack of September 11 the devastation was huge,

and people looked to the media [when] there was no other form of communication. It was the media that provided information, solidarity, and some level of comfort to folks. So that was a very unique role, and that was something that the media did that nobody else could do at the time.

The question became, What happens next? And with the country united in clear solidarity for the victims—as it would need to be [because] those were horrendous human rights violations that took place. . . . I think that it's true that at the very beginning there may have been some confusion. At the very beginning, the administration set out on a course that really would have put very significant restrictions on civil liberties in the United States. The very first legislation that the administration put forward was very broad in scope, and it was [questioned by] a group of 150 organizations that varied from Amnesty International to at one point the National Rifle Association. I think that at that point the media were looking to see what was going to happen but weren't exactly sure how to handle that particular initiative.

We went forward from there to the widespread detentions that took place, and there was excellent coverage from the media. It was extremely difficult to get information. There was an atmosphere of secrecy. Who was being detained? Why are they being detained? What are the criteria for detention? Where are they? Do they have access to counsel? And I believe the media were asking those questions under very difficult circumstances. And yet the responsibility that the United States has as a leader in the world is great. And in that sense I think that what we have found in our work is that we as a human rights organization have had to be probably more measured than we would otherwise be . . . [out of] a sense of responsibility in the current context.

Kalb: *You mean you held back to an extent because of your views about what most Americans are thinking about the war?*

Arriaga: Not that we've held back but [that] we've been extremely careful in how we present it. We've tried to identify very carefully what the issues are and to be specific. So that when we were looking at the detentions, for example, Amnesty International joined several other organizations, once again, in a Freedom of Information Act [suit] to get information. When it [comes] to the Geneva Conventions and the treatment of those in Guantanamo, why is it important? It's important because when the president of the United States says, This is the way we're going to treat individuals, it sets an example for other countries, and that will be how Americans are also treated. We want to hold other countries accountable to our own standards.

The military order that was issued in November [was] extremely problematic [President Bush issued an order on November 13, 2001, authorizing the use of military tribunals for suspected terrorists]. The order as written—not as the way it will be implemented, but as written—would allow for closed trials, would allow for trials in which with a simple majority you could sentence somebody to death, and that individual would have no right to appeal in the United States, in a foreign government, or in any international forum. Not that that's the way it would be implemented. I certainly would not like to see that happen. But any dictator around the world can hold that up and say, I'm going to apply the George Bush military order.

Siegel: I just wanted to add that in this case journalism is not providing the first draft of history. The Pentagon is providing the first draft. We get to do a second draft after the reporters come through the places that we have already heard accounts about, and they then get to see what happened. In most instances when we've spoken with reporters who got to Mazar-e-Sharif after the battle for Mazar-e-Sharif or got to Kabul after the Taliban evacuated Kabul, what we find is that claims of accuracy of bombing have generally been borne out. Nearly every reporter I've heard from has said [that] this is quite unlike other battlefields we've seen. These weapons are extraordinarily accurate. They tend to hit the targets that they're aimed at—we're in a new era of war. [But] they also uncover incidents where the U.S. weapons have hit things they shouldn't have hit. That tends to happen a month after the event, but it happens. Reporters have been reduced to rewriting what was originally reported out of various Pentagon briefings.

Jurkowitz: Obviously we're starting for the first time to get some kind of empirical accounts of what's going on. But having said that, I was listening to my local NPR affiliate one day fairly early on in the conflict, and I heard a BBC . . . interview with a man from the Kandahar area who had had his home accidentally hit, or at least was making that claim, making claims that some of his friends were killed. It was a fairly wrenching report.

It dawned on me that I hadn't heard anything like that on the American media. Now, that shouldn't dominate coverage, because it needs to be proportional—it's not the whole story of the war. But it struck me how nowhere in the mainstream of American media had I even seen a report like that. As a matter of fact, I remember watching CNN one morning when the anchor talking about Taliban-reported casualties simply passed it off by saying, "Well, we don't know, but we sure do know that whatever the Taliban says, they're notorious liars." You know what? She might be right, but that's not journalism. The other point I'd make is—and not to blame CNN solely—but let's not forget that this is also the network that sent out a memo to its staffers saying, When you're getting reports of U.S.-generated casualties from the Taliban, every time we report on that, we need to have a sentence in there that says, Let's not forget the Taliban are harboring the terrorists who killed 3,000 [or] 5,000 Americans. Now context in the story is crucial.

Overholser: It seems to me [that] there are so many reasons why the press reports may have been less comprehensive than they would otherwise have been. One important one is the degree to which this administration has been remarkably effective in containing information. Obviously for some good reasons. But they have been way better than most administrations have been.

I heard [journalist] Seymour Hersh the other day talking about . . . one of those early transcripts from a Rumsfeld press conference. Just look at the transcript: It goes question, answer, laughter. Question, answer, laughter. As Hersh said, "He's our new Woody Allen." He has been phenomenally effective.

So the degree of dissent has been very low. We cover dissent where it is. Hersh made another wonderful remark . . . [T]here is no one more cowardly in America today than a prospective Democratic candidate.

Kalb: *Often when I think of the word "dissent" I think of something large and philosophical, deeply personal, important. Is there anywhere in this country, anyone out there, any organization, that says, The prosecution of this war against terrorism is against my religious beliefs, my philosophical beliefs, and it must be stopped? Within that context of dissent, does it exist? Is there any reporting of it? Should there be any?*

Stephen Hess: *That's very interesting. What we've generally been talking about and have reached some degree of unanimity [on] is that the press will take on some questions of strategic opposition. Are they taking on any policy opposition? Now strangely enough, if you look at the Americans who are most [vocal] in policy dissent, people like Noam Chomsky, and you go to the world press, you see that they're all over the place. You can barely pick up a European paper or even an Asian paper without a small group of Americans, Edward Said and so forth, who are having op-ed pieces that you haven't seen, I don't think, in the American press. Have I got it wrong?*

Siegel: No, I do think there are voices of American dissent, perennial voices of American dissent, that get more circulation abroad than they do in the United States. . . . I got into radio and journalism as a student at Columbia in the '60s, where there was real protest and where there was real dissent. I never felt its growth had anything to do with how the mass media was covering it, ignoring it, or mischaracterizing it. I think there really is a culture in the country, including its politics, . . . and people come together around certain ideas, and it's not because it was on *60 Minutes* or on NPR or in the *New York Times*. So I don't feel that [the] media as a whole cause or are accountable for whether movements have legs.

In this case—unlike the Gulf war, when I used to get a lot of e-mail from people saying, Why aren't you covering our march; why aren't you doing this?—I don't hear it in this. And I don't think that it's my job as a journalist or the institution's job to create it. I just don't think that's what people in America of any sizable numbers are doing.

Kalb: *Is it your perception on the basis of your reporting or your letters to the editor, your e-mails, that everybody out there is quite content with the way in which the war is being prosecuted?*

Siegel: No. I think everybody's a false concept. We don't count up and see how many people are dissatisfied with U.S. policies. But you look around, and you say, Are there things happening on campuses? If there are, let's do a story about it. Are there demonstrations? Are there interesting writings about that? Let's interview the author of that article that is highly critical of what's happened. But if that's barely happening, then I [don't] think at a certain point we . . . say, Well, let's make sure that we've set aside a block of air time to a phenomenon that we can imagine taking place, but [that is] not happening.

Kalb: *Let it be noted that at the end of February of the year 2002, there was not enough dissent in the United States of America for major journalists to believe that the issue ought to be covered.*

Overholser: But I don't agree with that.

Siegel: I'm not saying it shouldn't be covered.

Overholser: You have to kind of scratch around to find it, which of course may go to your point, but it does exist. I looked online yesterday, and I found a site—I think it's peace911.org—which contends that it has some 500,000 signatures.

Kalb: *Peter Hart, you've been working on this problem of what the American people feel for decades. Is this an unprecedented moment then?*

Hart: It's a fascinating moment. And I don't know if everybody in the audience is having as good a time as I am because I think it's a juicy discussion. What makes it so delicious, I think, is the way in which we try and interpret American public opinion.

On the one hand, what is the pressure that an anchor on Channel 12 on Long Island feels [so much] that he must put an American flag on his lapel? Clearly there is something there. And I think you have to differentiate between what we would call support for the war effort and the ability to understand dissent.

I don't think the American public has lost its way. I think that the media may have lost its way. On the war we're very pro-American, we've very patriotic, but that does not mean that we're not unhappy with what goes on in the Office of Strategic Initiatives [an office the Pentagon created to coordinate and sell long-term policy issues; it was discredited after accusations that it might spread disinformation]. I want to pick up on a point where I think Geneva's absolutely right. Part of the reason this has been so successful and dissent has been stifled is because, I think, Secretary Rumsfeld has been a master communicator to the American public. He has been a very important filter and has changed the dynamics of the coverage because of the way in which he's done it. People are not reading transcripts; they're getting a sense of communication.

Jurkowitz: On the issue of how do you cover dissent in this country, there's something the media doesn't do well, which is complexity and shades of gray.

What are the issues? Well, they're more nuanced. Is it a military situation or is it a criminal action? Should we bomb or should we take it to the Hague [international court]? Now that doesn't represent a movement. There's no simple answer—we're against this, we think it's wrong. I think there are a lot of people in this country who may have had some qualms about the level of bombing but were thrilled when the burkhas fell off. I think there are a lot of people who are willing to stand in line forever in an airport and felt queasy about military tribunals. But you never saw coverage that dealt with this kind of layered response to what was going on because it was completely encapsulated in the broader [reaction]—We're angry and we have to do something. And there were a lot of people making individual nuanced judgments about how to react that didn't get covered. And I don't think that's just peace groups, I think that's a lot of people.

Overholser: A perfect example of what you're saying, Mark: Do you all remember when there were several thousand people demonstrating here on the Mall, it must have been early October? And what they were chanting was, Bring the terrorists to trial. Bring them to this country to trial instead of going to war. The headline in the *New York Times* the next day said, "Protestors ask to make peace with terrorists." That's a perfect example. There was no nuance.

Siegel: I would really want to return that to some context. This unanimity, near unanimity, about the war in Afghanistan seems to me to relate to the remarkable decision to attack both the World Trade Center Towers and the Pentagon. I honestly believe that if Osama bin Laden's people had decided to only hit the Pentagon but not the World Trade Center Towers—or only hit the World Trade Center Towers but not the Pentagon—various subcultures in American life would feel unaffected by this; they would think it was the other America that they were really getting at and not us. Something happened that united people in a sense of vulnerability . . . [T]hey had been attacked. I think the response of the country, the absence of the kind of opposition that you're talking about, isn't a very complicated problem. The country felt a sense of what they'd heard . . . happened at Pearl Harbor, only this wasn't an island way offshore from California. This was in two places that represented different centers of American power, culture, society. So every dissenting issue I've heard raised here I think we've done stories and interviews about on NPR. When you ask the basic question [whether] we've been covering what I think of as dissent—dissent from the policy that the U.S. should have gone in and attacked al Qaeda and the Taliban in Afghanistan and taken military action—yes, there was an issue about [whether] should it be prosecuted, but I think essentially the near unanimity that we have reported in this has been the near unanimity of the country.

Arriaga: Just a reminder once again of John Ashcroft. We've been talking about Secretary Rumsfeld, but the attorney general as well [with] his famous words about phantoms of lost liberty and fearmongers and [his remark] to those who scare peace-loving Americans, "Your tactics aid the terrorists." Those kinds of messages, also from the administration, fell into this whole atmosphere of secrecy, . . . and made it much more difficult to raise the question. I do think the media there did once again speak up very loudly in all of the major press, saying [that] this was not the way to go.

But I do want to return to one bigger issue, which is the one that you were talking about, which is the bigger policy question. Because what we have found is that where we do dissent we have to explain very clearly why we dissent and what the consequences are. One area that has been a concern of ours and I think of other organizations in the conduct of the war is, What are the long-term consequences? And I'm not sure that that has really gotten the coverage that it deserves. What are the long-term consequences of the types of alliances that we're currently forming, of the serious human rights violations that are committed in some of these countries. And what are the consequences for long-term peace if that is in fact what we're trying to seek. So I'd just like to throw that out as well.

Kalb: *I remember back in 1965–66 when the Vietnam War began to seem problematic. At that time people on Capitol Hill—not the press, the press was very much for the war—but people on Capitol Hill, individuals like Senator Fulbright, began to have hearings. The hearings then made respectable the very idea that what President Johnson was doing might not be in the best interest of the United States long term. Then other people, including James Reston of the* New York Times *and others of major journalistic institutions, began to raise questions about whether the president was doing the right thing. So Peter Hart, as you look in your crystal ball a year or two ahead, what is it that has to happen before the American people begin to think about the consequences of war, the sacrifices involved in the prosecution of war? Do we go down a war path without a discussion? Do journalists sit back and say, We've done a great job, we've reflected public opinion, and we've done that very well and that's enough?*

Hart: When you talk about the dissent of '65 or '66 or '67, remember that [that is a] three-year period, and we're five months into this, and we're assuming that American public opinion is going to remain stable. Events will change, and obviously if you start to go into Iraq or you start new incursions elsewhere I think that's going to change public opinion. But there's one other major difference between the '60s and this war. It was our brothers and sisters. It was our neighbors who were fighting. There's no sacrifice in this war. The sense in the community is very different from [what] it was. So I don't think you have the same kinds of grassroots feelings that went on back then.

Hess: *You have something else going on now that you didn't have then, and that's the homeland security issue. It may not be like our brothers and husbands being killed in Vietnam, but at the same time there is this worry that somebody may kill our neighbor when he gets on a plane and goes to San Francisco.*

Hart: And let me make the point that over 70 percent of the American public still believes that's a very real threat and essentially that also stifles the element of dissent. At that stage of the game, interestingly enough, the support for John Ashcroft, which was very divided in the first several months of the administration, suddenly went higher. Just one other thing. We touched on this partly talking about the brilliance of Rumsfeld as a spokesman or an icon for this administration, but a lot of other things they have done have really in retrospect been quite brilliant. The idea of turning it into a woman's issue and virtually neutralizing the normal opposition. That was a strategic decision. It didn't happen by accident. It happened when Karen Hughes set up a team at the White House.

Siegel: There's an assumption here that if the war against terrorism becomes burdensome to the public that it will become unpopular. Dan Schorr pointed out very astutely after the State of the Union address that President Bush in that speech called upon people to make a volunteer effort to the country as a response to what happened. And what Dan got right was that the president recognized that he'd gotten it wrong in September when he suggested that people should go shopping and that the response of September 11 was to act normal and spend your money so the economy doesn't take a hit. That wasn't what people wanted to do. They didn't feel after the country's been attacked that they should now go to the theater in New York.

So I think the idea that the American public is not going to respond favorably to a prolonged war effort—which, as Peter points out, is a war effort that will be fought by a small group of Americans who are professionals at it—I think it's quite possible that we could see a policy of the United States that involves military actions in a variety of places that we can't pronounce or spell, that go on for a number of years, and that never generate a broad movement. It's quite possible that it won't. I find it hard enough to get what's already happened right on the air rather than try to report the future, but I think it's very possible that there will not be a great political division over this policy.

Jurkowitz: If you think about what's down the road—and the most recent polls have shown that 75 percent of Americans are willing to now use ground troops to dislodge Saddam Hussein based on the Afghanistan experience—I think the one place where the media will never sort of lose is in the horse race aspects of this crisis. So let's not forget that it wasn't all that long ago before the Taliban left Kabul, that we did have a spate of coverage that suggested we might be headed for another Vietnam-like quagmire. If the Taliban were in Kabul today, that drumbeat would have gotten much louder; the president's numbers would have gone down, I'm convinced; and coverage would have been a lot more unpleasant and what we would consider to be dissent or adversarially oriented. When we talk about the factors that have led to [favorable] coverage—including no real debate in this country, the fact that the war was prosecuted so successfully, so quickly—[they are] another key element.

Arriaga: On the issues of public opinion and the climate for dissent more generally, as [a representative of] an organization that is often found to be dissenting, I have to say that often the Congress has been our ally on many of the human rights issues. It's very different in a wartime. So there, too, there are fewer who are speaking, and it doesn't have necessarily the amplification that it might have otherwise.

Overholser: This is just one moment in time. Our discussion today really looks at just a snapshot, five months after September 11, and that can change dramatically, and I assume it will based on what happens in Iraq, based on the alliances we make, based on whether a Fulbright of our time arises, whether, God forbid, we're attacked again. So many different elements can change in five months.

Siegel: We always start talking about what happens when Americans start dying in numbers in some future military action. A former military officer amended that in a conversation at our studio to say [that] it's not just a matter of suffering losses, it's suffering setbacks. What happens when a military strategy starts to fail? The problem in Vietnam wasn't just that people were dying. It was that nobody could demonstrate that the country was achieving what it said it was achieving. When that happens, I think that there will be possibly some dissent if the U.S. says it's achieving things through its use of military force that it is not. That we have to watch out for, that we have to cover, and I would imagine there could be more genuine dissent if there developed a true gap between the statement [that] we have defeated the regime in Afghanistan and the reality of whether we have actually done so.

PART FOUR

Reporting from the Field

Three Sites

11

Afghanistan

I t's one thing to talk about a war; it's another thing to cover one. According to the *American Journalism Review*, Afghanistan was "one of the most dangerous assignments in modern times." Eight reporters were killed there during the U.S.-led offensive against the Taliban in the fall of 2001, and Daniel Pearl of the *Wall Street Journal* was murdered in neighboring Pakistan. War in the first years of the twenty-first century emerged less as a conflict between states, the traditional form of warfare, than a conflict between stateless, rootless warriors and their proclaimed enemy, which could be a state, a combination of states, or a competing civilization. This came to be called asymmetrical warfare—for the journalist, an especially threatening kind of assignment.

On February 13, 2002, five correspondents, just back from Afghanistan, gave us their stories. They were

—**Michael Gordon**, an author and London-based correspondent for the *New York Times*

—**Carol Morello**, a *Washington Post* reporter with wide experience in the Middle East

—**Lois Raimondo**, a photographer for the *Washington Post* who gained special access to the Northern Alliance forces and wrote stories to go along with her pictures

—**Tom Squitieri**, who has covered many wars for *USA Today*

—**Kevin Whitelaw**, a *U.S. News & World Report* correspondent who arrived in Afghanistan to cover postwar reconstruction.

Each of them left the war zone with one indelibly memorable experience. Gordon was caught in the crossfire of Afghan warlords near Tora Bora. Raimondo accompanied Northern Alliance troops as they swooped down on the

Taliban. Morello felt trapped by Pentagon rules at Camp Rhino near Kandahar, unable to cover the fighting. Whitelaw was present at the reopening of a girl's school in Kabul, which, he said, was "the most heartening thing to see." Squitieri saw the sunrise at Bamiyan in central Afghanistan, where the Taliban had destroyed two monumental, centuries-old statues of Buddha.

The Pentagon's public affairs officers understood the importance of "feeding the beast"—providing the media with access to the troops and the action without jeopardizing lives or military missions. It was a tough balancing act, which the Pentagon thought it did quite well and which the reporters thought it did abysmally. "The Pentagon will always be the Pentagon," Gordon said, meaning it always would limit reporters' access to the story. Morello spoke of being "embedded" with troops for only four or five days, too brief a time to get to know them and write about them.

After a while, reporters realized that they could not depend on the U.S. military, and they started making their own arrangements, hiring their own interpreters, drivers, and bodyguards—a hit-and-miss operation that was extremely costly. Reliable information was precious, and almost impossible to come upon. Gordon regularly called the Pentagon for information unavailable in Afghanistan. Travel from one region to another was incredibly dangerous. "You just have to keep your fingers crossed," Squitieri remarked. On one side of a bend in the road, you're safe; on the other side, you're dead.

These journalists were brave professionals, afflicted with a rare disease reserved for war correspondents: they didn't think the bullets were meant for them. But in asymmetrical warfare, such as the war in Afghanistan, bullets hit troops, civilians—and journalists. They did not discriminate.

Marvin Kalb: *What was your single most memorable experience while covering the war in Afghanistan?*

Michael Gordon: The most interesting time I had was after the so-called fall of Tora Bora [a cave complex dug into the mountains of eastern Afghanistan and  the site of a fierce battle between U.S. forces and the remnants of the Taliban and al Qaeda], where Afghan forces allied with the United States had come down and declared victory and announced that the al Qaeda was gone and the area was cleared and basically the war aims had been achieved. At that point there was a lot of interest in the press to try to get into Tora Bora and see what it was really all about.

In retrospect, it probably wasn't the smartest thing to do—you try to do something that's not too dangerous. I hooked up with some of the local so-called Afghan commanders, paid some outrageous fee for a couple of body-guards, and went in there with a photographer and another *Times* reporter, Barry Bearak. The quest there was to see the so-called notorious caves, which may not have been so vast and complex as they were made out to be.

What I learned was just how lawless Afghanistan is—there are whole sectors of the country which are really under nobody's control—and how many of the various groups allied with the U.S. aren't allied with each other and quarrel among each other.

After getting a couple of miles into Tora Bora, perhaps somewhat naively we stumbled into a situation where we were with a group of fighters in a very smoky, dark outpost. We were trying to talk to them and interview them, and suddenly there was a message over the radio and everyone grabbed their guns, AK-47s, and went running outside. We thought, Okay, you know, al Qaeda. This is the real thing. The battle's supposedly won but okay, they're still fight-ing and we're going to see al Qaeda guys. It turned out that the crisis at hand was not al Qaeda, but another Afghan group—two forces that supposedly col-laborated with each other to cut off the exit of the al Qaeda forces from Tora Bora. We were in the middle of this thing. It was a period where it looked like there was going to be a firefight, not between the American-backed forces and the Taliban/al Qaeda forces but among the American-backed forces, probably over who was going to get to loot what cave.

I'll just sum up by saying our interpreters and so-called bodyguards became extremely apprehensive, and we dealt with the situation by flight, which was the only sensible thing to do under the circumstances, trying to very quickly get out of there. The problem was [that] the trespassers were also trying to get out of there. We were between these two groups, and we were trying to get around or to the side of one of these groups, in case they decided to settle their disputes the old-fashioned Afghan way. We got back, and we wrote a colorful story about it. My sense was in going from Jalalabad [in eastern Afghanistan on the border with Pakistan] into Tora Bora was going like from chaos into anarchy. It was an interesting illustration of the problems Afghanistan now faces, but I think it also shows the kind of problems that the correspondents ran into there. Many of the risks were not standard, classical battlefield risks, but the fact [was] that so much of the country was under nobody's control, or under this warlord's control, or under a bandit's control, which is a situation that still seems to be the case there.

Kalb: *I think your grandchildren are going to love that story. We'll go to Lois now.*

Lois Raimondo: When I first went into the north I got all the military maps that I could, knowing where the front lines are, which commander has which

post, how many men are there. I planned to stay for a long time. I was pretty much in the same region for two months.

I knew that the Ramadan offensive was about to begin. I had a couple of really good sources who were up on the front line, and they were relaying messages back to me through wireless. So once Mazar-e-Sharif fell [a small but strategically important city in the north that the Northern Alliance captured with the help of the U.S. bombing cam-

paign], we knew that to get to Mazar from where I was [we could take] a number of routes . . . but there were Taliban ridges in between. And, of course, there are no roads so we had to pick our route. I sat down with my translator and a number of commanders, and we plotted our route. My translator, myself, and the driver set out over the mountains.

We bunked in a number of bunkers along the way and used their wireless, and this is where the luck comes in. We figured, Okay, if we get here, maybe the troops, maybe they'll all converge on this point. So we went over the top of a hill, and we landed on this plain in the middle of the Hindu Kush. It was like landing in the middle of some epic film, because thousands of soldiers were pouring over the hills.

We ended up marching over the mountains with the army into Taloqan [a city in northern Afghanistan] the night that they liberated it. And that was quite remarkable because I had built up relationships with a number of the bunkers along the way, different front-line posts. It was quite remarkable because contrary to what I would have expected—most of these men hadn't seen uncovered women in probably eight years, [they] were posted to the north, they were away from their families [—] I was so well taken care of. When I got to a new town, they'd be fighting, they'd have their guns in one hand, and then they'd say, "Lois, do you want tea? Do you want sugar in your tea?" This is their life. They're so used to war. And I don't know whether I was a mascot or nobody had spoken to them in so long [that] they were just so happy to get the attention.

When you get there the first thing you do is you learn the name of the man who serves everyone tea, because in Asia nothing happens without tea. And if you know the guy who serves people tea, you'll always have your source. Every time we landed in a new town, as I moved with the army, generals would come by in jeeps and say, "We're heading this way. Come."

The other thing that happened was, they would be returning to their mothers, their sisters, their families, [whom] the soldiers hadn't seen in, say, four, six, sometimes eight years. So I would be invited into everybody's home, and I'd be ushered into the inner chamber with all the women. The women would be cooking all night long.

Carol Morello: I think the moment I remember the most is a moment of extreme frustration that in retrospect is almost comical, I guess. I was with a

group of reporters who were in a pool with the U.S. marines at Camp Rhino, which we were never allowed to call Camp Rhino. It was being called that in Pentagon briefings, but we always referred to it as "a remote desert air strip within striking distance of Kandahar."

We had spent five days there. We had gone out with grim resolve. We were going into a war zone, and the military had given us helmets, and flack jackets, and gas masks that we would strap onto our thighs, and biochem warsuits. We were told to sleep with all of it in case there was some sort of an emergency or an alert in the middle of the night. We spent five days sort of being shuttled from one feature story to the next. We had been taken to see church services. We had been taken almost on a guided tour. We had been taken to spend the night with Charlie Company in the foxhole, where the most exciting thing that happened was a camel came along and stuck its nose in a foxhole. We had been taken to promotion ceremonies. Any time news came anywhere within an inch of breaking out, we were told that we could not report it.

We had come back from a night with the grunts in the foxholes, and we had been told we were going to be replaced and they were rotating another pool in. So we're sitting there writing our feature stories in this large warehouse when a public affairs officer comes in and says, "Okay, everybody gather around, I have some news to tell you. There are casualties who are being brought in here to Camp Rhino. There are American casualties and there are Afghan casualties." Everybody hops up, and another public affairs officer goes to a computer he has set up, his laptop, and calls up a press release that has been written 7,000 miles away in Tampa, Florida. The casualties are being brought in to a medical tent that is literally 100 feet away from us, behind us. They are being brought in as we speak. And he's reading the press release written 7,000 miles away saying that this was a friendly-fire incident, that it involved a B-52 bomber.

So the reporters were like hungry dogs. What can we do? A photographer says, "Can I go take pictures?" He's told no. One of the print reporters says, "Can we at least go stand there and watch?" We're told no. The public affairs officer says, "What, you want to go see dead Americans?" We said, "No, we think this is our job." We said, "Can we talk to the pilots who flew them back?"

"No." "Can we talk to any of the medics when they're done?" "Well, they're too tired." "Can we talk to any of the Afghans who have minor injuries?" "No, we don't have a translator." News was breaking out 100 feet from where we were standing and we were ordered to stay in that warehouse. We did not get any of it. Pretty much all the information that came out came out from Washington. Half an hour later, we were out of there. That's what I remember. It was sort of a metaphor for what our entire trip was like. It was an incredible amount of press restrictions. It did improve the second time I went out, which was at Kandahar airport. Now the army is running Kandahar airport, and I have the impression that some of the restrictions are back. I saw a *Toronto Star* story that was published a few days ago, and it could have been written from my own first trip. Reporters are given briefings and told how many tons of cargo were coming in, but if they want to see anything or talk to anybody who has taken part in anything, those requests are basically denied.

It's a very difficult war to cover, at least covering the military. That's what I remember.

Kevin Whitelaw: I was in Kabul and Kandahar. [My story is] actually different than the other ones because I was mostly there for the post-conflict part, the

simmering that's going on now. I did a piece on the reopening of a girls' school, and it was really quite fascinating to see these classrooms in Kabul and [to] sit in class and listen to the teacher teach and watch the girls[—]many of them who hadn't been in school for five years, certainly not openly—learn and ask questions and be very enthusiastic. So it was very exciting to actually see the tangible results of what had been a long, protracted conflict. It might not have been the aim of the conflict from the U.S. point of view, but it certainly was at least an immediate and tangible result, and it was people trying to make the best of a very unusual situation. School usually is closed in the winter because it's so cold. Schools are unheated. [The students] have no chairs, they have no desks, they have no pens, they have no paper, and they're still there, sitting there every morning freezing and spontaneously going to school and trying to learn. That says a lot about the Afghan people and the strength of their spirit, people who have been at war for twenty-three years. So I think that was the most heartening thing to see.

Tom Squitieri: In central Afghanistan is Bamiyan, where there had been . . . two huge buddhas until they were destroyed about a year ago by the Taliban. And I went to Bamiyan to do some research, as well as check out reports that some of the Taliban had fled to that region.

One morning about 4:30 I was on the sat [satellite] phone from my desk talking about something else, and I felt something on my back, and it was the  sun coming up. The sun rose up in that valley and slowly illuminated the mountainside where the two buddhas and some of the smaller buddhas had been. The beauty of that moment just overwhelmed me, and I realized that years ago whoever chose that location to build those buddhas really knew what they were doing. I was mesmerized by the whole scene. I turned around and looked at an ancient fortress on another hill that had been destroyed by Genghis Khan. It just put my whole role in covering what was going on today in Afghanistan in a historical perspective.

Afghanistan has rebuilt cities destroyed by former invaders in the past, and towns have come back and the people have come back, and they have fallen prey to themselves and other invaders. And I wanted to make sure that as everyone talked about the new Afghanistan, the twenty-first-century Afghanistan, that I wanted to be inspired to write my little piece of the story. Shakespeare said [that] there are no small roles, just small actors. So I like to think there are no small stories, just small reporters. In *USA Today* we don't have that much space, but we have a mission, like we all do.

So that was the moment that probably sticks out among many. I'm glad this is being taped, by the way, because my daughter's only two years old today so I don't know if I will see my grandchildren, but they'll be able watch this on the tape.

Kalb: *To what extent did you feel that you were dependent upon the U.S. government to get the information that you needed? Obviously Carol did. What about the rest of you?*

Gordon: Initially my intention was to go and be part of some Pentagon pool and operation, and I tried to get my name on the various lists. They were taking names and putting them on lists, and talking about embedding reporters with ground forces. Not this week, maybe next week.

Kalb: *Explain this idea of embedding reporters.*

Gordon: I've actually never done it, but it's a logical idea. Instead of just throwing a bunch of guys in for an hour or so, you take a reporter and you put him with the unit. The way the Pentagon talked about it, you would live with the marines, you would live with the 10th Mountain [Division], or you would live with the 101st Airborne and be part of the unit, and maybe you wouldn't even be allowed to file during this period to maintain security. Then you would deploy with this unit, and you'd be subject to various security restrictions, but you would be an integral part of the unit. It was partly security, partly logistics, and partly would help you understand it. I said, Send me in, coach. I'm fine. I agree to all this, security guidelines, whatever you say. No problem. I'm eager to do this. Time went by. It became clear none of this was ever really going to happen. I think it finally happened in a minuscule way when they flew some guys in to be with the Special Forces for four days after almost everything was over.

Kalb: *Carol, you were what would be called embedded, however, right?*

Morello: I wouldn't call it embedded; the military called it embedded.

Kalb: *What is it that you would call it?*

Morello: My idea of embedded is very much what Michael's talking about. You go and spend weeks, maybe in some cases several months with them. And, in fact, when I went out with a group of reporters, we went out by military convoy. It was our understanding we would be there for weeks and maybe months if we wanted to. However, while we were there, the public affairs officers kept saying, You're embedded. To me, being there for four or five days is not embedded. You are just starting to sort of get to know people and interview them.

Gordon: It became clear it wasn't going to really happen in any time frame that was relevant to the war. I got offers of far greater cooperation from the British military. Finally, I just went in with a UN flight and just started going around.

The new type of war—these so-called proxy wars, where the U.S. relies on other people to do the brunt of the ground fighting—is a very good thing for journalists because it offers up new possibilities for covering these kinds of conflicts. The people who stuck with the U.S. military in Rhino, including our own *New York Times* correspondent, didn't see very much both because of the press restrictions and also because the U.S. forces in Rhino didn't do very much. But the people who went with the Northern Alliance or who somehow got lashed up with some of the Pashtun [the largest ethnic group in Afghanistan] guys in the south actually ended up seeing more of the conflict.

The moral I take from this is that if there are future proxy wars, the Pentagon will always be the Pentagon, they'll always have these restrictions, and the way to cover the war is just don't work with the Pentagon. Just go in independently and work with the proxy forces the Pentagon is going to enlist to do its fighting.

Kalb: *Lois, you didn't have any dealings with the U.S. government. You were dealing with the Northern Alliance.*

Raimondo: By choice. I was on the phone with the director of photography, and he said, "You can go south to Kabul, the U.S. is moving in, or you can stay in the north." My response was that I'm really well sourced here. I want to do the contextual story. I'm in Afghanistan. I didn't want to go to Afghanistan to write about what Washington was doing; I wanted to go and cover it from the Afghan perspective, which means you dive in deep, as hard as you can, as fast as you can, and spread the branches wide. So he totally backed me and said, You stay in the north.

As it worked out for us, we had a number of reporters who were in the south. It was difficult getting into the north, so I was in a position to both take pictures and write for the paper, so it worked out well for us.

Kalb: *You also mentioned the fact earlier that you had "very good sources" in the north. How did you know that you had a good source in the north?*

Raimondo: Because of the ways that he gave me information. I trusted him completely. He was incredibly honest with me. Another story I remember that hit me hard was after working together, [when] we became quite close and I thought things were moving along well, he turned to me and said, You are a total sinner, and I have to pray very hard at the end of the day. And no one in the Foreign Ministry wants foreigners here because we think that you're decadent, we don't like your culture, and all of this. . . . We'd go to the market, and he would tell me, This is what they said. Some of this is gossip, but on a much broader level, he got me into conversations with commanders where they talked about globalization and things like this. I was led into safe houses when we took new towns. There were still snipers all about, and I was in the safe house with the top commanders and we would be talking about these things. But I could sit there and listen to them, to what they were saying. There were many times I couldn't ask questions because it would be inappropriate. I wasn't supposed to be there at all. I could listen and use it as background information. So he walked me into any number of situations that were incredibly rare, and also he was just a really, really good person. He was my translator. And it was luck. I went through a series of bad translators. And . . . no matter where we were in the war, when the sun was rising or setting, he would stop to pray, and I would sit and watch the sunset. I saw more varieties of sunsets in the last two months than I have in my entire life. He calls me now on his satellite phone to report on what he's doing.

Stephen Hess: *Can I ask a very basic question? Tom mentioned his sat phone; you did too. We've come a long way from, I guess, the Crimean War and carrier pigeons. How actually, technically, did you get your story back, get your photographs back, deal with your editors?*

Squitieri: We have a lot of great equipment. Afghanistan was really trying on equipment because of the dust and the dirt. It knocked out a lot of computers and phones. I thought the irony of having great communications and satellite phones which [allowed us] to transmit stories and photographs is that there's no phones within Afghanistan. So you had twenty-first-century technology, but it was almost like the eighteenth and nineteenth century to arrange interviews. You'd send a note over and arrange an interview that way.

So you had this wonderful contrast in using this great equipment [which allowed you to] file from anywhere in Afghanistan if you hit that satellite and you had power to, but not being able to communicate within the country.

Kalb: *Tom, you've covered a number of other wars. How was Afghanistan different from those?*

Squitieri: It's similar—these proxy wars where you don't have front lines as such. . . . Now the fighting is going on within parts of the whole country. That's like Bosnia and like Haiti in the sense that stuff would erupt in different parts that would seem calm the day before. How it's different, however, is [that] I didn't feel that sort of overshadow of danger lurking about in Kabul after the fighting had subsided. I think outside the city there was more uneasiness that you could feel, but in Kabul itself, unlike, say, Sarajevo or Port-au-Prince, you didn't really feel that danger existed in the day time.

Kalb: *Kevin, you were nodding a moment ago. Did you have that same experience?*

Whitelaw: By January Kabul felt very safe. Kandahar felt very safe as well, actually. You could move around. You could move around in the city, a little bit outside the city. It's when you get to the more remote provinces that things got a little bit more risky and reporters had to make a lot of choices. A good example is the story about the U.S. airstrike up in Oruzgan, which is in central Afghanistan, about two or three weeks ago. And reporters wanted to go up there. We were hearing reports in Kandahar that [the target] was not Taliban, not al Qaeda. And it was a very difficult choice for them to figure out whether to go or not.

Kalb: *A difficult choice because?*

Whitelaw: A difficult choice because no one had any information about the safety. No one had been there. Who do you ask? How do you know if it's safe for an American reporter and a photographer to go to a place that no one's been to?

Kalb: *Mike was talking about some kind of protection to go into an area. How do you work that out? How do you know whether you've got somebody who's not going to point a gun at you rather than protect you from someone else?*

Whitelaw: You don't.

Squitieri: It's trial and error a lot of times. Unless Carol had been using somebody and was leaving and hands him or her off to me, you know. Because few reporters—and there have been reporters who have been in Afghanistan prior to this—but a lot of those people, unless they were with the Northern Alliance, who they had connections with, didn't really have anyone in the south or in Kabul to sort of go back to. So you have to just learn.

The Northern Alliance assigned a lot of translators to people up north, so you were stuck with them initially until you could find somebody else. Some of them turned out to be okay, and some of them didn't. The issue of translating is one thing, but the issue of trust and confidence in that person is another, and that's just a trial-and-error thing.

Gordon: Afghanistan is not really a country. It's a mosaic of different tribes. Whenever you move from one area to another, you need a representative of the power in that area. So when I went down to the south, I had a Northern Alliance translator, a Tajik who was of limited value in the south and arguably a liability. A bodyguard is not just a guy with a gun, because everybody has a gun. It's a guy who's tied in to the local power structure. They recognize him; they say, "Okay, you're with this guy. You must be all right." They know a lot of the customs.

Kalb: *It's still not clear to me how you find somebody, though. I still don't understand how you find a bodyguard. Do you look in an ad?*

Raimondo: The way it happened in the north was all the journalists who came in through the north landed in Koshiba Hoadin, which was the temporary headquarters of the Northern Alliance. And they had set up a whole list of translators. You had to go and register, and they would assign somebody to you. And there were so few people who spoke English that 70 percent of the time you'd get somebody who hardly understood what was happening.

Gordon: I thought the most important hire was the driver/bodyguard, and that turned out to be our best hire, by luck of the draw. We happened to get somebody who had been the driver and a bodyguard for General Massoud [the leader of Afghan resistance to the Taliban], who had been assassinated a couple of days before [9/11]—

Kalb: *Didn't do a very good job.*

Gordon: He must have been off that day, or else he might have been killed. But this guy was really terrific, and he was a straight shooter in more ways than one. I remember one instance: we were chasing down a rumor that bin Laden had been sighted in Pakistan, and it came out of the Defense Ministry, which is located in the presidential grounds in Kabul. We got there, curfew was at 10:00 p.m., and we were there by 8:00 o'clock, and the rumor proved to be bogus. So we were leaving the compound, like leaving the White House from the front of the White House, going out to Pennsylvania Avenue, and a guard that served at the checkpoint raises his rifle and cocks it and runs over to me, screaming that we were out after curfew. Well, it was 8:00 o'clock. This is one of the problems with an illiterate population. A lot of the guys can't tell time, so they just guess that it's after curfew. [The guard] was about to fire, and the driver just calmly looked at him and just said whatever he said to him and barked something out. I heard the name Massoud several times. The guy just put his rifle down and apologized and walked away. And repeatedly at checkpoints, our driver would just calmly talk to these guys. He had this aura of authority about him, and also confidence, but he was calm. I respected him and admired him for that and thanked him a lot because he got us to places because of that ability.

Hess: *When I wrote about this in an earlier study, I would always ask reporters, What are the tricks of the trade for staying alive? For instance, John Pomfret from the* Washington Post *said, "Never wash your car." I said, "Never wash your car, why?" He said, "If somebody's going to put a bomb under your car, [you could spot their] fingerprints." From all your past wars, do you get any training before you go in? Eight reporters have been killed in this. Tell us about how you prepare to stay alive. Or are you just fatalists and think, "When my time's up, my time's up?"*

Morello: I think the killing of those four reporters spooked a lot of other reporters, because they seem to have done everything right. When you heard about the three, I think it was three, who were killed riding on top of an APC [armored personnel carrier], you could say, Well, that was sort of a dumb thing to do. But the four who were killed, they were part of a convoy. They didn't go in on the first day; they went in on the second day. They weren't in the first car; they were in the second or third car. They had a local driver. They had someone with them who was Afghan. They did everything right. I had made those decisions before. It's sort of like a gut thing. You try to minimize the risks to a point where you feel, Okay, it's safe enough; I'm willing to risk it. I've heard a lot of foreign correspondents . . . talking about the deaths of these four because everybody's made that same calculation before. They did everything "right," and they still ended up getting killed.

I think there's a certain level when you can say, Okay, it now feels safe enough. And I think the more you do this, the more cautious you become. The ones who leap in and say, I'll be in the first day in the first car, are the people who are just starting out as foreign correspondents. You sort of develop a feel, I think, for various areas when you've covered it and you go back several times.

Squitieri: One of the most frustrating feelings [is that] you're doing everything right. You're going down the road. It starts off feeling right, and all of a sudden you go around that bend and you're stuck, and that good feeling in your gut that was legitimate that morning turns to a bad feeling, and there's nothing you can do. You can't get out of it. You just have to keep your fingers crossed. That's the worst feeling I've ever had, and that happens too often.

Kalb: *Whom did you end up trusting as you went on covering this war?*

Whitelaw: Nobody.

Gordon: This was the strangest conflict for me to cover because it was the first time where I felt I actually knew less about what was going on when I was inside Afghanistan than when I was in Washington. Information was very, very hard to come by. You'd get conflicting [information]. You'd go from commander to commander or ministry to ministry or office to office, and you'd get a different story. Then you'd have to sit and try to pick through all these different stories and figure out which one was right.

Raimondo: The other complication is that the Afghans were dependent upon the Americans. I mean, all the people that I met in the north, all the commanders were waiting to hear from the Americans with the airstrike. My sense of it was that they kept them in the dark for so long. I mean, I had generals on the front line saying to me, When are the Americans coming? So the people on the ground knew very little. You would know more about this, but what we were being told was [that] the Americans couldn't decide who they actually trusted on the ground and they were trying to work all that out. A lot of the key Afghan people didn't know what was happening, I think.

Squitieri: I found it very frustrating, repeatedly, that among the Afghans there seemed to be a propensity among men not to admit that they didn't have the answer. That's fine. If someone says, I don't know, that's fine with me. And this is a silly example, but it sort of made it all come together near the end. The lion at the Afghan zoo, Marjan, died after a long and not very healthy life thanks to a hand grenade thrown at him once. But they were going to bury him and have a funeral for him at the zoo. So all the reporters went to cover it. It was a particularly slow day. I was waiting for the funeral service to begin, and I was talking to the zoo caretaker and Marjan was being buried on the zoo grounds, so I asked him, Is this the first animal from the zoo to be buried on the zoo grounds? That's a pretty direct question. He said yes. Okay, fine. First one. So as the service gets under way, the mayor's office mentioned . . . how Marjan now joins Vamboo the elephant being buried on the zoo grounds. So after the service I went up to him. I said, Didn't you tell me Marjan was the first one to be buried here? Yes, I did. What about the elephant? I tried to cut him slack. Did he die before you worked here? Oh, no. But I forgot where he's buried, so I didn't want to tell you.

It's a silly story, but to me it was sort of typical of the problem we had in getting accurate information. Because he was ashamed to admit that he didn't know where the elephant was buried—I mean, how do you lose an elephant?

Whitelaw: You had the same problem with eyewitness accounts. Whenever you were trying to figure out what happened somewhere—for instance, the assault on the hospital in Kandahar, when the U.S. Special Forces and the Afghans went in to finally get these six al Qaeda guys who had been threatening to blow themselves up for two months. . . . Everybody we talked to had a different story. They were all right there, they all saw it unfold, and they all had literally a different story. They blew themselves up. None of them blew themselves up. One of them blew himself up. They were shot. They were not shot.

Hess: *Michael, you were there largely to do the military strategy part of the story. Wouldn't your sources be importantly Americans? Were they giving you anything that you wouldn't have gotten in Tampa and the Pentagon? What was the relationship?*

Gordon: I had no relationship with the American military despite repeated efforts to establish one. But what I did have was my sat phone and I had e-mail, and I could kind of call back to the Pentagon and say, "Look, this is what I see here. How does this fit with what's supposedly happening?" I'd gotten all the briefings at the Pentagon; I heard all of that stuff.

From just a military standpoint, the dependence on these proxy forces was both a strong point in the strategy and an Achilles heel. It's why bin Laden got away, because they didn't share the same ardor for chasing him that General Franks [coordinator of U.S. operations in Afghanistan] had. And their war aims and the American war aims didn't entirely coincide. That's what you could see at Tora Bora. And it was the perspective of the war you could never get from the Pentagon.

And just to sum up quickly, I remember one day, talk about sourcing problems, the commanders come down off the hill, and they say, It's over, we won. We won? It's over? Yeah, we won, they're gone, al Qaeda's gone and we've got Tora Bora. Finished. Victory.

The next day General Franks says on one of the talk shows, We're fighting, we've still got a long way to go, there's shooting in Tora Bora, it's by no means over. Hmmm. The guys who are doing the fighting for the Americans say it's over, and they're not even fighting anymore. They've taken their guys out of the hills. It's over, gone; peace is at hand. The American commander in charge says it's not over and he's continuing the fight.

That to me was not so much a sourcing issue. [Instead], it showed that the Afghan conception of the war—which [was that] we've got our towns back, we've got our loot back, we're in charge here, so it's over—was different than the American concept. It's a view I would never have gotten if I'd hung around the Pentagon briefing room.

Squitieri: One of the chilling things that emerged from a reporter's point of view is the way the U.S. Special Forces and those guys in the field felt towards journalism. The attitude towards journalists that some Special Forces showed, letting the locals hold them at gunpoint [and] saying, Oh, don't worry, they won't kill you, and taking equipment away. This sends a really bad signal to the local militia. Part of the U.S. mission and UN mission is nation building, including freedom of the press and respect for opinions. The idea that journalists could be manhandled and their stuff taken away and it's okay—we're sending out the signal [that] it's okay to do this, Special Forces, U.S. Special Forces doing this to U.S. reporters or other journalists—the local people see that, the local gunmen see that, [and] they think it's okay. That's a dangerous path to begin to go down.

Kalb: *Within the last week or so we have had a rush of reporting about civilian casualties. My memory may be faulty, but I don't remember that kind of report-*

ing taking place at the time that the casualties were inflicted. Now did any of you know about this story of civilian casualties [and feel that] you shouldn't be reporting?

Squitieri: I think Kevin and I were both in a briefing in Kabul when they spoke of one incident in eastern Afghanistan. The U.S. allegedly strafed civilians fleeing in the middle of the night. Reporters questioned the UN spokespeople on that. Who told you this? What's the sourcing on it?

A few days after that, some reporters were able to get down to that part of Afghanistan and do some reporting to determine whether there was a munitions cache there or not. There was an attempt at reporting of these allegations. It was very difficult then because of the safety and ability to get to places. I think the roads have opened up a little bit more now; people are coming out more. So the timing is better to do some of the on-ground reporting.

Whitelaw: Most of these sites were pretty remote . . . in remote central and eastern Afghanistan. They were very hard to get to at that point. The UN had come out of their briefing, and they said [that] there were no Taliban, there were no al Qaeda; we have a reliable source. Okay, who's your source? Can't tell you. Well, what do you do with that? There's not much you can do with that. If you find a villager three days later who's just come from there, had been taken through the dead bodies, and he said, Yeah, there were a lot of Taliban guys and a lot of innocent villagers. Okay, what do you do with that? There were still innocent people. There might have been Taliban; there might not have been. We couldn't get there.

Hess: *Lois, as a photographer you had to be, by definition, closest to where people were killing other people. Did you see any of this?*

Raimondo: Every town that I was in, one of the first things I did was to go to the local hospital and meet the doctors. So whenever there were civilian injuries, somebody would come and find me. So I spent quite a bit of time photographing that. I did a number of stories out of the hospitals. If there was some hard news happening, there was the war; but when there wasn't, I would work through the hospitals. I sort of wove some of that into what I was doing.

Question (from the audience): *Did you ever get a chance to confer with your counterparts from al Jazeera or other Arab or oriental media outlets that might have a different perspective on what was going on out there?*

Kalb: *Were there Saudi reporters, were there Jordanian reporters, Egyptian?*

Squitieri: I don't remember that many, do you Kevin?

Whitelaw: I don't remember very many either. A couple of al Jazeera and one or two of the other networks.

Kalb: *So where do they get their information?*

Hess: *And let's go beyond that. One of the things that reporters do with each other is share information. Not their scoops, but general information. You said you passed them on the streets, you had conversations and so forth. Did they tell you anything that was useful to you from a different point of view that you weren't otherwise getting on your own or from Western reporters?*

Morello: When I was based in Cairo and I covered the Middle East for the *Philadelphia Inquirer*, there were many local correspondents who were not only colleagues but friends of mine and they would sometimes pass on story ideas. We would have dinner and drinks some nights. I think when you're based in a region, you get to know a lot of the local correspondents and socialize with them and share story ideas and perspectives. I think those influence each other, more so than when you sort of parachute in.

Whitelaw: There weren't that many local correspondents. Afghan television did have at least one team, which almost got run over during a violent game of buzkashi [a traditional Afghan sport in which riders on horseback try to drag a calf carcass from a hole and place it in a designated spot].

Hess: *Michael, you had been stationed in Moscow for years. Did you run across your old friends from Russia there and share any information?*

Gordon: Well, Afghanistan was a bit of a reunion for the Moscow Western press corps because they all came down there through Tajikistan, so I saw a lot of Americans and Spanish and European reporters.

Kalb: *What about Russian reporters?*

Gordon: There were Russian reporters there, and I'd gone around with the Russian press in Chechnya, actually. I'm sure they were there, but I didn't encounter them.

Raimondo: I took one trip with a guy who was a Russian. He spoke four different Afghan languages, and he was teaching at a military institute in Moscow. He had been in Afghanistan a decade earlier working as a translator for the Afghan army. We spent four days together and went up to different front lines, and it was interesting because it was a whole other dimension of Afghanistan and how people reacted to him. He was basically terrified the whole time he was there, and he left in about a week.

Question (from the audience): *I was wondering, as journalists, what is the farthest extent that you will go to to get a story in a war-torn area?*

Hess: *How much risk will you take?*

Gordon: There was a moral issue in Afghanistan. It's that you have to imagine, especially in the south, a place that's utterly corrupt. You have to pay for everything. You have to pay for a bodyguard, you have to pay for a driver, and depending on what area you're in, he's under the influence of a warlord, the warlord's taking a cut. They were selling accommodations in Tora Bora on the top of the mountain for $300 a night to a wire service, a news magazine, and a photographer, and a major American network was paying $600 a night. They wanted to be up there for the day when bin Laden was caught to do the stand-up. The accommodations weren't great. Some of the guys had to live in an unheated bus. But they were on the plain where it happened.

There were prisoners picked up in Tora Bora, and they displayed them for the Western press. I was offered access to them for $900. You can do an interview with them. Well, we don't really do that. We're not going to pay for a story. I think some people did pay.

The *Wall Street Journal* bought a computer in Kabul for their new Kabul bureau, and then discovered that the computer had been looted from an al Qaeda house in Kabul and that the hard drive contained al Qaeda stuff. So they didn't buy it; it wasn't a case of that. But this sort of thing did happen, especially with journalists from other countries. So that I think, in addition to the risk factor, [there] was [an ethical] factor. We'd pay for a bodyguard, and maybe the bodyguard would be expensive, but he guaranteed you some protection. But we wouldn't pay for information. That's where we drew the line.

Hess: *Mike Getler called reporters in Afghanistan walking ATM machines. The idea was you had to carry an awful lot of money and that was one reason why you were so much in danger. Tell us, How much money were you guys carrying?*

Gordon: Thousands. In hundred dollar bills.

Squitieri: I would wrap all my hundreds and fifties in ones, the dirtiest ones and fives I could scrounge up, because that would immediately turn off people. They didn't want small bills.

Morello: Even with the marines, I think I carried $5,000 in hundreds and fifties, the idea being that I didn't know what was going to happen, and I could easily find myself in a situation where I'd turn around and the marines [would be] gone and I'd have to figure how to get out myself. So I went to the ATM and American Express and got 5,000 bucks before I went in.

Raimondo: I think this is also one of the reasons why there were certain countries that just couldn't be represented because it was too expensive. I worked for a while with a woman from Irish TV and radio, and they lasted a week and a half because it was $300 a day, and she said, We're busted. So they just left.

The other thing that drove prices up every place were the . . . television networks. I was at one refugee camp where a Japanese minibus pulled up, and these guys threw dollar bills out the windows so they could have 3,000 refugees run with the camera pointed out the window of the minibus. That's one example. It was a Japanese television network. I don't know which one. I also know there was an American wire service reporter who paid a woman to take her burkha off in a refugee camp. This is when my translator came and said, "They hate you. You're destroying our culture." So these single incidents become so huge, and they all happened out of money. He paid her, I think, $20 to take off her burkha.

Question (from the audience): *I wanted to go back to the question about the proliferation of stories over the past week on civilian casualties. You all make a point that there is greater access now to these remote areas, but also [that] there is greater legitimacy for what you are already hearing. I get the sense that some of the other nations' presses, the Irish press, the Australian press, maybe the English press, earlier gave greater legitimacy to those reports. I don't know if that's right. But it raises the issue about, Have we been sort of the home team covering it?*

Whitelaw: The best answer I could give you on that would be to say that I think some of the European media were running those reports a lot earlier, but they were running on what the UN said, quoting an unnamed source; they found one villager who'd traveled to Kabul from the area. They weren't for the most part able to get to a lot of the villages either, so they were relying on piecemeal accounts. A lot of us felt that wasn't enough to base a whole story on when you can't actually get there and you can only talk to whoever happens to pass through somewhere. So I think there might be a different level of sourcing that maybe I felt comfortable with versus what other reporters might have.

Kalb: *But the larger point is, Did you hold back because of the rush of patriotism?*

Squitieri: Not at all, no.

Raimondo: It was the opposite, if anything. It makes me more vigilant.

Squitieri: The rush to be first is not always the best way to approach journalism. The rush to be accurate is probably better, especially in such [an] intense area as civilian casualties caused by flagrant U.S. bombing attacks.

Whitelaw: Especially when it's so hard to tell the difference between Taliban and non-Taliban. Who do you believe when someone says there were Taliban and there weren't Taliban? It takes a long time to get to the bottom of who these people actually were and how a strike unfolded and what happened. You don't get that from talking to the one or two villagers who happened to walk through somewhere.

Gordon: I think that an interesting, just an interesting fact, [is that] the Pentagon always acknowledged its mistakes reluctantly after the fact, and I don't think these incidents would have been on the public record had not correspondents from the newspapers gone to these sites, talked to these people, asked them what happened, and begun to raise questions about it. My impression is that only then, and as kind of a public relations reaction, would the Pentagon begin seriously investigating.

Squitieri: I really reject the idea that people in Kabul didn't want to move on it. I think at the time we did as much as we could, and I think the circumstances have now opened up to permit deeper and better coverage of that.

Whitelaw: Keep in mind that what these reporters have done—the ones who have gone to these sites—it's very dangerous. It's very risky reporting. They're taking a lot of bodyguards with them, and they're taking risks. They're going to places that no one's been to. There are difficult choices for reporters to make in those situations to evaluate whether [they're] going to survive or not.

12

The Middle East

Almost from September 11, 2001, day one of the war against terrorism, the Israeli-Palestinian war has struggled to find its place in this conflict. Is it distinct, entirely separate from the larger, global war against terrorism, or is it part of it? If it is, how does it fit, and how is it to be managed? To the reader of a newspaper, one war often becomes hopelessly entwined with the other. The Bush administration has tried valiantly to keep them in separate files, but that has been a losing proposition. When Israelis retaliated for suicide bombings by terrorists associated with Islamic Jihad or Hamas, they argued that they were only doing to the Palestinian Authority what the United States had done to the Taliban and al Qaeda in Afghanistan. The State Department squirmed, but did little. Everyone understood that for decades Israeli-Palestinian violence has marked the reality of the Middle East and that U.S. policy has played a central role in the unfolding drama.

For U.S. diplomats and journalists, certain questions naturally rose to the surface, more after 9/11 than before. How to sort truth from propaganda in a world of conflicting accusations? How to resist adopting a pro-Israeli or pro-Palestinian viewpoint? What effect does anti-American sentiment in the region have on a journalist's ability to report this complex story? And, on a very basic level, how does a reporter stay alive in this dangerous environment—the same question he or she faced covering the war in Afghanistan?

On April 24, 2002, we invited four highly experienced reporters, three of whom had worked earlier in the Middle East, to answer these questions—or at least to try to. They were

—**Glenn Frankel**, a foreign correspondent for the *Washington Post* who won a Pulitzer Prize in 1989 for his coverage of the first Palestinian intifada

—**Todd Purdum**, a correspondent for the *New York Times* who had visited the Middle East twice in his career—to accompany President Clinton while covering the White House and to cover Secretary of State Powell's visits to the region

—**David Shipler**, a former Jerusalem bureau chief for the *New York Times* who won a Pulitzer Prize for his book *Arab and Jew: Wounded Spirits in a Promised Land*

—**Robin Wright**, an author and chief diplomatic correspondent for the *Los Angeles Times* who covered the Israeli invasion of southern Lebanon in the early 1980s.

No reporter who has ever covered the Middle East leaves the scene indifferent to the competing passions of the people in the region. One reporter may be drawn to the Israeli side, another to the Palestinian; but both end up feeling sympathy for the Israeli cry for security and acceptance and the Palestinian desire for national identity and, more recently, a degree of economic and political reform. Frankel spoke of the need for the reporter to be "morally careful," this being a story that "really has an enduring, important, and moral meaning." In the last few years of unrelenting violence and terrorist assaults, American reporters have been bombarded with extraordinary criticism, hardly a day passing without pro-Israeli supporters denouncing them for betraying the Jewish people and pro-Palestinian supporters denouncing them for twisting or ignoring the plight of the Palestinian people. Never before has the reporter felt as exposed to sharp, barbed criticism from both sides.

Frankel noted that American journalism seemed relatively objective to him, "aspir[ing] to a certain degree of proof or information," whereas in his view the European press seemed slanted toward an anti-Israeli, pro-Palestinian stance. Wright remarked that al Jazeera, the Arab cable network, has become an extremely important force, carrying brutal anti-Israeli pictures into Arab living rooms night after night—"the constant stream . . . is really quite overwhelming." Up until the 1982 war in Lebanon, Wright said, the world press was essentially pro-Israeli; since then, it has changed dramatically. Even though Arab governments and sources have tended to inflate figures and distort reality, Shipler argued that, from his perspective, the thrust of Middle East coverage has portrayed Israel as the conquering but dreaded Goliath and the Palestinians as the embattled but tough David. There is no escape from the journalists who, with a laptop and a satellite phone, are helping to shape policy and diplomacy.

Marvin Kalb: *How do you get information, and how do you come to believe that the information is reliable enough to put into your paper?*

Glenn Frankel: I just spent two weeks in Israel, in the occupied territories—spent most of my time in Israel proper and just literally a few hours in Tulkarm  in the West Bank. A few hours because it took all of the day basically to get into Tulkarm and get out of there.

I was the Jerusalem correspondent during the first intifada, and the differences are quite striking in terms of the intensity, the difficulty of working there, and the amount of attention. The first intifada was a slow-building, organic development where the people involved did not realize really what they were involved in and where it was going, and it took a long time for anyone to recognize that. It was amazing at the time how everyone failed to see what was going on, including the PLO, the Israeli government, the Israeli army especially, and the media. We were all way behind the curve.

This is much different. It is a war—Clausewitz said [that] war was diplomacy by other means. This is war by many, many means. Diplomacy is part of the war, media is part of the war, and so it makes it extremely difficult for us to sort through or to get basic raw material.

One big difference, I think, between the American press—and by the American press I mean the *New York Times* and the *Washington Post* and a handful of other papers and media outlets—and what's going on in Europe is that at least we aspire to a certain standard of proof or information before we'll print something or before we'll get behind something. I noticed, certainly in the British press, pretty much anything someone will say to them will end up in the paper, oftentimes as fact. The *Independent* correspondent last week said, "Someone told me there were twelve bodies or fifteen bodies or thirty bodies buried in this house, and I wouldn't have believed it two weeks ago, but now I do." There may be thirty bodies buried under that rubble, there may not be, but for the correspondent to put his endorsement on that is very different than what we would do.

We are in a war. Each side is attempting to use us, to enlist us if you will, to convince us, to cajole us into accepting their version of reality, and their version of reality is based on their strategic needs. It's much more two organized groups, two organized nation states—though you can't call Palestine exactly a nation state—but certainly two organized nations using every means available. And I just take my hat off to the people who are there on the ground for us and the *New York Times* and the other news outlets who have to face this every day, who have to sometimes strap themselves up with bullet-proof vests, who are renting armored cars and thinking about buying them, who are facing a shooting war literally on both sides where they are potentially juicy targets. It's a dramatic difference from my time there.

Robin Wright: My only experience, and I shared it with Todd, was [when] we were with Secretary Powell on this last shuttle, and our access actually was

framed by the diplomacy, not by the action on the ground. Our one little expedition into the West Bank was to see Arafat and Ramallah. It was fascinating; it was a kind of microcosm. We were the only ones to get into Arafat's compound, and yet we had incredible limitations on what kind of information we could get. We had to rely on the few Palestinians who were allowed to talk to us, . . . and the Israelis didn't even allow our cameras to swing around to take pictures of their deployment. We didn't know, for example, that the five people who allegedly murdered the Israeli tourism minister were actually in the basement of the building that we were in until after both of the trips there.

I've been covering wars in the Middle East since the 1973 war. This one is so different, most of all, because of al Jazeera, which beams these pictures constantly into Arab homes. We see very little of it comparatively in the United States. There's a bit more on CNN International. But the constant stream of pictures in the Arab world is really quite overwhelming. And it's not only become an issue in terms of turning people out into the streets, it's become an issue for governments. It's created a political dynamic where the people who are angry, either on the streets or in the public editorials—even Saudi Arabia has had its own little demonstration, which is almost unheard of—[have] led to a kind of alarm among leaders like they've never felt before in the history of the Arab-Israeli conflict. I think al Jazeera has created a phenomenon we have yet to fully appreciate.

David Shipler: My experience there as a correspondent was from '79 to '84. I did go back to Israel for three weeks a year ago, so I did get exposed to the

early stages of this intifada. It was not as vicious, of course, as the last few weeks have been, and the Israeli army was perfectly willing to let reporters go anywhere they were stupid enough to want to go. I was going to Hebron—this was in early May last year—from Jerusalem. I showed the eighteen-year-old Israeli soldier my Israeli press card, and he looked at me and sort of shrugged and said, "All right, the fighting is to the right." You . . . had to be picked up by a Palestinian driver or Palestinian friends and go in a car with Palestinian plates. And the best was to get a Palestinian taxi driver who knew the back roads, which is what we did that day, and avoid the main road down to Hebron, where there was always the possibility of clashes between settlers and Palestinians and between the army and Palestinians. We went the back way, around to little villages where there were no Israeli settlers, no Israeli troops, and that felt safe, but it took a long time. I would like to draw one parallel with the Lebanon war. There is a pattern here that seems to have been repeated. It is true that this is an unusual war in many respects. The Israeli army's approach to the press, it's much more severe this time than it was in Lebanon. There is one underlying problem which existed in Lebanon, namely the exclusion of reporters from areas of battle so they can't really see what's going on. In 1982, the correspondents based in Jerusalem were not allowed into southern Lebanon until the fighting was essentially over, that is, until the Israelis got to the edge of Beirut and were in east Beirut. There was no way for reporters to get into Tyre, Sidon, other areas where the fighting was taking place.

One result was the exaggerated casualty statistics that were circulated. I don't remember the numbers now, but if my recollection is correct they may have originated [with] the Palestine Red Crescent, [been] transmitted to the ICRC [International Committee of the Red Cross] in Beirut and then picked up by them, and then therefore became fact. The number of homeless was in the hundreds of thousands, which I think was almost as many people as lived in southern Lebanon. As soon as correspondents got in, we could see quite clearly that certainly the homeless statistics were way off. There were some people whose homes were destroyed, but the numbers were nowhere near what was being reported. The Israelis spent the whole summer trying to knock down those statistics. It became a big issue in the States apparently. I was not aware of how much of an issue it was because statistics in the middle of a war are never reliable. We know the first numbers are not going to be proved to be accurate anyway.

But in the States the number of dead, the number of wounded, the number of homeless apparently became a major issue for pro-Israel people, and they were fighting this propaganda war all summer until the *Times* finally asked me, "Please, can you try to do a piece on this and try to nail it down as well as you can?" And I did.

I went around. The Israelis wouldn't let us into refugee camps, for example. After the fighting we had to go with an Israeli army escort every time, a reserve officer who was mobilized to ride shotgun literally in the passenger seat of our car. I was lucky enough one day to draw by chance a colonel, a reserve colonel named Mordechai Baron. He later became a member of the Knesset. He was very active in the Peace Now movement, and he spoke Arabic. His nickname is Morelai. Morelai said, "Well, where do you want to go?" I said, "I'll tell you where I'd really like to go. I'd like to go into some of the refugee camps where there was a lot of fighting and the Israeli army will not let us go." And he said, "I'd love to do that."

So we cross the border. We pull up to Rashadiyah camp, and there's this Israeli armored personnel carrier out front, and Israeli soldiers with their shirts off kind of lounging in the sun on top of it, and the Israeli army had said, These camps are dangerous. There are unexploded ordnance. Does that ring a bell? Does that sound familiar? Unexploded ordnance. You shouldn't go in there. There may still be fighting. Things may be booby trapped. It's like Sharon had this little script that he pulled out this year from '82—it worked so well then.

So we get up to this APC, and these guys look startled and they stop us. Morelai has this discussion in Hebrew with them. He used to be the chief education officer of the army. He knows a lot of these soldiers anyway. So they shrug and wave us in. We spent most of the day in Rashadiyah with people crowding around us—no reporter had been in there before—and telling us about what had happened there.

I started asking them, Who knows how many people were killed? Some hands would go up. We'd start to get a sense of people killed. Of course, this is a very unscientific approach, but the fact was that in this camp there were not a huge number of deaths as it turned out. A lot of the civilians there said, "Well, most of the destruction is from the army coming in and blowing up bunkers after the fight." The camp was full of bunkers . . . [T]hey would put a bunker at the intersection of four houses; if you blow up a bunker, you blow up four houses. There was a lot of destruction, but not a lot of deaths. There were some people still buried under the rubble, they felt, but it was not a wholesale massacre certainly. And after doing that for a while, and going to hospitals, talking to doctors, talking to some religious leaders, I began to assemble some kind of a picture that demonstrated that the casualty figures first put out were exaggerated. That doesn't necessarily mean that it was a picnic by any means, but still the point I'm making is that the Israelis, if they're behaving themselves in a fairly decent way, make a big mistake by keeping the press out.

Kalb: *At this particular point, if we jump ahead to what is happening these days and you think about the headlines out of Jenin, the headlines have already created a kind of reality. The reality creates a working supposition that there was a massacre. Words like "war crimes" are being used. The press participates in this. When you were traveling there with the secretary of state, you were in a kind of flying cocoon. How reliable, do you feel, is the information you're getting within the cocoon?*

Todd Purdum: The difficulty that I face and my colleagues who cover the State Department face right now is in covering the sort of bureaucratic war that's  going on here and in trying to get reliable information about who is for what policy, who's arguing against it, why it changes. Obviously, when we were traveling with the secretary—as you say, in this flying cocoon—a lot was happening back here in Washington that had the effect of undermining his efforts in the region. Ari Fleischer, the White House press secretary, called Sharon "a man of peace," adopted the Israeli phrase "homicide bomber," and emphasized [that] it had been Powell's decision to meet with Arafat. At the same time, the big pro-Israel rally happened on the Hill, and they sent the deputy defense secretary Paul Wolfowitz to make an appearance. The Israelis and Palestinians both were taking ample note and reflecting it back to Secretary Powell in their meetings with him and in their discussions with us.

I found [that] it's very difficult to get reliable information from an administration whose basic posture is to be very closed down. And even when it's arguing, which it clearly is doing now, this administration doesn't argue like other administrations. It doesn't argue openly and nastily; it argues quietly and happily. But it's very hard for me to be sure what is happening. I have some suppositions about it, and I think they're informed suppositions and they're based on some reporting, but it's not an ironclad analysis. Powell does regularly brief the flying press corps. His preference seems to be to come back and do a straight-ahead, on-the-record briefing.

Stephen Hess: *One problem when we had the group of reporters just back from Afghanistan was that they had never been to Afghanistan before. They were "parachuted" in there. So isn't it a little different covering this war? Because I suspect even when you're dropping in new people, [you're] dealing with a much more knowledgeable press corps.*

Purdum: I can answer that as the person who knows least about it on the panel. My previous trip to Israel with President Clinton was for about sixteen hours in the midst of the 1996 wave of bombings, and that seemed a sort of fraught moment, which now seems like happier days by comparison. But when I got to Jerusalem, we had on the ground there not only our current bureau chief, James Bennet, but two prior bureau chiefs, Joel Brinkley and Serge Schmemann, and two or three other reporters, a couple of whom had just recently been in Afghanistan, and John Kifner. Every day was a collaborative effort with them on the story, and I think the readers were much better served by that than they would be with some wet-behind-the-ears person who was just at the mercy of the State Department.

Shipler: I think Israel is unique in this regard. I had Todd's job some years ago when George Shultz was the secretary of state, and my experience was that going to Israel was fine because I knew a lot of people and we had the resources, and Cairo was the same way. But when we went to Damascus, where we did not have a bureau, or Saudi Arabia, where we did not have a bureau—and where in both cases the governments restricted the traveling press corps to very pleasant hotels and would not let us get out really to talk to people—it was just like going to Kenya or Liberia. For me anyway. I don't know if this is still the case.

Purdum: I think it's even more the case.

Hess: *And it raises another interesting question. Now we're talking about a part of the world, where particularly in Arabic, we've got a press corps that is totally illiterate. What do you do? You get an interpreter, and then you rely on this person being honest? How does it work?*

Shipler: It's a great handicap. If I had known [that] I was going to be there for five years when I arrived, I think I would have studied Arabic. I did try to study Hebrew. I was canceling lessons all the time and not doing my homework because I was too busy covering the story. But if the *Times* had given me some time before I went to get Arabic, I think it would have been a great advantage.

You do rely on interpreters, and sometimes that's an advantage in the sense that a good interpreter who knows people opens doors, makes people relax and trust you, and gives you entrée. That is, to some extent, perhaps true in the West Bank and Gaza as well. I think an American speaking fluent Arabic, dropping into, say, Dheishe Camp near Bethlehem, might arouse some suspicion, whereas if you have a Palestinian who knows people in the camp, who gets you in, you have a kind of entrée. So it's a toss-up. There are pluses and minuses, I guess.

Kalb: *In terms of a comparison now between one intifada and the other, what has changed about the Palestinian public relations operation?*

Frankel: I happen to be one of those who believes that public relations operations on both sides aren't anywhere near as good as they're reputed to be. The Palestinians had an advantage in the first intifada and they have one now, and that's being the underdog and being able to cast themselves as David against the Goliath. They get a bit more sympathy going in, but they're not terribly good at organizing anything. The Israelis are vaunted to be really good at PR, and I've never really found that to be the case.

Of course, it's a terrible disadvantage not to speak the language, but finding people who can help you, who can negotiate your way, and finding people who you trust and who trust you, that hasn't changed from last time to this time. Last time in Gaza, I remember meeting someone outside Shifa Hospital in the first week of the intifada and developing a relationship that helped me for a year and a half. It's not just a question of somebody with Gaza license plates and someone who really knows the terrain, but [someone who] also has to understand who you are and what you're there for.

When we finally got into Tulkarm the other week, we eventually made our way to the house of the family of the man who was the bomber in Netanya, the guy who blew up the Park Hotel on the first night of Passover, which really sparked this new incursion [nineteen people were killed when the bomber detonated forty pounds of explosives]. We found the older brother of the bomber, a thirty-five-year-old man who himself had lived and worked in Israel for ten years. We sat there, and I asked some questions, and he made it clear to me right at the beginning. He said, "You know, this is not a democracy. I can't really tell you how I feel about what happened." I took that in and said, "What about your brother? What was he like? Tell me a little about his life." He showed me his brother's room. We took about an hour and a half, and gradually he started talking about the event and his feelings. I just wanted to sit with this family member. The first take you get when you talk to [the family of] someone who has been killed in the conflict is always, "Well, we're so proud that they did this. We'd sacrifice all our children for this." It takes a while of sitting there and listening carefully and maybe not even asking questions for a while to try to get to some deeper emotion, something that feels more genuinely human, and you need a translator who's going to sit there with you and is going to honestly interpret and who understands what you're there for.

Kalb: *Robin, what is your sense about the reliability of the information that you're getting about the Middle East from the U.S. government?*

Wright: I think we only get a very tiny bit of the picture. I think it's an enormous problem. I often find that the first leaks traditionally have come from Israel, whether it's what Powell's schedule is going to be [or] the terms of the peace plan.

The Tenet plan, which they say is the foundation for getting to a final settlement, still has not been announced by the United States. But if you look on the Israeli Foreign Ministry website, there it is. So the United States is never the first source of information on the Arab-Israeli conflict. The fact is the United States is often the last recourse. They don't want to say anything until they think it's a deal, until there's something positive.

Can I add one point to this whole issue of public relations? When you look at the history of Middle East wars up until 1982, we always saw the war from the perspective of the Israeli side, in large part because that was where information was, where the press corps was allowed to be based. You didn't see it from the Syrian side. But because there were so many bureaus in Beirut, this was the first time, in 1982, that you saw a war from the Arab perspective. Because the Israelis cut off access by the Israel-based correspondents, it was the Beirut-based correspondents who had the dateline, who had information. They had the on-scene reporting. We could get to the camps. We could see the fighting, or we were in some cases underneath it. And it was a fascinating transition. I think that was the point at which the Palestinians particularly and the Arabs in general learned [that] there's something to getting their information out. I think that's influenced everyone, even including Saddam Hussein, including the Iranians. The Iranians began to see after 1982, during [the] war between Iran and Iraq, began giving access to journalists to the war front because they saw the benefit of seeing those who were dying under bombardment. It was a really important turning point in terms of media coverage in the Middle East.

Hess: *Robin, can I ask a question that only you on the panel can answer? That, of course, is being a woman correspondent in the Middle East and in Arab countries. You have maneuvered it for years and know how to do it. When you started in Africa, you were one out of 100, if I remember correctly.*

Wright: You have a good memory. When I went to Beirut, I remember I was the first correspondent to go in. There were a couple of wives of correspondents who were stringers. But the interesting thing about Beirut, again, it was a turning point; when some of the male correspondents started being taken hostage, news organizations, bless their altruistic souls, began to see a role for women. So in particular the networks were sending in women producers, women correspondents, and suddenly there were lots of us. It was very striking.

I think there's a bit of a myth about women in the Middle East. When I look at my contemporaries, Elaine Sciolino and Judy Miller from the *New York Times*, Caryle Murphy from the *Washington Post*, there are a lot of us who actually went there and didn't find obstacles. There's one, and I won't name her, who wrote an article about having to make up a fictional husband named

George and wear a wedding ring. I never had that problem. I was often surprised that . . . it was accepted that we had different standards [being Western
women]. I think that's true in the Muslim world in general. I was in
Afghanistan under the Taliban a couple of years ago and had access to officials,
was treated as an equal of my peers. I'll never forget going to Saudi Arabia in
1981 with Lord Carrington, who was then the British foreign secretary. I
worked for the *Sunday Times of London* then. And I remember King Khalid,
the predecessor to the current king, came over and shook my hand first, at
which point Lord Carrington said, "That's the last time I take you any place
with me." Now, King Khalid would not have shaken hands with any woman to
whom he was not related in Saudi Arabia. But because I was a foreign woman
he was honoring foreign customs.

When I think of the number of women today, there are clearly far more. In
the *Los Angeles Times* case both of our correspondents in Jerusalem are
females. That was true of the last two correspondents. And one of the women
who is about to be replaced is going to be replaced by another female. I don't
think there are any limitations at all on women covering the Middle East today.

Kalb: *Glenn, a question for you on the differences that one perceives in the coverage, what one reads in a British, French, German newspaper about the same
event and what one reads in an American newspaper. How do you account for
that?*

Frankel: I can take the chauvinistic view that they're just not as good as we are,
but I won't do that. I think there's a different mindset and a different set of
assumptions going in. Again, we're based on the assumption—for the most
part, I think—that we're in a war with two sides who are striving to make their
case at the same time that they are in combat with each other. Therefore the
information coming from those two sides immediately has to be examined
critically and closely. It's an imperfect process, and we don't always get it right,
heaven knows, but there is a presumption of at least an attempt to critically
examine both sides.

Hess: *Is there something else? I've read a lot of the* Guardian, *a lot of the* Independent *in Britain, and they look so different than the* Times *and the* Post.

Frankel: I don't want to overgeneralize, but the European press tends to look
at this as a liberation struggle. Maybe because there's a more established left in
Europe compared to this country. There is a natural sympathy for the liberation struggle and for the Palestinians as a result, but things are seen through
that prism I think in a way that they aren't in this country. But the TV cameras

from every country tend to root for the underdog. So there is a presumption, if you will, a definition that tends to put the European press much more on the Palestinian end of things.

When you see the photos of Jenin and you go to Jenin, obviously there's been damage done and terrible things have happened. If you don't juxtapose that in your mind with the Passover bombing, with the suicide bombers, and with the question of whether the Israelis have a military, political, moral justification for going into a place like Jenin—I mean, once you're in Jenin, bad things are going to happen. There are fighters mixed among civilians, and if you're going there, if your mission is to root out the fighters, you are by definition going to do damage to civilians. The parallel that everyone talks about is with Afghanistan, where the same kinds of things happened and maybe worse things happened to civilians, but because the press wasn't there at all, never mind only much later, it was much harder to sort through what happened.

What happened in Jenin, the press wasn't there, but we got in fairly quickly afterwards. If you just work on the presumption that killing civilians is by definition a war crime, then it's pretty easy to find the evidence to support that view. If you believe there is a right of self-defense that includes going into places like Jenin and rooting out the fighters who are there, then you draw different conclusions. We see our job in the American press to navigate between that and to try to come to some understanding both of motives and events and to look for some proof. A European correspondent would give you his or her specifications.

Purdum: There is a greater tradition in the European press of contentiousness and of journalistic opinion, even in mainstream daily newspapers, that there isn't really in America today. I think it's fair to say that many major European newspapers have known points of view which the American press would have had fifty, sixty years ago—Colonel McCormick's *Chicago Tribune* was a certain kind of world view, the Chandlers' *LA Times* was a certain kind of world view, and for that matter the Sulzbergers' *New York Times* was a certain kind of world view. My impression is that that tradition and that gestalt endures in Europe in a way that it doesn't so much here.

Shipler: I just wanted to add, as a reporter, the Israeli analysis of this, which I've heard for twenty-five years. You can take it or leave it. Which is essentially that there are very strong strains of anti-Semitism that exist in Europe. I think we've seen those coming to the surface recently. And that, by and large, Jews are liked when they're victims but not when they're powerful. . . . Israel was an underdog until the '67 War, in which it was celebrated for triumphing in six days over the Arab armies and then became the occupier and ceased to be the underdog.

This raises another issue. That is, that one of the things that we always do badly is to write about history in the course of covering current events. This is an area of the world where history is so important that people in prisons buy [history books]. Every paragraph of history is a paragraph less that you can devote to what happened today. Editors are very impatient with historical digressions. If you try it, you won't find it in type.

The other issue that I think is often lacking from reporting from the Middle East is the acknowledgement of what does not change. News is by definition what is new, what is different, what has changed, but what is durable and what is constant in these situations is equally important.

And the final point—things that happen to people where no one is hurt, no one is killed, but that inflict wounds inside minds that are going to be long lasting. Now both the *Post* and the *Times* have had recent pieces about Jenin, about Ramallah, that do get at some of this stuff. Those of us who are in e-mail contact with Palestinians, as I am, hear every day about things like this. One eighteen-year-old Palestinian high school student e-mailed me the other day about getting kicked out of her house for a couple of days by the Israeli army. She described a scene where these little kids were crying and the Israeli soldiers pointed guns at them, and she said of the little kids, "What kind of people are they going to grow up to be?" Nobody got hurt, nobody got killed, but something happened in that incident that will have echoes. That's the kind of reporting after the dust settles that is desperately needed.

Kalb: *This is so emotional a moment in the Israeli-Palestinian conflict, it has created a tremendous backlash. A lot of people are upset by some of the things that you may be writing. Do you feel any pressure from the American public?*

Wright: Probably only in the sense of the kind of e-mails or letters or feedback that we get, and I frankly get more in terms of what television coverage I participate in, being interviewed on CNN, than I get in the newspaper.

On no other issue do you get the kind of reaction as you do on the Middle East. I think we all are aware that there is something very special about Israel. We have had for a half-century a moral commitment to Israel's existence that doesn't exist in Europe, and I think that begins to shade the kind of perceptions, in terms of our coverage, our attitude. I was born the same year Israel was, going out there and having very strong pro-Israeli sentiments and thinking, Oops, I got stuck in Beirut, and suddenly discovering, Wait a minute, there's another side to this story. It's jolting. There's no other part of the world that I think we as Americans or as American journalists go out and cover with kind of a set opinion or acceptance of a certain moral value and importance.

Purdum: It's been an interesting education for me. This is my twentieth year at the *New York Times*. It's my first real immersion in this story, which for better or worse is probably the single most important, most durable, most covered story in any part of the *New York Times*. The *New York Times* covers this with a constancy and an intensity that it doesn't really give to City Hall or the White House. I can't think of any ongoing story which has over time gotten more ink, more consistent attention in the *New York Times*. I got a letter yesterday from some person thanking me for all my work to preserve the state of Israel, and then a letter from someone else saying how could I take these blatant pro-Palestinian views.

Frankel: I think anybody who signs up to go to Jerusalem, say as a bureau chief, has to understand going in that they're going to be scrutinized and they're going to be in contact with the public in a way that they've never been before and probably never will be again—and that it can be abrasive, it can be really difficult. But I got used to it and kind of liked that aspect of it, because it made me very closely examine what I was doing and made me perhaps more evenhanded or more [aware of] the assumptions of my own work and [of] the implications of the things I wrote. It made me more careful, frankly, and not just careful with the facts, but morally careful about what I was doing. It's a standard I've aspired to in all the work I've done since then, in a way that I don't think I did before I went there.

I now write everything, rightly or wrongly, with the presumption that it's going to be read really closely by people who know something about it. As I say, that's often not the case in newspapers. But it's part and parcel of being part of a story that really has an enduring, important, and moral meaning. The state of these people tied together on this very small piece of property trying to work out history and destiny and whether [they] can live together is a pretty basic story.

Shipler: You develop a thick skin pretty quickly, although I think the criticism can be helpful if you can sort of filter out hysteria from what is in fact legitimate criticism. I had the same experience that Glenn did in terms of learning from some of the letters I got, although some of them were kind of hopeless. I had a pen pal from New York who used to write me all the time. Every time I did a story on the West Bank he sent me a letter. He was incensed every time. The first letter he sent me had a little bar of soap in it, and he said, "Sorry, no lamp shade." He continued to write to me. I wrote back the first time—that was kind of my policy. I would answer the first time. But then after that I would just file these letters away.

Hess: *Following up on that, what about being a Jewish journalist in the Middle East? Is it a great asset? Is it a liability?*

Shipler: I can't speak to what it's like to be a Jewish correspondent in Israel. I will say that when I arrived in Jerusalem, Zev Chafets, who was then the head of the Israeli government press office, told me he was relieved to learn that I was not Jewish. I said why? He said because in his experience Jewish correspondents tended to bend over backwards to prove that they were not partisan toward Israel. Now frankly, I never really saw that. I don't believe that's correct.

Wright: Covering the Arab world and being based in Beirut I was there with Tom Friedman, and I always envied Friedman for being Jewish because he could cover that issue with particular credibility. Anything he said that appeared to reflect the Palestinian side of the story had legitimacy because he would take Jewish issues into account.

Frankel: I find on the Israeli side it's a relatively easier task to understand motives, to understand decisionmaking. You're helped enormously by the Israeli press, which is a very muscular, aggressive press, lots of knowledgeable people who are also willing to sit with you and explain to you what's going on within the government, within the society. It's a fairly open society.

On the Palestinian side, they are less well equipped to give you that from the government, but there are all kinds of sources, of places you can go and people you can talk to. I do find that in spite of the fact you've got to strap on a bullet-proof vest now if you want to go to Jenin and that it's much harder to work in the territories in these conditions, nonetheless there isn't any story that's more accessible . . . where you [can] get at people and their emotions and their motivations and their background [better] than this story. It's really quite accessible in a quite fascinating way.

13

Foreign Correspondents in Washington

Even if there were no war against terrorism, the world would still be wired; and the report of a foreign correspondent in Washington would have clout not only in his or her own capital but in others around the world. But in this war against terrorism, Washington is the key beat, the place where news is made and public opinion formed, almost on the hour. The views of foreign correspondents therefore are of crucial importance. How do they go about getting the news they transmit to the world? Are there angles of special interest in Russia, Mexico, France, Turkey, or Saudi Arabia? How do they adjust to the awkward fact that their editors are able to read the *New York Times* on the Internet before they even wake up to go to work in Washington? Are they inundated with too much information? And do they do original journalistic legwork, or do they simply copy what the American reporters have already done?

To answer these questions, we assembled two panels of foreign correspondents. The first, consisting of four journalists from non-European countries, convened on December 5, 2001. The second, consisting of three European journalists, convened on March 6, 2002. The journalists were

—**Hafez Al-Mirazi**, Washington bureau chief for al Jazeera, the Arab News Network

—**José Carreño**, Washington bureau chief for Mexico City's *El Universal* newspaper

—**Yasemin Çongar**, Washington bureau chief of the Turkish newspaper *Milliyet* and of the radio-TV network CNN-Turk

—**Toby Harnden**, Washington bureau chief of London's *Daily Telegraph*

—**Rudiger Lentz**, Washington bureau chief of Germany's Deutsche Welle Radio and Television

—**Jean-Jacques Mevel**, U.S. bureau chief of the French newspaper *Le Figaro*

—**Andrei Sitov**, former Tass correspondent at the United Nations, now Washington bureau chief of ITAR-TASS, the Information Agency of Russia.

What was clear was that all foreign correspondents in Washington work very hard, all realize their beat is the most important in the world, all reflect Washington through the cultural lens of their home country, and all must depend to a degree on the published or broadcast product of their American colleagues. They are both prisoners and beneficiaries of the modern technological revolution that is transforming the world. The "CNN effect," which has been questioned by many American students, is of central importance to them. So too is the Internet. Their product is a result of the new technology, filtered through both their organization's perspective and that of the American media.

Carreño explained that his editor is always tuned into CNN. "They see something developing on CNN," he said, "and [they say] 'What do you have on that?'" Indirectly, CNN determines his news agenda for the day. "Absolutely the same," echoed Sitov and Al-Mirazi. Mevel added a percentage to his comment: "Eighty percent of my production," he said, "is basically rehashing what the American media is doing." But then, said Harnden, "We have to constantly justify why we're here and give added value."

December 5, 2001

Marvin Kalb: *I would like to ask each of you—and start with you, Andrei—for a sentence or two on your relationship to your government. Do you get your weekly paycheck from the Russian government, and do you feel that you have, therefore, an obligation to convey essentially a Russian government point of view?*

Andrei Sitov: Basically, the answer is, Yes, ITAR-TASS is still funded by the government, especially in its international operations. And as for my obligation to cover the government, the longer I live, the less I like governments, whether my own or other people's. So I try to be reasonably skeptical about the motives of any government in the world.

José Carreño: None whatsoever.

Kalb: *"None whatsoever" meaning no connection to the government?*

Carreño: No connections at all. *El Universal* is one of the most representative newspapers of the media [which] has been reinventing itself after the fall of the PRI [the Partido Revolucionario Institucional was the ruling party in Mexico from 1917 to 2000]. I think that it has been healthy.

Yasemin Çongar: The newspaper and also the TV I work for have no connection to the government at all. And I must say that being a foreign correspondent makes it even easier to stay more independent. I have worked in the Ankara office of the diplomatic correspondents, and you're covering the Turkish foreign ministry on a daily basis, and then their influence or their spin, you know, can get to you more than now . . . when I'm so far away.

Hafez Al-Mirazi: I used to get the check directly from the U.S. government when I worked with the Voice of America. But, after I moved to the BBC, and now at al Jazeera—al Jazeera is modeled after the BBC example. It is a public corporation. It receives grants from the government. It has its own independent board of directors.

Kalb: *But, to be clear, all of the money for al Jazeera does come from the Qatar government?*

Al-Mirazi: And advertising; it is both.

Kalb: *Now, to help us understand the way in which a foreign correspondent would cover this war, which is out there in Afghanistan at the moment: What is the central issue for you? Is it the covering of the war in much the same way as, say, a* New York Times *or a CBS reporter would do it, or do you have, for example, Yasemin, a Turkish angle that you are obliged to cover almost on a daily basis?*

Çongar: I would say both. It's such a major story that you have to cover the big picture: whatever [the] *New York Times* or CNN is covering on a day-to-day basis—questions like, Is there going to be an international peace force? Or, Is there going to be a second front, let's say, in Iraq? These are major questions which we all deal with.

   Then, of course, there is a Turkish angle, especially for the newspaper, less for the TV. For the newspaper, if it has anything to do with Iraq, then it's a more important story than, say, Americans being killed in Afghanistan today. So there is always the national angle. In other stories, on a day-to-day basis in Washington covering Washington, almost every story I write has a Turkish angle to it, almost every story. But since September 11, I find myself writing more and more about international events and American concerns, even if it didn't have anything to do with Turkey or Turks.

Kalb: *Andrei, the Russian government angle—for example, when President Putin was here, that was your focus, was it not, not the war?*

Sitov: Obviously. That was the biggest event of the year for us. And, as for the war itself, I would say [that] we are a news agency. We have to cover hard news.  That's what we do. And we do cover everything, including the sources that Yasemin just mentioned. We do try to find Russian angles in all those stories. And I personally also always pay attention to a sort of a lesson. Even if a story doesn't really have a direct bearing on Russia or Russia's role in international politics, I also look for a moral lesson for Russia—[for example] if single standards or double standards are employed; or maybe a better example [is] the controversy of whether we call the opposition terrorists or not.

Kalb: *What do you call them?*

Sitov: In Russia, all Chechens who fight the Russian government and who have arms in their hands are automatically labeled terrorists.

Kalb: *What about the Taliban?*

Sitov: And the Taliban, we try to refrain from that, although it's even linguistically sometimes difficult.

Kalb: *You will, on the Taliban, not call them terrorists, but the Chechen opposition you do?*

Sitov: No. We call all of them terrorists. Of necessity, we do not have those restrictions. What I'm trying to say is that I am trying to show in our reporting that it is not a given, it should not be taken for granted, that whoever fights against you is a terrorist.

Stephen Hess: *Hafez, you don't have a Qatar angle, or do you, on everyday stories?*

Al-Mirazi: No. It's an Arab angle, an Arab perspective, that's the main perspective for al Jazeera, and especially in this crisis and during this war. Al Jazeera had a unique position in which we had exclusive coverage from Kabul, the only camera and only TV team internationally to be in Kabul and to cover the war. At some points, people mixed the message with the messenger and wanted to shoot—they literally shot—the messenger. Our office had been bombed in Kabul by U.S. jets almost during the hours of the Northern Alliance storming into Kabul.

Kalb: *You believe that was done deliberately?*

Al-Mirazi: Until now we haven't heard deliberately or not deliberately. The emphasis for us in the Washington office was to make the balance as much as possible, to give the American perspective, because we already have the other side of the story. And that really put a lot of pressure on us covering "live coverage" of most of the major news conferences, live Arabic interpretation.

Kalb: *Do you run Secretary Rumsfeld's briefings every day?*

Al-Mirazi: Most of the time, unless we have a special program that we cannot interrupt or we feel that the briefing doesn't have something important today, just a routine one. But during the war, most of it we do. Even when most of the U.S. networks, except CNN, decided not to carry President Bush's speech from Atlanta, Georgia, about two weeks ago, al Jazeera was covering that and carrying it live with no taxpayer's money involved. Yet, we have been criticized.

Kalb: *You have been criticized for being a strongly anti-American Arab voice.*

Al-Mirazi: Yes. We have also been criticized as being anti-Saudi, anti-Egyptian. Al Jazeera puts on people who hold the views against the policies of the U.S. government as well as [invites] U.S. government officials to talk and to give their side of the story.

Kalb: *José, I want to give you an opportunity to explain, from a Mexican point of view, how the coverage runs.*

Carreño: There is a Mexican angle in this whole thing: for instance, What is the impact of this conflict on the U.S. borders with Mexico, in terms of vigilance, in terms of trade, in terms of immigration, in terms of the people that are already here, illegal aliens. Most of them are Mexicans, or at least a big part of them. And what is the effect on the U.S. economy? Mexico is a country that is extremely intertwined with the U.S. economy, so there is a very big impact for us there.

Kalb: *Yasemin, what has been [your] biggest story in the war coverage?*

Çongar: The biggest [story] within the war with a Turkish angle [is] the second front. Even from the first day on, [the story has been] What's going to be the second target? Because this is the only thing Turkey is so much concerned about. So, it's not happened yet. It's just up in the air. It's just speculative, but

I think it's the issue I wrote most about. I wouldn't say it's the most important one, but it's the issue I wrote most about.

Kalb: *Hafez, for you, what has been the single largest theme in this war?*

Al-Mirazi: I mean, if the war started September 11, it should be October 7, with the military action itself, and the airing of the bin Laden tape.

Kalb: *How did you work out that deal to get bin Laden exclusively?*

Al-Mirazi: We had an office in Kabul, and Kabul was under the control of Taliban, so it was very easy for anyone to deliver a tape to a news station in Kabul.

Kalb: *So, it went from bin Laden to your office in Kabul?*

Al-Mirazi: Of course, it's layers of people in the middle until they get it to you. And I always ask people, If it had been delivered to our Washington bureau, then you would have come and arrested me? But in Kabul—that's why you were bombing Kabul, because those people can deliver tapes like that to a TV station.

Kalb: *What was the last one you had?*

Al-Mirazi: The last one was, I believe, November 1, [when] we waited for a representative from the U.S. government with a statement from the White House to read in Arabic. Ambassador Christopher Ross, and he did a rebuttal live immediately after that tape was aired.

Kalb: *José, what has been the biggest story that you've covered in this war?*

Carreño: I think the beginning of the bombing itself; all the rest of the stories sort of pale next to it. The other side is that many of the consequences that I was talking about are still very much in the air. So there is not a definitive issue in terms of immigration or trade; it's very, very much still going on, a developing story.

Kalb: *And for ITAR, is this the largest story?*

Sitov: It is definitely one of the largest. It's not the largest. Obviously, the big story for us is the Russian angle in this story, the Russian participation, the Russian willingness to be partners, the Russian willingness to support the American advances to the Central Asian countries and to station troops there. And the Central Asian angle in general. In recent days, the biggest story was probably the introduction of the Russian presence in Kabul, although it's the emergency ministry's personnel rather than the military.

Hess: *Many years ago, it would have been unusual for you to talk on the international telephone to your office; it was expensive, cables were as well. Now, of course, with the technology, with your e-mail—tell us about your relationship to your home office. How is it different? Are they telling you what they want? Are you arguing with them about the angle? Yasemin, what's going on between you and Istanbul?*

Çongar: The biggest difference is the Internet. Now my editor in Istanbul reads [the] *New York Times* before I do or reads all kinds of Internet sites, web-

sites, and sees all these really weird stories which I have never heard of. Here you are sitting in Washington, watching all the TVs and talking to all your sources, and you don't hear that. And then they find this little story somewhere buried in there and say, "You know, this is happening, are you aware?" "What are you talking about?" So it's really so much more interactive.

In a way it's very advantageous that they are so much aware. But sometimes there is such an imbalanced view that they get from just Internet, from certain websites, and they think it is the fact. It just sounds perfect, and [they say] Let's do something on it. And then it's difficult for us to talk against it and to try to prove that this is not the case, [that] so and so said this, [but] so and so said [that]. And it's a livelier discussion.

Carreño: CNN effect, again. [M]y managing editor and the international editor of the newspaper have CNN all the time on their TV sets. So they see CNN, they see something developing on CNN, and [they say], "What do you have on that?" That is the fact. And they also have the *New York Times*. We also have all these stories. But I'm all the time under pressure to try to come up with the stories [when] sometimes I have no access [to sources] at all.

Sitov: Absolutely the same—a very important fact for us based in Europe is the time difference. We do not have any deadlines, being a news service, so the Moscow head office carries on during the night while we are away. I would say, again agreeing with what José has just said, we try to find some additional angles that are inaccessible to them in Moscow, and to probably show how this influences Russia or reflects on Russia or [has] some additional importance for the Russian audience.

Al-Mirazi: When you have to decide on interrupting regular programming to carry a news conference, for example, there are decisions to be taken. Usually it should be taken by the home office or the editor in chief. But, in this case, they would rely more on us in Washington to decide—Yes, interrupt your pro-gram and carry that, or, Don't carry that; there's not much you should expect from that news conference. And that would put more burden on your judgment, that you decided from Washington to interrupt an important show over there or a talk show, [maybe] creat[ing] some sensitivities with the host of the show. And then you sit and watch the news conference with your fingers crossed, hoping that something major [will] be in it because someone else will come and say, Why did you decide to carry it? So more responsibility first.

And then, as I'm saying, the American angle. Sometimes even you take the risk of sounding like an American mouthpiece, just because you feel that someone already did the other side of the story. So you feel that for the balance for the whole station you need to do it this way or to get a guest that you feel is giving the extreme [view]. Although in normal circumstances you wouldn't bring that guest to give the American story, you would get someone in the middle.

Hess: *Now, all of you are quite experienced in the United States. You've seen the country. You have some notion of the American character. Do you find it differs a great deal from how your editors and consumers see the American character, and are you working against that?*

Sitov: Sure. There is this great myth that Americans and Russians are very much alike. And I do not agree with that at all. The biggest difference that I see, and the biggest change that is happening in my country ever since the fall of the Soviet Union, is this mental shift in the attitude of my countrymen towards something closer resembling the American model, and that is reliance on oneself. I do believe this is of unbelievable importance for the Russian people to finally make people free in their own minds, in their own hearts.

Carreño: I would say that both the Mexican society and American society are two societies that are bent to ignore each other. So I do not claim that Mexicans understand even minimally what the American psyche is. We have had for too many years this image of an imperial American. And this is something that is an image that remains with us. The country is starting to know the United States, but I do not think that the old images have disappeared at all.

Çongar: I think this war and everything that's happened since September 11 has taught me that there is so much anti-American bias and so much anti-

American cynicism in Turkey. On paper, Turkey is a NATO country. We're very good allies. There's so much cooperation in every field. And actually the country itself, the way of life itself, although it's very different economically from here, but the importance of family—on a day-to-day basis, many things are very common between Turkish society and American society. But, there are very strong, very intrinsic negative feelings about America and Americans in general. And at the time when sympathy for Americans should be at the highest, since September 11, I have seen that there is so much questioning, so much cynicism, so much bias. And it's something I have to work against.

Al-Mirazi: I don't understand quite well the question about American [character]; what do you mean by that? Although, for example, I would make an effort to [clarify] President Bush's characterization of the war as a crusade, and I would try to put that into the American perspective in saying that [as] he's using the word, it means an all-out effort, it does not have anything to do with the historical Crusades. And yet, you would also have to [point out for balance] that unfortunately the American media would pick up a statement [for example, when] Arafat . . . would use the word "jihad," and [make] the same mistake that we do when Bush uses the word "crusade." For an Arab leader to use the word jihad, it doesn't have the same meaning, or political load, that it would have with the audience. Jihad is the same exact translation of crusade. It's an all-out effort; it doesn't have to have any violence in it, or a crusade or a fight between two religions.

These are the things that at times you feel that you would like to put into context so people would not just snatch the word and play with it. But in the meantime you find difficulty in explaining the American media, in trying to caution people not to judge what the U.S. government sometimes does or does not do by what the media put out—[you have to explain] that there is no media control. However, the media itself is pro-establishment. The media does not question the government in foreign policy. Even the Congress does not question the government in the U.S. in foreign policy.

Kalb: *When you pick up the* New York Times *or the* Washington Post *or you watch CNN, do you feel that you are getting just an American view of an event?*

Çongar: Of course it's an American view. I think the *New York Times* and *Washington Post* are really good newspapers, so in a way they still manage to be critical and to be objective in my own personal view. So it's not necessarily what the Bush administration is saying [that] is given to me in that paper. But it is an American angle, of course, and being a Washington correspondent I feel my job is to reflect that American angle, not necessarily to write from a

Turkish angle. Being a Turk and having all the Turkish background, of course I bring it somehow into my columns or my stories. But I try to reflect, Okay, the American media is saying this, American officials are saying that, and American commentators have been saying that. Former Clinton administration officials are saying that. So my aim is to arrive at a balanced representation of what the American view is, not only the Bush administration, not only the Congress, and not only the media, but overall the opinion makers in Washington in general.

Sitov: I agree on the high degree of professionalism of the American press. At the same time, I do believe this is an American point of view. I stand for a variety of points of view, as many as possible. That's why the Soviet Union collapse was probably good, because there are fifteen different points of view instead of one old one. And in terms of looking at the American press, I work at a news agency, and we cover news. At most what I do is maybe just explain what an American means when he says something, if it needs such context.

Other than that, we do have hardcore ideological stereotypes, both in my country about America, and in America about my country. In Russia it is mostly the communist press that keeps saying that Americans are to be suspected in everything, Americans basically have evil intentions.

Carreño: The United States for the first time ever has been the object of terrorist hate in its own land. So there is a very emotional side to it. The American press presents the American view of things; I mean, if you want to see American propaganda, go to the briefings, and you will see what is real propaganda. No matter how truthful they are, there is a huge bias there.

I do believe that the American press has done a very good job in this sense, at least. It has been the American press, the one that has made a ruckus in terms of civil rights, that has been airing the proposals to use torture as a method of [extracting] information, the one that has aired the problems of the inaccuracy of bombs in the bombing of Afghanistan. So I think that they have made a good job. Is there a built-in bias? Yes, there is a built-in bias, absolutely. You have to account for it. We have to realize that there is no way to avoid it. But once you are aware that there is a bias, you can discount it, and work with what is left.

Hess: *Say a little about being a foreign correspondent in the United States. What are your opportunities, what are your constraints, what's your access,* *what are your problems of filing or otherwise? How does this rate as a beat? What are the frustrations of working here? What are the pleasures?*

Sitov: It's the talk of the world. It's the best beat. And I feel it is a personal and professional privilege to work here. I started my American work in New York, and coming to Washington was a very big cultural shock. Bureaucracies, as I learned, are the same the world over. The American bureaucracy is probably similar to the Soviet one. I did encounter some of that in terms of access. I did have people reluctant to talk to me, probably for no other reason than I was Russian. But, I also met some wonderful people, made some very good friends.

I think after September 11, the government has started to realize the importance of talking to the international audience directly. And one of the changes that we are all seeing is that people from the State Department, people from the Treasury, people from the White House are coming regularly to the Foreign Press Center and talking to us. We appreciate that. We think it's very good for them, and it's certainly very good for us.

Carreño: To be in Washington is like to be a mosquito in a nudist camp. You know what to do, but not where to begin. There's such a wealth of information that you really can get lost trying to do it. There is so much information you're lacking eyes and hands to do everything, so you have to be very narrow. And in that sense I would say that I feel sometimes like if I were a reporter from a Texan newspaper dedicated to what is the Texas—or in this case Mexican— side of the story. So you have to narrow yourself, otherwise you get lost.

Çongar: I should add two things. First of all, of course, at least for the company I represent, we have a Washington office, we have a New York office, but we don't have offices all around the country. And this is such a big country to cover, and there are so many stories, it's really overwhelming at times. And it's not fair to America to have only Washington and New York correspondents, and no one in, let's say, San Francisco or Chicago.

On your question about the access, I would say actually this is a very welcoming capital for foreign journalists. I've been here for almost seven years now, and I've worked in other capitals, Western European capitals, and Middle Eastern capitals, and believe me, although I agree with Andrei that there is bureaucracy in this town, believe me, I have seen worse, including the Turkish capital itself. It's still easier to get by, still easier to have access to people. If you have a question they will try to answer it somehow. I mean, it may take time, but they will return your calls. I feel personally very welcome since the first day on.

Al-Mirazi: For me, the problem is not the lack of information, but the flood of information that you need to [review to] figure out what is really of substance [and then] put out [a] report of three minutes or an interview of three or four minutes. That's the first challenge. The second one is that if you work for [the] Arab media, you know that some of your colleagues in other capitals might step over the line and they might go to jail for whatever they say in criticizing the government. You feel privileged that you are in Washington. You can say whatever you want. Though you try not to take advantage of that. . . . to be responsible as a credible journalist.

Question (from the audience): *Do you have a policy when it comes to describing a suicide bombing which results in significant destruction and death? Do you describe this in political, religious, or criminal terms? Do you call this murder, an act of terrorism, an act of martyrdom? Does it matter where it's taking place as to how it may be defined or described?*

Sitov: We don't have a policy like that. Again, for me personally, the biggest challenge here, is that a single standard be applied to such cases everywhere. Terrorists are terrorists everywhere; that's what the Russians have been saying for years now.

Çongar: We don't have a policy either. And personally for me the definition of terrorism is very easy. Whenever civilians are attacked for any purpose, that is terrorism. So I don't really buy this difference between freedom fighters and terrorists. If it is against civilians first and foremost, it's a terrorist attack.

Carreño: There is no policy about that; however, a terrorist is a terrorist wherever.

Al-Mirazi: I try to avoid the whole term. I believe Reuters puts quotation marks on terrorist, because it's a controversial term. However, if we are talking about September 11, all the Arab media agreed this is a terrorist act. But there is a debate now because of what's going on between the Palestinians and the Israelis in the Arab media. For the Western media, when Palestinians kill Israeli civilians, they are terrorists; when Israelis kill Palestinian civilians, they are called soldiers. If you cannot call an Israeli a terrorist who is killing Palestinian civilians or innocent children, then you'd better not call the Palestinians terrorists, unless you can use the same term for both. Or try to quote the other, saying "what the Americans call [terrorists]," "what the Israelis call [terrorists]," and just attribute that.

Kalb: *Hafez, do you factor into that intent? In other words, was it intended to kill civilians or was it an accident that civilians were killed?*

Al-Mirazi: I think that when it happens under occupation, the struggle and the violence takes a different angle. That happened during the War of Independence in the American history, and with many other nations.

Question (from the audience): *I'm a reporter for a website publication on African news and events. I would like to know, on the responses you receive from the readers, whether proximity to the war, as your countries [have], except Mexico, does that matter in the responses in general? Because what I find is that in Africa, from the responses I receive the Africans take the war quite lightly.*

Carreño: I believe that there is a very ideological side of it. If you are anti-American, as it happens in many cases in many Latin American countries, you will find people that will proclaim . . . , "We are all Osama bin Laden." That has happened in Brazil, in Mexico, and even in France. That is an ideological view against the United States.

Now, the fact is also that we have had some people who died in the towers and that has informed in a way the Mexican response to it. However, at the same time we have had a very long story of friction with the United States, and . . . this is another component of the answer. So there is not a clear answer. But, it is a very mixed bag of different things.

Kalb: *Yasemin, Turkey, a member of NATO, a Muslim country, right smack in the middle.*

Çongar: Yes, and proximity plays a role, a very big role. As I said, although the story in Afghanistan is a very major story in Turkey, if there is a war in Iraq, again it's going to be a much bigger story. The closer it gets to home, the bigger the story gets, the more real the story gets for readers. It's interesting, because [if there is] a war in Iraq, of course Turkey will be more involved, and there will be a Turkish angle on everything. So it will be more real, like the war in Kosovo, for example, in Bosnia; I feel that they were more real for the Turkish audience. They understood it more, and they were interested in it more, because there [are] some ethnic ties. We have so many immigrants from those countries.

As for Afghanistan, for us, it's a very remote country. The language is totally different. The culture is to a certain extent different. Although, there is the same religion, we're a Muslim country as well. Still, it's far out there. But if it happens in our own region, in the Balkans or in the Gulf, then it's much more real.

Question (from the audience): *My question to Andrei and Hafez: in your work, do you get the perception or the assumption that you are an old enemy, in the case of Andrei, and a new enemy, in the case of Hafez?*

Sitov: Frankly, I don't feel that. What I feel on the part of the Americans is a sincere inability sometimes to see the world any other way than the American way. They seem to not understand how people have different viewpoints; it's so clear to them. It's not necessarily seeing you as the enemy, it's just that maybe if you are big and powerful, you can disregard other people's opinions. I think this question touches on the responsibility of journalists, because we know that here very many people believe what they hear on television and what they read in the newspapers, and that puts a greater onus on us to try and report things straight.

Al-Mirazi: The new enemy? Well, I believe it's a very valid question because until now, I believe, [on] the application for a visa to the U.S., you are still asked, "Have you ever joined the Communist Party?" And I believe the question should be now modified, [to] an Islamist party or something like that, because that's really perceived as the new enemy.

The rhetoric from the administration is very clear, we are not against Arabs and Muslims. However, during the last month, at least with the new legislation, the U.S. Patriot Act, the talk about tribunals, the detainees, and also the limit on the visa—twenty-five-days require[d] delay for Arab males, [for] Arab Muslim males from [the] age of eighteen until thirty-five, including the editor in chief of my station, who was supposed to be tomorrow in New York for a conference sponsored by the UN . . . [T]hey had to replace him, because he found out when he applied to the American embassy that as [an] Arab Muslim in the age of eighteen to thirty-five he has to wait . . . twenty extra days for security reasons. All of that hopefully is just temporary because of what happened on September 11, which would justify any temporary security measures. But we hope this is not the trend. It will be very difficult for the government to sponsor officially discriminatory policies and ask the people not to discriminate.

So far we are still in the mix. Everybody is worried about that. There is a feeling among the community, Muslim Americans, and also overseas, that we might become the new enemy. But so far nobody knows whether it is just because of the war or it's going to last.

March 6, 2002

Kalb: *Turning now to the perspectives of European correspondents in Washington, are you getting cooperation from the administration in trying to* *understand American policy? Where do you get information from? How dependent are you on the American press in getting your information?*

Toby Harnden: Well, I think there's one very practical day-to-day factor, which is the time difference. We have to file stories by lunch time, which doesn't give

us very much time to go out and go to seminars and go to these conferences. And we can't follow the U.S. daily newspaper cycle. So there's no doubt that we draw heavily on the American press, but also we've got two people in Washington, we've got one in New York, and one in LA. That's not very many people to cover the whole gamut of politics and life in America. It's an open society. We get briefings from British officials; certainly it's harder to get

them from American officials, certainly on the time scale we'd sometimes like them.

Kalb: *If you had a better time scale, would you be able to rely on U.S. sourcing?*

Harnden: I think "rely" would be too strong a word; it would be easier. You live in Washington, you develop your own sources. If you follow up with the State Department, you'll get the line. That's the line that you can hear in the briefings every day and you can read in the papers, and you can sort of write the line yourself, really. What you want to do is get behind the line, and the way to do that is to get to know people. And so the people that I draw most of my information from are not people who are spokesmen.

Rudy Lentz: Let me add, I think [sourcing is] a mix of everything. The think tanks play an important role insofar as they are sometimes translating and expressing [views more clearly] because they are more independent, [while with] spokesmen, I absolutely agree, you have to know them personally to be able to read between the lines. And that sometimes gives you also a hint where the direction is. I have a television studio with twelve people working for me; three are Americans—two technicians and one administration person. They are also sources, because they are plain people; they are coming in the morning and they have seen the news, but maybe they perceived the news in a different way than I did, and we talk about it. If I file a television report or give a comment, they react to it, because I ask for it. So I want them to be part of the decision process, the building of my own opinion. But, after all, I think it's a broad mix of where we get our information from.

Jean-Jacques Mevel: I hope that Toby won't take it badly, but the deadline is a poor excuse; nothing prevents you to work your sources in the afternoon for the day after. If you asked for a proportion, I would say that 80 percent of my production is basically rehashing what the American media is doing.

Kalb: *80 percent?*

Mevel: Yes. I put it really flatly. And so maybe in the European media we are allowed to put more of our analysis or judgment—I'm not speaking of propaganda, that's totally different—than the average American reporter. And luckily enough, now.

Harnden: I think on the practical business of reporting, the last place I was in was Northern Ireland, which was the biggest domestic news story in the UK and a big world story as well. And I found that regularly, if something big happened, I'd have, broadly speaking, three pieces to write. I'd have the splash, the main news story; I'd have an insight color piece on the bomb going off and what happened to people or to victims; and I'd have an analysis piece. What I've found in America regularly is that all those three elements have to be in one piece. There's a different kind of journalism; you're having to mix up those different strands. You've got to sort of translate that information and guide people much more than you have to on a domestic story.

Kalb: *In terms of the new technology, what is your relationship to your home office? I ask the question because "in my time" we were really quite detached from New York. In Moscow I didn't have much to do with New York. But with the new technology it would seem to me that you would be at the other end of an umbilical cord, being fed ideas, editing of your copy, that sort of thing.*

Harnden: Yes, it's a strange sort of relationship, in fact. We still have to dial into the *Telegraph* system—so it's still slightly antiquated. But in terms of the flow of information, what it means, I think, is that vast amounts of the information that I've got access to here, they've also got access to. And what we find is that before we've got off, the foreign desk has already read or at least scanned the *New York Times* and the *Washington Post*, and they've drawn up an initial [story list]. Rather than asking what we wanted or what we think should be done, they'll say, This should be done, because it's the lead in the *New York Times.* So we have to sort of grapple with that and there are a number of ways to do it. You can stay up late and get the first editions and then file your overnight so you get it in ahead, or you can just be quick on your feet in the morning.

But the other thing we've certainly found since September 11 is that everybody is an expert on America now because there are websites. Even the British domestic papers all have links to U.S. websites and U.S. articles. Professionally speaking, it was a relief in the immediate aftermath of September 11 that nobody else could get into the country in terms of journalistic reinforcements because what you often get is monstered by the big guns from the paper. But even so that didn't stop the flow of information. So large amounts of . . . it were being written from London, even though they were quoting Americans and it was all about America.

Mevel: I totally agree with Toby on the fact that people in the French department have read the newspaper before [I have] my coffee in the morning. There  are two sides to the problem. One is to consider that since you can get access to the U.S. press earlier in Paris, why don't we shut down the Washington office? . . . On the other hand, I think it pushes the [Washington] correspondent to provide what he is really able to do, which is local sources, local experience, local background. I mean, the correspondent is supposed to know what he's talking about, and that's the big difference between writing about the country you live in and a country you read about every morning on the website of the *Washington Post*. But it's true, it's new, and it's provocative, and it pushes us to a change in our trade.

Hess: *Does the Internet mean that you're more likely rewriting the* Washington Post *or the* New York Times?

Harnden: No, I think it's actually less because I think what it does is it challenges us to add value. [Now that our editors read the U.S. press in real time] we have to constantly justify why we're here and give added value, and go and get our own stories, and go to our own places. So I think it's an antidote against lazy foreign journalists.

Mevel: It's also a help in the sense that for a factual story they no longer need me. What they will ask me is, What does it mean, what are the implications, how did the American people react to this? And I must say, in a way, it's a much more interesting job to do now than it was fifteen years ago.

Kalb: *Rudy, might you now be pushed into adding value to your news production that is not straight reporting but is much more news analysis? And if you have to do news analysis, do you feel that you're being pushed to say things that you're not all that comfortable with?*

Lentz: Let's put it this way, I think we are closer to commenting about things and events than ever before. In former times it was enough for a television producer or reporter to stay in front of a building in telling a story. But the agencies like Reuters or AP, they have more crews than we have out there. Sometimes they have the pictures earlier than we because we are not on the spot. So our only advantage is to put it into context, to analyze it, to give added value to it. One difficulty for a television guy like I am is the news breaks, the small reports, don't leave you space many times to give more value, more background, analysis. So if there are not other slots where you can give that value and that deeper information, then I think really you can give up foreign correspondents all over the world, because the pictures are much easier to get and cheaper from news organizations like Reuters or AP or others.

Hess: *Could I ask one question about anti-Americanism? And I separate that from somebody who is against some American policy. Is it just a myth that Americans have created?*

Harnden: No, I certainly don't think it's a myth. When I was in high school, I remember Ronald Reagan. There was a television program called *Spitting Image*, and they had an item, "The President's Brain is Missing." This became part of the lore over there. And amongst, again, elites, the upper reaches of the newspapers, the media, there's a very strong sense in Europe—perhaps in continental Europe a bit more than Britain, which is, I think, more instinctively pro-American—that Europeans are more sophisticated and more thoughtful and more reasonable and [that] Americans eat too much, are very fat, and just make loads of money, and don't read books, and don't have passports, and don't travel. And I feel that this is under the surface the whole time. After September 11, for most people, there was sort of a decent period of mourning, and now it's rising to the surface again. And you saw that with the reaction to the axis of evil speech, just as you saw it with reaction to the evil empire under Reagan.

Hess: *So how do you then deal with it, if you deal with it at all, in your reporting?*

Harnden: Well, you try to counter it—I mean, the whole time really. All through the election Bush was portrayed in most of the British press as a complete idiot who would certainly lose to Al Gore. So throughout all my coverage—I hadn't been here that long, I was initially fairly sensitive—I was saying, Hang on a minute, I think there's more to this guy than meets the eye. He may very well win, and you should take him seriously. And looking back, I wish I had done that a bit more strongly at the outset because you really have to correct this misperception.

Lentz: We call it the Kohl effect in Germany because we had underestimated that candidate beforehand as well, especially by the press. When [Helmut] Kohl was elected chancellor first, and public opinion was for him, the media thought this guy is plain stupid, and it turned out he was not plain stupid. And we give you the benefit of the doubt as well.

To come back to the clichés, I think anti-Americanism has been existing for a long time. . . . [T]hose mindsets are there and you can call them up. And I think this is the problem. You can easily play on those images and perceptions, and we might see more of those in the upcoming months. But we can only give our input from this side and try to calm the tensions and to explain a little in a broader framework.

Mevel: My own view on that is to talk about France, which is usually a good target when one talks about anti-Americanism. I would say the historical French anti-Americanism is on the go. Maybe I'm one of the last who has gone to universities where teachers were either Gaullists or communists, and both of them for obvious reasons had some interest in understating the American mission through the centuries. Fortunately, people do travel, young people especially; they come to the U.S. and they see.

So I would say that the French people reacting, for example, to 9/11 in New York City was the reaction of people, many of them, who had been to New York and knew what was going on. They had the Twin Towers in their pictures in their photo album. At the same time, George Bush, I'm sorry to say, is an excellent excuse for those bursts of anti-Americanism. I mean, we don't have any affinity with him. I'm not talking about myself. I'm talking about the average feeling of the French people or the way they perceive George Bush through what I write. Maybe they don't understand what I write, but maybe I'm going native now.

Hess: *Do you feel you're going native?*

Harnden: You sometimes get accused of it. It's strange. I left Britain for my last holiday on September 10. I haven't been back there since then. If it had been a day later, I would have been stranded at Heathrow and wouldn't have gotten here for about ten days. So I speak to people in Britain the whole time, obviously, every day, and I have to write for the British audience, and I think it's important to go back every so often. I'm going back in a couple weeks' time to sort of soak up what the differences are. But you certainly have to avoid the danger of going native. It's very easy to do. You have American friends, you watch American TV, you enjoy America, and all the rest of it. So you have to be careful to take a step back, because you are writing for a foreign audience.

Hess: *How often do you go back, Rudy, to remind yourself of from whence you came?*

Lentz: Four to six times a year, so this is pretty often. But I have an additional threat to face. My daughter is attending an American school. And this is really an impact on the family, because she brings back all the cultural influences which she is facing. So I think this is a nice struggle in the family. We try to keep her European or German, and she is forcing us to get even more closely involved in [the] American lifestyle. But to make a differentiation: I was stationed here between '88 and '91, and Washington has changed very much for the better in the time in between. And it has become, from a European point of view, much more European, more international, more affluent. Even the restaurants have become far better than they have been ten or twelve years ago.

Question (from the audience): *How much of the differences between Europe and the United States is really context? The term "war" I think is very important to talk about, because if you mention war in Europe, you have a totally different context than you have in the United States.*

Harnden: Well, I think there's a great difference at the moment between the language that's used in America and in Europe, and also I think there was a very severe psychological shock that America experienced and is still experiencing that people in Europe didn't experience to the same extent. And I think if you look at this, the rise in popularity of Donald Rumsfeld, I think, is a very interesting example of this. This guy stands up before the American press and talks joyously about the number of enemy troops that are being killed and smiles about it and uses the verb "to kill" the whole time. There were none of these old American Clintonian terms, if you like, about collateral damage and euphemisms. I think part of that is because it's a different administration. A big part of it is September 11.

Also, the use of the word "evil." Now, clearly, Ronald Reagan did it; he used that as well. But that's not a word that is fashionable in Europe, to talk about the fight between good and bad, good and evil, and right and wrong. But it's very deeply embedded in the American psyche, particularly after September 11, and I find that that's one of the big disconnects at the moment.

Kalb: *Do you agree with that?*

Mevel: Yes. I think it goes further than just the speeches. When I talk to American friends saying to me that America is at war—that's the country where I live, and I have the feeling that I'm missing something and I don't know what they're talking about. I mean, the U.S. is obviously at war with terrorism, but the country itself, is it really at war? I mean, maybe it was at war one day, on September 11.

Lentz: I think that that touched a very, very important point. After the First World War, but especially after the Second World War, we have been trying to convince not only ourselves but also the public and the rest of the world [that] political goals have to be achieved by diplomatic or political means and not by war, not by force. This is the whole concept of the European Union. And here comes a nation after 9/11 which takes the challenge of a new threat on globally and says, "We only can root that out by force, and by tremendous force and overwhelming force," and all the vocabularies which are involved are very, very far away from what we use in our talks, in our political talks amongst ourselves in Europe. And there's a certain form of actual cultural differences.

Kalb: *How do you reason with Osama bin Laden? You seem to be suggesting that if the president uses the word "evil" to describe Osama bin Laden that there's something naive and Texan cronyish about him.*

Harnden: I agree with him, actually. Since September 11, I feel like I'm more like an American than a European. British people don't really say they're European. They talk about themselves as being British, and we've got the whole legacy of a shared language and culture and UK-American relations. So I don't have a problem with it at all. I find myself more and more having a problem with people in Europe. At least what you get here is people saying what they mean, which is what I find refreshing. And I think a lot of ordinary people in Britain do as well.

Mevel: That's the big difference between Osama bin Laden and Saddam Hussein. I mean, as long as the problem is to deal with bands of terrorist gangs, networks, there's no discussion, not with the Europeans, not with the U.S. No problem, just watch what happened on September 11. But when you're dealing with states, I mean, there's something called diplomacy, and war is the last resort of diplomacy. But you have to try diplomacy first. That's the way the world works now.

Hess: *It's a very big country, and you all have relatively small bureaus. How much opportunity do you have within your budgets to see places that are off the coasts?*

Mevel: It depends on the intensity of the news. And, unfortunately, for the past three years, between America, the Florida election, and September 11, I've been quite busy. And actually, it didn't leave us much time to go abroad. But the last year, I was able to travel. I would say I would go ten times a year out of Washington reporting, physically doing my job.

Lentz: Less than we would, but it's still enough. I mean, this country is a large country compared to where we all come from. But it's so different. Everyone of us, and I think this is a common belief amongst all foreign correspondents, love to go out and see and feel and smell the country and not get stuck here on the East Coast, especially in Washington. There's lots of things to offer, and we're going to experience and try to explore it.

Harnden: It's possible to do. I'm actually taking part in a competition with a colleague on the BBC as to how many states we can report from. And in two years I've actually written stories from thirty-five different states. And you do find excuses. Even after September 11, I thought it was very, very important to get out of Washington because it's a business city where the business is government in many respects, and 87 percent of the population of D.C. voted for Al Gore. It's very different from the rest of the country. It's very important to get out. And you can find excuses to do it. I mean, leisurely after September 11, I went to South Dakota and Nebraska to write about the economy and how people felt in middle America. And those are the pieces that often get into the paper, rather than a sort of academic piece about the economy from Washington.

PART FIVE

From Different Perspectives

14

Public Diplomacy or Propaganda?

T hroughout the cold war, the United States and the USSR were engaged in many battles. One of them was for "the hearts and minds of the people." Critics undercut and undervalued that battle, describing it as nothing more than "propaganda." By attaching a pejorative connotation to the word, they displayed their distaste for the effort.

When the war against terrorism erupted on 9/11, the United States found itself in another war for the hearts and minds of the people—this time, of the Arab and Muslim peoples. The U.S. government tried to sanitize the process by describing it as "public diplomacy" and by establishing a high-visibility bureau of public diplomacy at the State Department, but at the end of the day it might still have seemed to be propaganda to its intended audience. To define this new war between "propaganda" and "public diplomacy," we invited four experts on January 16, 2002, to discuss their different approaches to and perspectives on this problem. They were

—**Karen DeYoung**, a veteran foreign correspondent and associate editor of the *Washington Post*

—**Thomas A. Dine**, president of Radio Free Europe/Radio Liberty, based in Prague, capital of the Czech Republic

—**Joseph Duffey**, former director of the United States Information Agency

—**Christopher Ross**, former U.S. ambassador to Syria and Algeria and special coordinator for the assistant secretary of state for public diplomacy.

The central problem, it soon became clear, was one of definition. Ross saw in public diplomacy something distinctly different from propaganda. It was, he said, "the public face of traditional diplomacy." Did it include propaganda? Did it allow for lying? His answer: "We don't deliberately look to state things that are not true. We may couch them in a certain way, but we deal with the truth." Duffey put it less obliquely. Public diplomacy was "to speak directly to the public," to interpret and explain U.S. "values and policies," and not to lie. Dine spoke to the unshakable importance of truth-telling. DeYoung thought the United States was selling its antiterrorism message well to the American people but "not very well at all overseas."

Were people "overseas" not buying the American position because they no longer admired America's democratic values or because they disagreed with American policy in the Middle East? "With some exceptions," Ross didn't think that "people hate America," though they might disagree strongly with certain "concrete policies," such as U.S. support of Israel. Dine was more optimistic and direct. "Deep down, underneath the rage, underneath the hate," he said, "is this admiration for the American system." DeYoung provided a journalistic response. Secretary of Defense Rumsfeld's apparent candor at his almost daily briefings beamed to countries around the world eased the problem of explaining American policy considerably, but in her view the Pentagon's PR "apparatus" often undermined his performance by being less than candid about military operations, leaving journalists with the feeling that once again they were being misled.

In conclusion, the experts tangled not with differing definitions of "public diplomacy" but with the usual collision between the Pentagon and the press over trade-offs on how much information should be given to the public. DeYoung expressed a commonly held view: "Sometimes we lose, sometimes they lose." The key question was, Who controls the flow of information in wartime? On this, the Pentagon undoubtedly won much more than it lost.

Marvin Kalb: *I have an article that [former U.S. representative to the UN] Dick Holbrooke did for the* Washington Post *two months ago, saying, "Call it public diplomacy, call it public affairs, psychological warfare, if you really want to be blunt, propaganda." Ambassador Ross, is it simply propaganda? And if it is, that's fine. Just explain it to us.*

Christopher Ross: I conceive of public diplomacy as being the public face of traditional diplomacy. Traditional diplomacy seeks to advance the interests of the United States through private exchanges with foreign governments. Public diplomacy seeks to support traditional diplomacy by addressing nongovernmental audiences, in addition to governmental audiences, both mass and elite. It works very much in coordination with and in parallel to the traditional diplomatic effort. When I hear the word "propaganda," I imagine a much more manipulative kind of process than I would like to think that public diplomacy is.

Kalb: *Is propaganda providing lies, trying to put a bad thing in a good light?*

Ross: Much propaganda contains lies and does not shy away from them. In public diplomacy we don't deliberately look to state things that are not true. We may couch them a certain way, but we deal with the truth.

Joseph Duffey: I think the issue now is credibility. You can't get away with lies very much. They damage your credibility. Maybe the sharpest way that I came to understand public diplomacy is [that] it's an attempt to get over the heads or around the diplomats and official spokesmen of countries and sometimes around the press to speak directly to the public in other countries and to provide an interpretation, explanation of U.S. values and policies.

Kalb: *Do you regard Radio Free Europe/Radio Liberty as being involved in propaganda, public diplomacy, or what?*

Thomas A. Dine: In the case of a news gathering and news disseminating organization like ourselves, you try to gather facts, you try to understand the  difference between important news and nonimportant news, and then disseminate [it] with the belief that in a democracy, in a society of pluralistic ideas and situations, that you will be informing people of news and information so they can make decisions.

The negative view of propaganda is that it is a methodological way of either being in favor of something or against something. From a news and information point of view, we're trying to fulfill the first responsibility of our freedom—the freedom of speech, freedom of press. That's how we conduct ourselves in putting together our programs every day.

Kalb: *Karen, as a reporter, how do you think the United States is doing in the dissemination of truth to the rest of the world?*

Karen DeYoung: I'm going to go to definition briefly, because I think the word "propaganda" has come to have a pejorative connotation, but in fact in terms of definition [it] just deals with the dissemination of information to further one's purpose. I think that where it is the same as public diplomacy is in how you choose your information, what information you choose to make public. Obviously you choose to make public information that furthers your own aims, which is not the same as telling lies. And I don't think one would expect necessarily any administration to do differently.

How have they been doing? I think that they've been doing very well in this country, because I think people are very much disposed to agree with them. We have found that when you write things that don't necessarily agree with them or at least are seen as not agreeing with them, you get a whole lot of response very quickly.

I think they're not doing very well at all overseas. Not because they've been derelict somehow in putting out information, but just because people are not disposed to believe this particular brand of information. They're getting other information from other sources, and when they balance it, according to what their own beliefs are, it doesn't necessarily measure up.

Kalb: *Ambassador Ross, do you see major difficulties in getting the position of the United States across?*

Ross: It is not an easy task, but it's somewhat different from what has been portrayed in the media since September 11. If you recall, since September 11  there has been a theme to the effect that the world hates us, or at least certain important segments of the world hate America, and that somehow public diplomacy must affect that hate and transform it into something else.

From my perspective, having worked overseas a number of years, I don't think that people hate America, with some exceptions. What you see overseas in most cases is a mixture of admiration and envy and a certain amount of dislike for the fact that we are the sole remaining superpower. But that doesn't translate into the kinds of extreme actions that we saw on September 11.

I think what people react to most abroad is concrete policies that they don't agree with. And that is the focus of their attention. As we try to address all of this, our first task is to make sure that our government's policies are understood for what they are and not for what other people are saying they are. So there's a process of explication here which is useful. It does not change many minds when people are truly not in sync with our policies. But beyond that there is a much-longer-term effort needed to put those policies in a context, a context of American values.

Kalb: *Could you provide a single element of success?*

Ross: One of the main accusations that was hurled at us in the aftermath of September 11 and in the lead-up [to] and the execution of the war in Afghanistan was that we were not really fighting terrorism, we were fighting Islam. I think we've been fairly successful over the weeks in countering that to the point where no serious commentator at this point in the Arab world or the Muslim world is harping on that theme. I think there's been acceptance of the notion that the war was in fact against the al Qaeda organization and against the Taliban regime that was harboring the al Qaeda in Afghanistan. So on that particular theme, I think there has been a shift in the way people are viewing our efforts.

Dine: I think deeds are more important than the rhetoric, although the rhetoric by the president of the United States has been excellent. Simple, direct, and consistent. But the deeds are even more important. Living in Europe you feel the love and the hate. Living in Europe before September 11, you felt the love and the hate. Nothing is really new. The French have been irritated at us for a long, long, long, long time.

The fact that we can criticize ourselves on a constant basis [and] we do—that is our glory. That is our exceptionalism to the world.

Kalb: *But that was true before September 11 also.*

Dine: Correct. That's why they love us. Down deep, underneath the rage, underneath the hate, is this admiration for the American system being able to work.

Stephen Hess: *Recently, Sandy Ungar, the former director of the Voice of America [VOA], said, "The Voice of America has really made an effort over a period of time to present all sides of these extremely difficult stories. The State Department has tried to end the objective role of the Voice of America, tried to turn it into a propaganda agency, I hope without success." What in heaven's name was Sandy Ungar talking about, Chris Ross?*

Ross: I think the issue was the tussle over coverage of [an interview the VOA aired with Taliban leader] Mullah Omar. I was not in government at the time of that tussle so I don't really know all the details. By general agreement, the State Department does look over VOA editorials that are quite clearly meant to reflect official U.S. government views. And as for the rest of the VOA's operations, the State Department like anybody is free to suggest, to propose, et cetera, and the VOA is free to dispose. I think what happened with the coverage of Mullah Omar's interview was an exception to that rule, which at least as far as I'm concerned should not happen again.

DeYoung: But again, this is a perennial situation with VOA. I remember in Argentina in the late '70s covering the U.S. human rights campaign that started with the Carter administration. I think it's healthy. There are a lot of people, particularly in Congress, who believe that VOA should be a propaganda arm of the United States. Under its charter, it's not supposed to be. I think most of the people who work there believe it is not supposed to be. And whenever there is a foreign policy issue that the United States is deeply involved in, this question comes up. It's argued out, and sometimes the victory is on the side of more information and sometimes it's on the side of less; but I think it's a relatively healthy argument that's not necessarily unique to this situation.

Kalb: *Karen, how important is it all? Tom Dine said [that] deeds, not words, are what people around the world [use to] measure the success or failure of the United States. If the United States did not appear to win in Afghanistan militarily, would all of the eloquence of Ambassador Ross been worth, forgive me, much?*

DeYoung: Sure. Obviously it's important to win. You don't get into something like this unless you win. The importance of deeds, at least deeds that we consider positive, is that someone covers them, that someone talks about them, that they're written about, that they're broadcast. All of us are kind of scrambling for stories now in Afghanistan. The well seems to be a little dry at the moment.

On the other hand, it's important to cover things like civilian casualties from American bombing. Part of Secretary Rumsfeld's brilliance is [that] he says things like, "I don't know." "I'm not going to tell you." "War is hell"— things that everybody already knows and [that] kind of stop you short. Whereas the Pentagon itself and the Pentagon's public information apparatus is very poor when it comes to responding to things like that. Their instant attitude is number one, "It didn't happen." Then when there is information that shows that perhaps it did happen, they say, "We're investigating." Then, they fall back on [the claim that] our technology is so good and our targeting is so good that it couldn't have happened. Then you say, "Did you go there to see?" They say, "We can't tell you that, because we can't tell you about movements on the ground." So they're kind of stuck, but they don't present it very well.

Kalb: *Chris, your professional experience has been largely in the Middle East, and you speak Arabic and you know a lot about Islam. How valuable is public diplomacy to this country at this time?*

Ross: I think in its broadest sense—that is, including all of the aspects of what we have considered public diplomacy, both on the information side and on the educational and cultural exchange side in the past—it has been very valuable. When you look at the number of people who have been brought to this country to be exposed to American values, to return to their own country [to] take up positions of leadership, I would posit that had that kind of activity not existed, attitudes in the Middle East would be even worse than they are today. So the world is better for public diplomacy. The great dilemma is that there are very few concrete barometers, very few concrete ways to measure the effectiveness of any particular activity.

Hess: *One measurement always has to be the truth of what we're saying. The State Department's public diplomacy program is very proud of an advertising campaign that it put out called Rewards for Justice, an advertisement which showed [9/11 hijacker] Mohammed Atta. Then, underneath [his picture], the text said, "He wanted to learn to fly but didn't need to take off and land." "He was interested in crop dusting, an obviously risky behavior, when he couldn't even get a plane off the ground." Both of those statements were wrong, of course. He wasn't the one who made the first statement; it was [suspected hijacker accomplice Zacarias] Moussaoui who made the first statement. And in terms of the second statement, we know he had a pilot's license and he did fly small planes. So isn't one of the ways that we're judged ourselves the scrupulousness with which we tell our own story?*

Ross: Preparation of the text, in retrospect, could have been done differently. The audience for that poster and other similar posters was not the legal profession; this was not a legal document. The audience was a mass audience. And what had been intended at the time was a series of statements that would describe situations that one might find oneself in [in] daily life. Why is this [person] asking to fly, but not to take off or land, et cetera. And we could have put up a generic picture of a terrorist above, but that wouldn't have had the same effect as a face that was immediately recognizable.

DeYoung: But I think that that's part of the point. [Y]ou say it wasn't for a legal audience, it was for a broad public audience so then it was okay that it wasn't totally accurate because putting those quotes with those pictures made a better point. People knew that picture because it had been all over the place. Those quotes were particularly stark. You put them together, and it's designed to create a reaction. Is it then okay that in fact those quotes don't go with that picture, just because it's for a broad audience?

Duffey: On the other hand, it was advertising, and we don't always expect truth in advertising. Public diplomacy shouldn't be advertisements.

Dine: All of this points to a certain disarray in our public diplomacy. From my perspective, one of our brilliances is the ability of successful candidates to put on campaigns, rhetoric, presence, images, substance. Why can't we do this in public diplomacy? If the right hand and the left hand, in this case public diplomacy and the security operation of the State Department, are going in opposite directions, you immediately undermine yourself with untruthfulness. That's the worst thing you can do in either diplomacy or public affairs. Hans Morgenthau once said that there are five elements of national security—military, intelligence, diplomacy, economics, and information. We spend a pittance on information. We don't know what the left and right hands are doing sometimes, and it's not a campaign. It's not systematic. Therefore we are not as good as we could be.

Kalb: *Tom, tell us a little bit about what you do. For example, during the cold war, Radio Free Europe and Radio Liberty were literally front-line operations in the fight against communism.*

Dine: Our mission is the promotion of freedom and democracy. Our mission is to help build democratic institutions, democratic processes in countries that used to be communist, totalitarian. We broadcast to twenty-seven countries, and at the end of this month we'll add a twenty-eighth, Afghanistan. We're now up to twenty-eight languages. We'll [have] thirty when we start Dhari and Pashtu. Then, next month, on February 28, we'll be on the air to the northern Caucasus, a very troubled part of Russia, and programs will be in Avar, Czechen, and Caucasian languages.

The point is [that] in these languages we report news, and we have people on the ground. Right now today—and I just talked to our headquarters in Prague before this session began—we have twenty people on the ground in Afghanistan, not just in Kabul but all over the country, collecting news, putting it together in terms of stories. It goes back to Prague. Then all of our language services pick it up. But it has to be factual, it has to be accurate, it has to be balanced, and it has to be what's important.

Kalb: *Are you getting any instructions from Washington as to what you put on the air?*

Dine: We're not a government agency.

Kalb: *But you're getting government money.*

Dine: Thanks to the taxpayers of America, we are a private, nonprofit organization incorporated in the state of Delaware. But the appropriation does come from Congress, therefore I have to keep Congress informed of what we're doing.

Hess: *Tom, on civilian casualties in Afghanistan: you've got twenty reporters on the ground in Afghanistan. Are you looking into that question?*

Dine: Absolutely. The degree of destruction, the constant interviewing of the interim government ministers and their people on the difficulty of starting [a new government], the role of the United States, the role of the Western Alliance, the role of the grand coalition in this case—so everything is fair game. We're going to report what is happening and what is not happening in terms of nation building.

Kalb: *Chris, you said earlier that a lot of it goes back to American policy. There isn't very much that you can do about that with respect to public diplomacy, I imagine, except explain it better.*

Ross: That's true, to explain it in our own terms and not in the terms of third parties that may have one interest or another in presenting a slightly different version of our policy. But also—at least on the principal conflict of the region, one on which much of this antipathy has hinged, the Arab-Israeli conflict—also to keep hammering away at the fact that we have been involved in efforts to solve that conflict for decades, that no one else has stepped up to the plate in quite the same relatively effective way, and to make the point that peace has, after all, become an interest of everyone in the region, again with the exception of some extremist fringe elements.

Hess: *We come back to the question of what you are doing other than explaining what is already out there. Do you have a ten-point program? You've mentioned one—to explain that this is not a war against Islam—that you said you've had some success in. What's point two, three, four? What is it that you are stressing that turns American policy into a separate division called public diplomacy as opposed to public affairs, where a spokesman gets up and gives a statement in order to respond to reporters every day?*

Ross: One is to represent the basic American values that unite this country. The second theme is to present democratization and openness as a vision for a better future, a future which does not require people to resort to terrorism. And a third theme which hits at what we are coming to consider increasingly to be perhaps the most important audience for our work: young people, those who are going to create the future, whose world views and mind sets are not yet fully formed. The third theme focuses on them through a look at educational systems and how they are structured. So you have values, you have democratization and openness, [and] you have education as three focal points of a total communications plan that would mobilize the resources of public diplomacy in all their aspects, both on the information side and on the educational and cultural exchange side.

Hess: *Karen DeYoung is taking notes like mad. What's your lead going to be?*

DeYoung: What would be the lead on that? I think the lead would be how they're going to go about trying to influence the education systems in other countries. Senator Levin made a statement the other day about something that's not new, but about Saudi Arabia, saying that in their education systems they teach people to hate. He said some fairly extreme things. The Saudi ambassador, Prince Bandar, issued a statement this morning and said, We don't teach anybody to hate in our schools; our schools conform to our own values and our own traditions. And basically said, I like Senator Levin, but he's completely off base, and please stay out of our education system. And I guess my question would be, How are you going to do that? How is that a matter of public diplomacy? I would ask more about how you're going to go about that.

Ross: The resources available are minuscule compared to the task. So part of this strategy involves encouraging other agencies within the U.S. government that have much greater resources to work along a common task to focus on this problem. It's essentially an effort to make sure that educational systems— particularly in the current campaign against terrorism, particularly in the Muslim and Arab countries—evolve in a way that provides to young people the tools needed for modern life so that they are not attracted to the apocalyptic kind of vision that Osama bin Laden and others have proffered. We recognize it's an enormous task, but the fact that it's enormous doesn't make it not worth pursuing. As a matter of fact, there are some government officials in the region who have already expressed an interest in seeking our help on this point.

Dine: The interesting thing about Bandar's statement is that it gets at one of the problems we've all faced since September 11. The Arab-Israeli conflict is what it is, and everybody blames that as the reason for the hate and the rage in the streets against America. But in fact bin Laden's rage and hate is really about the system of Saudi Arabia, and so [is the rage of] many others who see the

United States, the Western allies, as in favor of protecting and furthering oppressive regimes.

I'm a person who believes not in the top down but in the bottom up, and what has happened in the authoritarian Arab countries is that there's no bottom up, and people have had it. You can't stop information any more because of television, radio, and [the] Internet. It's sort of like the communist society when they began to see blue jeans and movies, more than jazz—they had it with communist rule. I think that's what's beginning to creep, if not run, in Saudi Arabia, Egypt, and other places.

So monarchies don't have a bright future. And if the United States can have a long-run strategy of getting the word out that you can only progress with great substance as long as your societies are open, pluralistic—these values, which are universal, they're not just Anglo-Saxon—then we've got an interesting future ahead of us which will be quite troubled, filled with turmoil, but [also with] important needed change.

DeYoung: How do you deal with the fact that to the extent [that] there is opposition in those societies it almost inevitably is channeled into Muslim extremism?

Dine: That's always the excuse. Give it a chance. It doesn't have to be that way. It doesn't have to be bin Laden who comes to power. It may be one of the products of our educational/cultural affairs [programs], somebody who spent more than two weeks in the United States, somebody who may have had an education at Oxford or Cambridge.

Kalb: *Chris, put yourself back to the time that you were our ambassador in Syria. You got the word from Washington: We're going to talk about education. Be practical, realistic, professional. How do you do that in Syria, for example?*

Ross: I think as in most countries you would hit a variety of bases. You would go see the ministers of education and open a dialogue with them on the state of education in a given country.

Kalb: *And they say to you that we have our culture, our system, and, in effect, keep your hands off?*

Ross: And I think we would respond in a given country [that] we're not here to question your values. We're here to help if you wish us to help develop a curriculum in which the kids receive the tools needed for life in the modern world, in the modern global economy, and go at it that way.

Just to come back to something Tom said. One of the problems in the region, which is by and large governed by authoritarian regimes, is that civil society as we know it here is very weak. There are no intermediary organizations between government and citizens. I once served in a country where a government official said rather proudly to me that "we have turned our people into dust." And one of the tasks at hand under the second rubric I mentioned, democratization and openness, is to encourage those budding examples of civil society, nongovernmental organizations, to begin appearing to fill that void between government and people in many of these countries and to create a different kind of political culture.

Hess: *While we're dealing with these positive values, they're dealing with propaganda. How are we responding to that? What is the machinery in our government that is analyzing this and disseminating this and making the rest of the world aware of the disinformation, the lies, the innuendos that we've heard about?*

Ross: This is done on a daily basis through our press guidance operation. The world press is surveyed on themes that come out, whether they be true or false. And if something is an outright lie, we will say so. That's one part of it. Another part of it is to make oneself available for media appearances in which these lies come out. This has certainly happened to me on al Jazeera. I don't think I will ever forget one session I had with an American-trained Jordanian academic on a panel who insisted to me that a handful of corporations in this country, controlled by a certain minority, ran everything in government and outside of government here, and he could not be shaken off that view. It was a rather sad commentary. Those things exist, and all you can do is counter them with facts and say right up front, This is simply not true.

Question (from the audience): *I'm Gil Robinson with the Center for the Study of the Presidency. We have a project called Communicating America. One of the panels came up with a recommendation to have a coordinator in the White House, everything stems from the White House, similar to Governor Ridge, for information policy. And that would be able to coordinate NIH [National Institutes of Health] and HHS [Department of Health and Human Services] and Defense, public diplomacy at the State Department, the White House itself, and have it coordinated.*

Duffey: I can't imagine the American government would stand for that. It would sound to me like it's totally inconsistent with our whole tradition, and I would think that a united front of American journalists would oppose that.

Kalb: *Isn't this person Karen Hughes?*

DeYoung: I think that theoretically exists now. This administration has tried to centralize information in a way that has been displeasing to journalists.

If you are the head of HHS or FEMA [Federal Emergency Management Agency] or the FBI, you can say, "Oh, no, that information comes from Tom Ridge's office; I'm not giving you that information." Does that work? Maybe for a while, but I think it irritates people, and I think it's not the best way to get information out.

Does it also result in an uncoordinated message? Sure. The other night, I was sort of bemoaning the reticence of the current administration to disseminate information, and a fairly senior person in the Clinton administration said, "You know, we have learned a great lesson from these people. It works not to be available on the phone. It works to shift responsibility to another office. That's what we're going to do if we ever come back." You could call up people any time you wanted to in the Clinton administration, and they would pick up the phone. They see that as having caused them a lot of problems. That particular problem is one that doesn't affect this administration quite so much.

It's a trade-off. It's a trade-off between our argument that the more information we have the better we are able to reflect the truth and all parts of the truth, and their belief that if [they] limit the information that's available to you and funnel it through one source, then [they] have control over that information. And sometimes we lose; sometimes they lose. Hopefully in the end everybody wins.

Ross: As the war in Afghanistan has wound down and policymakers have had more time to think systemically, there are discussions under way to create some kind of coordinating body in the realm of public diplomacy—messages addressed to foreign audiences. This is still very much at the preliminary stage, but the need is recognized to coordinate the activities of the main agencies involved in providing information to foreign audiences.

Duffey: Your point sounds strategic and that's what I would argue, but it just won't work. It won't work in this society, which has no tradition of centralization of news and information, plus the energy and resourcefulness of our press would break this apart pretty quickly.

Question (from the audience): *How would you evaluate how propaganda and truth have been presented and communicated, looking at religion? We hear it coming from our president that Islam is simply a religion of peace and tolerance. I'm wondering how those that are facing a reality of terror by terrorists in* *the name of Islam—particularly those in India, those in the Philippines, those in Israel, those in Somalia, those in the Sudan—do you think they're buying into that?*

Ross: The first point I would make is that acts of terrorism have been committed by followers of virtually every faith in the world. This is not uniquely a Muslim problem. But it is clear, and this goes back to the early history of Islam, that Islam is a religion open to many different interpretations. Scholars over the centuries have evolved very intricate rules to try and determine what Islam has to say on a wide range of societal points. What has happened in the Osama bin Laden phenomenon is that a group of extremists with a very precise agenda, coming out of a very fundamentalist branch of modern Islam, have begun to speak in the name of Islam as if that is Islam. The fact is that the vast majority of Muslims do not identify with the kinds of positions that Osama bin Laden and his Taliban protectors would take on how you live a good Muslim life.

I have yet to find someone who, in the Arab world at least, who was eager to move to Afghanistan to live under the Taliban regime and its interpretation of Islam. So there is some work to be done to try to promote within the Muslim population a discussion about where to center Islam, [about] what is Islam today. That's not a discussion for the U.S. government to lead. It's perhaps a discussion for the U.S. government to encourage. But it is clear that there is a silent majority out there that has not reacted in any forceful or effective way to what we loosely call the hijacking of Islam by Osama bin Laden. At some point it's going to be in the interest of that silent majority to begin taking a more active role in countering that very narrow, very extreme vision of Islam that Osama bin Laden espouses.

15

Congress

uring the Vietnam War, Congress played a major role in debating and directing the policies of the Johnson and Nixon administrations. On several occasions, it even played a crucial role. For example, in 1964, Congress passed the Tonkin Gulf resolution, granting almost unlimited power to the president to fight the war in Vietnam. Almost ten years later, after a decade of bloody conflict, frustration, and domestic demonstrations, Congress passed another resolution, which had the effect of restricting the president's ability to continue the war.

So it was not surprising that immediately after 9/11, Congress passed a resolution similar to the Tonkin Gulf resolution, empowering the president to take retaliatory action against al Qaeda, and a month later it enacted legislation, the Patriot Act, authorizing the administration to take a series of drastic measures to combat terrorism in the United States. But then, except for an occasional speech or hearing that got little more than a day's worth of publicity, Congress fell into a period of essentially silent acquiescence to the president's leadership that stretched deep into 2002. Instead of the rhetorical thunder from Capitol Hill reminiscent of the Vietnam era, there was barely a peep, with everyone along Pennsylvania Avenue seemingly in lockstep agreement with administration policy. Patriotism dominated the scene, with the president leading the red-white-and-blue parade and the Democrats following his lead, rarely raising any questions suggesting a difference of opinion.

On op-ed pages and in think tanks, differences did surface, as pundits and professors wondered whether Congress was fulfilling its role as a co-equal branch of government and whether its unusual reticence was in fact helpful to the country's success in fighting terrorism. People asked, Where was Congress? Was it perhaps premature for a serious congressional debate? Was Congress intimidated by the White House? Was there a role for the press that was being ignored? To help answer these questions, on April 17, 2002, we invited four experienced and thoughtful "Congress-watchers." They were

—**Candy Crowley**, senior political correspondent for CNN and winner of the coveted Dirksen Award in 1998 for her reporting from Capitol Hill

—**Tom Donilon**, assistant secretary of state for public affairs in the Clinton administration, an official in the Office of Congressional Relations at the White House in the Carter administration, and executive vice president of Fannie Mae

—**Mort Kondracke**, one-half of the Beltway Boys on FOX-TV and executive editor of *Roll Call*, a newspaper that covers Capitol Hill

—**James Lindsay**, a senior fellow at the Brookings Institution and author of *Congress and the Politics of U.S. Foreign Policy*.

If there was one answer to the broad question of "What happened to Congress?" it was that for the period immediately following 9/11 Congress was in essential agreement with the White House on the war against terrorism. There was no reason for a contentious debate, especially since the public overwhelmingly supported the president, who for a time appeared to be invulnerable, with public approval ratings hovering near 90 percent. Still, our Congress-watchers believed that as the capital's agenda got crowded with such pressing issues as the budget, homeland security, and the true nature of the terrorist threat, debate would begin, slowly but surely. The president's position would gradually weaken as his poll numbers dipped, and Democratic politicians, thus encouraged, would rise in cautious opposition. This in turn would spark the media (and eventually the public) into a more critical frame of mind—that was the panel's judgment.

Kondracke argued that the public was "a little bit stunned still," too shocked by the 9/11 attacks to criticize the president's response. Moreover, if the Democrats thought, after checking the public's pulse, that the president had the terrorist situation "under control," then, in Kondracke's view, there would be no debate. No reason for one. No one wanted to jeopardize ongoing intelligence gathering, which public hearings would almost certainly do.

The overall question, however, was considered broader than terrorism alone. For example, Crowley picked up criticism of administration policy toward nation building in Afghanistan and the Israeli-Palestinian crisis. Donilon sensed criticism-in-waiting on the homeland security budget. "You'll see a much more aggressive congressional reaction," he predicted. Lindsay, widening his historical lens, cast his eye back to the *Federalist Papers* to prove that "during wartime, power naturally flows from the legislature towards the presidency."

In that case, Kalb wondered, could the media be at fault for not focusing sufficient attention on the issue of domestic terrorism? Perhaps, Crowley replied, but "if you want to be fully informed, there's a chance to do it, but you're going to have to go out and look for it." The information required for sound judgment in a democracy was available to everyone—you just had to make the effort to find it. Kondracke had another explanation. Citing Harvard professor Thomas Patterson's research, he pointed to the media's role in converting all issues, including terrorism, into political games, in which someone won and someone lost. Questions raised in relative innocence became criticism with a hard political edge. Donilon felt that if the media had not cut back on its foreign coverage during the '90's, the U.S. would have been better prepared to face the threat of terrorism—and much more.

Marvin Kalb: *One hears a great deal about a historic turning point in American foreign policy. Just the other day the national security adviser, Condoleezza Rice, spoke of a "tipping point," suggesting that on one side there was one kind of a world, [then] it tips, and on the other side we have another. Why is it that one has the impression today that the Congress has removed itself from the debate, if indeed there is a debate on the war against terrorism?*

Mort Kondracke: I think there was a tipping point. Prior to September 11 we thought we were living in a post–cold war world where the future was going to  be some sort of straight line, where there might be difficulties in the world but we didn't imagine that the survival of civilization was at stake. And suddenly it occurred to us that we are vulnerable: we were attacked for the first time on the mainland, the potential exists for our enemies to develop weapons of mass destruction, technology could mean that they could be miniaturized. Our cities are vulnerable to the worst kind of attack imaginable. So I think the world did change.

Eight months since it all happened, and I think everybody is a little bit stunned still. There haven't been any more attacks and therefore a relative calm has imposed itself on us, but there's still a lot of tension. So it's a slow start, and it would be a slow start under any circumstances. Part of it is political. The Democrats are worried about criticizing the president when a war is under way that the public overwhelmingly supports and [when] his approval ratings are high.

The bottom line is, it depends on how it goes. If we keep winning and the president seems to have the program under control and in hand and is successful, then I think you'll hear less of the kind of debate that I think you should have.

Kalb: *Candy, you're up there on Capitol Hill every day. Is there any direction, does one have a sense of an organized effort to debate where we are in this war against terrorism?*

Candy Crowley: No, not at the moment. People were stunned, so that sort of set everybody back, including people on Capitol Hill, who not only watched  what went on in New York, but really sort of feared for their own lives. So everybody sort of was in a stunned silence. After that you have sort of a natural tendency to allow the administration to do something simply because it can move more quickly than Congress ever can. And third, you've got a nation that seems to be largely in favor of it. So those are three very powerful things that sort of stifle a huge outcry of criticism. But around the margins they've begun to do this, like [asking], What are we going to do in Afghanistan now that we've won the war? Are we going to stay there?

I think Congress doesn't seem reticent to criticize the administration's policy in the Middle East, so it's not an across-the-board thing. It just has to do with the war on terrorism. I think you're going to see more [criticism].

But what if there is another attack? What does that do? Does that again rally people around, and do those ratings go back up to 90? So I'm not really sure what happens if there is another attack, in terms of whether this brings up debate.

Thomas Donilon: It's emphatically the duty of the president to fight a war, and I think that's recognized by both sides of the aisle on the Hill. It was a stunning event, and there was a compelling thrust to unite.

Kalb: *But wasn't the Congress supposed to be part of this from the very beginning, if you're fighting a war?*

Donilon: Absolutely. Number one: [initially], given the stunning nature of the attack on the United States, it was emphatically [clear] that we do look to our president in America in the twenty-first century to lead our efforts against an external threat. That is the way the government has become organized, and that's the expectation of the American people. Congress has affirmed this decision, particularly among the Democrats, to indicate essential unity behind him and not to indicate any cracks in the unity.

Number two, I think as you get distanced from those events and as you add things like the budget, the structure of the government, the nature of future

threats, I think the congressional role starts to become more prominent with the longer-term issues, and I think you'll see that. Again, the system just demands it. The president submitted for 2003 a doubling of the homeland security budget from $20 billion to $40 billion. It will now be up to the Congress to review that budget and decide what those priorities are.

And I think the odds are, given technology, given the dynamics, given the history of al Qaeda, I think that the odds are that we will face another domestic attack. I think we need to be prepared for that.

Kalb: *Are you, Jim, as you look back, are you surprised by the relative silence from the Hill or is this something that , given the track record, you would have expected?*

James Lindsay: This is exactly what I would have expected. We're seeing the playing out of a dynamic that goes back to the earliest days of the republic. The

notion that Congress would quiet down, particularly in the beginning of a war when the United States was attacked, is a very old one. In fact, if we go back to Federalist [Papers] number 8 and read Alexander Hamilton, he writes about this. That during war time, power naturally flows away from the legislature towards the presidency because of what's expected of the president and what he's capable of doing. It's partly driven by the belief that we must rally around the president and partly driven by politics. When the president's at 80 percent in the public opinion polls, it's pretty difficult to go out and start criticizing him. In some sense for Democrats to go out and criticize the president would be playing to the worst stereotypes about Democrats on these issues; for political reasons, they don't want to get very far away from the president.

Having said that, I think there are a couple of things to keep in mind. One, I don't think we should exaggerate the breadth of the congressional surrender to the president. One of the really remarkable things is, on a number of issues where you would have expected a president in the 80 percent range to be able to get his way, he has not been getting his way, most notably on trade.

If you had told me [that] you had a president who [had] 90 percent public opinion approval ratings and you went up to the Hill for trade promotion authority, I would have thought it would have been a slam dunk. On some of the procedural aspects of the war on terrorism, whether we're talking about INS reorganization, the duties of Mr. Ridge, whether we should have a Homeland Security Agency, the issues to do with civil liberties and what have you, Congress hasn't gone along with the administration. They've been fighting with [it]. So I don't think we should exaggerate. When are we likely to see Congress revert back to becoming more critical of the administration? We're not going to see it until 2003. It takes some time.

Donilon: Jim, I guess what you're describing is a dynamic where there's kind of an appropriate protected zone around the president with respect to the direct fight against al Qaeda and its offshoots in the war on terrorism, but as you get further away from that protected zone, both in terms of issues and then in terms of distance from the event, you'll see a much more aggressive congressional reaction.

Stephen Hess: *I think you're being just a bit generous to Congress. It strikes me that this is a congressional election year, where uniquely all members of the House and a third of the Senate are thinking about themselves. You've had up to now a popular president. I don't know how it will change, but it strikes me that you have an awful lot of folks that don't want to raise their heads above the foxhole and get shot at.*

As far as the leadership, hey, where are the Fulbrights? I haven't really noticed. Now all of you are saying, Yeah, things will change over time, and I'm sure you're right one way or another, but we're eight months into it. Where is that great investigation on what happened with the intelligence failure on 9/11? This was set up about a month ago, given money, to have a joint session of the two intelligence committees. What happened? Where are they?

Kalb: *I keep on wondering who is the person, persons up on the Hill, with the courage—and that's the word I think is advisable—with the political courage to come forth, as Fulbright did in '65 and '66, and blow a whistle.*

Donilon: First of all, you should entertain the possibility that on the merits [of his actions] members of Congress support the president in the actions that he took against the Taliban and taking down the Taliban government and everything that's been done in Afghanistan. So that lack of criticism shouldn't automatically be described as lack of courage. There actually could have been, and I think there was, widespread agreement that what the president did was the right thing to do. Now there are questions. But I think we shouldn't, in an academic discussion, dismiss the fact that people were acting in good faith and on the merits.

The problem is you would be asking the intelligence community to give information publicly about the very people and institutions and entities that they have an ongoing operation against. And that's an exceedingly difficult thing to do.

Hess: *But Tom, when you were at the State Department, wouldn't you have been happy to have found the Hill as quiescent as they are now? Take the budget question you raised. Well, where are those hearings in that committee that are asking some pretty serious questions about the nature of this huge increase that the president has asked for in defense?*

Donilon: With respect to the Congress and the budget, Steve, I think you're exactly right. There's a tremendous amount of oversight the Congress has to do to ensure that in fact they're meeting real threats and agencies haven't tried to dump things into homeland security as they would have in other parts of the budget. I think it's an appropriate role for Congress and should be an aggressive role for Congress since they're overseeing the public's money.

Kalb: *Candy, is this an example of the president's popularity stifling even an honest desire on the part of some to stand up, blow the whistle, and say, "Wait a second, before we plunge further, let's figure out direction?"*

Crowley: I think a couple of things. One, I think you're absolutely right. Let's not take lack of criticism to be lack of courage. They did agree with him. Early on they said, I think this guy is doing the exact right thing. But the fact of the matter is that when you question something now, it is taken as criticism, and it's not necessarily criticism. I mean, what's wrong with a question about where [we are] going to go next? But the minute you become that person you're a critic, as opposed to [someone] just [asking], Shouldn't we at least ask what we're going to need to go in and take out Saddam Hussein? Shouldn't we at least ask what we're going to do about Afghanistan after the Taliban are all gone?

So what's happened here is that a hearing is taken as a criticism. I think somehow that needs to be turned around; [it needs to be recognized] that questions aren't criticisms, they're just questions.

Kalb: *Explain to me why a question is regarded as criticism, and even if it be criticism, what's wrong with that? Why must it be that way? Is there no capacity in Congress to pull back a moment and ask, If we are indeed at a historic moment in our history, why doesn't it sound like a historic moment?*

Lindsay: Two quick points. One, I think that a question sounding like criticism is in the context of who's asking the question. Part of the problem Democrats face is that they don't have public credibility on these issues. So when they ask questions the presumption is they're asking questions because they're really weak on foreign policy. . . . There's an assumption here that the reason we got September 11 was [that] somebody inside the CIA must have screwed something up really badly, and it's not clear to me that that is true.

Number two, if there were screw-ups, a lot of it happened out in public, and they have been discussed. All the talk about fixing INS, about trying to find some way to coordinate state and local law enforcement, federal law enforcement authorities, all [are] things that have been discussed in the press. Often I think they really don't know what they're talking about, but they're nonetheless still talking about it. We are addressing these things.

Donilon: Marvin, can I interrupt? You asked, Are the larger questions being asked? and that's a fair question. There are hearings. Senator Biden's holding a set of really historic hearings asking the question, Are we addressing ourselves to the right threat? Now, he got on the front page once when he had a scientist talking about dirty bombs, but he has these hearings week after week, and the media doesn't show a lot of interest in it. But a lot of that work is going on. What are the threats? Are we organized to deal with them? Have we thought correctly about them? Go through the list of other policy issues.

Afghanistan, yes. There was broad agreement that we should go in and support the president and take down the Taliban. There are lots of questions being asked now about what happens after that. There are big questions being asked about what our policy is in the Middle East, especially from the Republican side. There are a lot of questions being asked about the adequacy of our nonproliferation efforts. If you think about the real ultimate threat, it would be a nexus between terrorism and weapons of mass destruction. There would be today, I think, a big debate going on about Iraq if the Middle East hadn't blown up over the last few weeks and taken all the efforts and attention of the administration and policymakers there.

So I don't think it's fair to say that there's silence. I think as you get a distance away from the major events of September 11 and as these much more complicated, less black-and-white issues emerge, I think you do see debate and interest in the Congress on these issues.

Kalb: *Let me ask the question this way: is the problem then not to be seen in Congress, not to be seen as a matter of political courage, but rather to be seen in the way in which the media handled this ongoing supposedly serious debate about foreign policy that you've just outlined for us? Why isn't CNN carrying* *these hearings live? They carry just about everything else live. What about the media's role in all of this?*

Crowley: Obviously where you choose to shine the spotlight is an editorial decision, and what goes on live at CNN is certainly above my pay grade. Right now, we're looking at a war in the Middle East and that's where all the attention is going to go.

Look, CNN and Fox and MSNBC and ABC and NBC don't put on everything. It gets back to my cry constantly, which is [that] if you want to be fully informed, there's a chance to do it but you're going to have to go out and look for it. These hearings are getting covered. Are they covered live on CNN? I'm assuming some of them have been and others haven't.

Hess: *Maybe it goes back to the people keeping their head down in the foxhole; more likely, doesn't this start to play out in electoral terms as the president starts to be attacked? Makes mistakes? The Middle East perhaps is the entry to that. But aren't we about to have everybody soon shouting again? Isn't that really what we're soon into? The idea that we at Brookings have been worrying about for some years, this permanent campaign [of politicians to be elected] just is on hold now, but we're going to have these issues discussed soon, but in the crudest form. Is that a bad look at the future?*

Kondracke: Tom Patterson wrote the book *Out of Order* some years ago, I guess it was before the '92 campaign, and he said that the press used all of politics and public affairs as a strategic game. I'm not sure whether it was the media that imposed this framework on the politicians or whether the politicians were doing it all along and the press suddenly discovered it. But in fact what everybody seems to calculate is, How is what I say today going to play into my chances of winning the next election? and, Am I going to improve my party's chances of taking over Congress or am I going to give an opening to the other side?

So in this context, and the press plays into it by reporting, as Candy said, questions as criticism, and plays it into the context of the next election . . . Is Bush up, is Bush down? Is Daschle up, is Daschle down? And everybody is constantly fighting. So the questions are going to be taken in an election context. It's an election year and seats are on the line. So as Ross Perot once said, These are very nice people caught in a lousy system, and the system is one of intense partisanship and strategic gaming.

Donilon: That's not new then. If you're working in the executive branch for a cabinet secretary or for a member of the Congress, before you give a major speech or appear on a network television show, you'll get a call from a producer or the reporter saying, . . . "Where is the hit?" You're likely to get attention if you go on a Sunday show and attack somebody much more than you will if you call a set of reporters into your office on the Hill and say, "I'm going to have a set of historic hearings, there's going to be twelve hearings. The Joint Chiefs, the CIA have said these are the real threats we have over the next decade." The chances of getting the item in the newspaper the next day are zero, and the chances of you getting in the newspaper the next day if you have three sentences in a 3,000 word speech that attack the administration is high— that's the way it works in terms of press coverage of these issues, I fear.

Lindsay: That also colors what people think Congress should do, because what people know is what the spotlight is shined on and how the story is framed by journalists. So I would say it's actually both. There clearly is often a lack of political coverage on Capitol Hill. There's nothing new about that; it's as old as the republic. At the same time it's encouraged by journalists. Let's face it, going to a hearing on INS reform does not make for really good television, unless somebody gets out and wags a finger and attacks an administration official.

Kalb: *Jim, for the last fifteen years up at Harvard we have had probably thousands of officials coming up to discuss hundreds of issues. When it's impossible to define a problem and when it's impossible to state that politicians don't take the lead, the blame is always placed on the press, the media. "If you guys covered it right, if you guys had the courage to point the spotlight at the hearings that Senator Biden is conducting, then the American people would be wiser and we'd have a better democracy." That's a cheap way of handling the discussion.*

Donilon: Let me come back at that though. Would we have been better off as a country and would policymakers have been better off if the news divisions of the major networks hadn't pulled back radically on international coverage over the last decade? Would we have known more about the world? Would we have known more in particular about the Arab Middle East? Would we have known that something was going on out there that we should be paying attention to?

Kalb: *Absolutely.*

Donilon: So these decisions by the media I do think, Marvin, make a difference.

Kalb: *I think it makes a huge difference.*

Question (from the audience): *Mr. Donilon, you've talked about the media not covering anything, maybe it's a news media problem. So do you really think that the news media is not covering things that are going on around the war, the efforts of Congress? And if not, is it possible that that's because Congress, the individual congressmen, have decided not to?*

Donilon: I think there has been tremendous media coverage of the war on terrorism. I think, as a general matter, though, the media is interested in the most immediate issues. They're interested in conflict issues more than they're interested in long-term policy issues, and . . . my only point was that it's harder to get coverage of the kind of consideration of longer-term policy issues, the kinds of issues that Marvin was asking about, [such as], Where's American foreign policy going? Are we addressing the right threats? It is harder to get coverage of those than it is to get an immediate day story about a conflict between two politicians.

The last thing I'll say is, I hope as we do get some distance away from events like September 11th, I hope that the media would not retreat into its aversion to international coverage and kind of [revert] to the Gary Condit stories of pre-9/11 and will learn the lesson that it's important for Americans to understand what goes on around the world, given really what one writer [has]called the death of distance.

Hess: *Many years ago I wrote a book about Washington reporters in which it was possible to trace the fact that although stories looked terribly presidential if you looked at the headlines and so forth, when reporters filled out this log of mine daily on where they were getting the information, it was fascinating to see how many of these stories were actually circulating through the Congress and coming out that way. Even though they might have been coded presidential, the sources, the best sources, were often in Congress. There were a lot of people up there who love to talk to reporters. I really don't think that has been happening. For some reason I think there was blockage in this either because, as Tom rightly pointed out, they agreed with the president, or as others pointed out, you keep your head down because it's bad politics, the president's rating is up there. Or for a third reason, they have nothing to say, there's no solution to this problem or that problem.*

But for some reason I do think that part of this that we've been worrying about—Marvin has asked, Where are these great hearings?—can be traced to the fact that Congress really hasn't been in the loop in the same way on this issue for one reason or another that they usually are in everything that goes on in the city.

Lindsay: I think we also have to avoid romanticizing the past. I think it's important to keep in mind that while the Fulbright hearings came out—and they were striking because here you had the man who had been the floor manager of the Gulf of Tonkin resolution, William Fulbright, all of a sudden raising questions about his president's policies—[they] had very little effect on Congress as a whole. [They] had very little effect on American policy towards the war. And it wouldn't be until Johnson's policies of manifest failure after the Tet offensive that you all of a sudden see members of Congress coming out in very large numbers being critical of the war. Indeed, what's striking when you look at the evolution of congressional comment in the Vietnam War versus public opinion [is] that in many ways the public led members of Congress.

In the fall of '67 the war becomes increasingly unpopular, so much so that the Johnson administration in the late fall of '67 launches a conscious public relations campaign, persuades the American public that we're doing well and that the light is near the end of the tunnel. They even bring [General William] Westmoreland back to go on a public speaking tour to assure Americans. Then, all of a sudden, you have two months later the Tet offensive, which gives lie to what the administration's been saying. Then all of a sudden everybody's freed up; you've got people like Bobby Kennedy coming out, and all of a sudden the shifting tone becomes one of, Maybe we ought to rethink what we're doing—which wasn't really what Fulbright had been arguing in '66. So I don't think we should romanticize how it worked in the past.

Kondracke: Historically also you could argue that it was the press that led the way, that led Congress. The first doubts about the Vietnam War that I remember were from David Halberstam and other reporters who were saying, The way we're doing this is not working. We are not winning battles that we claim that we're winning. Tet remains a very controversial moment. Did we really lose Tet? The press all reported that we lost, when in fact we really decimated the Viet Cong. That's a case where public opinion I think may have been mismolded. Somebody holding hearings might have corrected that widespread impression.

Lindsay: There's something else important here, which is why the Fulbright memory is not really relevant here. You said it's important to have someone like Fulbright come out because he has stature, [that] legitimates criticism. . . . Well, if I picked up the op-ed pages of a variety of newspapers, there's actually a fairly robust debate going on. Some of my colleagues have written extensively, taking issue with various things that have been happening. So in that sense if there's been a legacy of Fulbright or a legacy of Vietnam, it's the extent to which a lot of this in the broader public already [has] happened. These debates are being had. I've been on numerous call-in radio shows. People get on and air their very thoughtful, very passionately held views. So I think in some sense our internal domestic politics are quite different, and you don't really need to have a senator come out and legitimate it. I think in many ways Congress is likely to lag behind their constituents on this.

Question (from the audience): *Should we expect Congress to take action when the issue resonates more with the voters?*

Lindsay: I think it's the fundamental dynamics of American politics—that is, politicians tend to worry about issues that directly affect their constituents, and the less it directly affects their constituents or some subset of their constituency, the less likely they are to pay attention to it. It's the nature of an electoral system.

Donilon: I think Jim outlined the reasons for congressional action or inaction pretty clearly. I do think that it just is a fact of the American system that the presidency is emphatically the institution that we look to to fight a war. I think, as you get some distance, you'll get much more congressional involvement. I do think you need to entertain the possibility that in fact Congress did support the president on the merits of these things and as the issues become less black and white and more complicated, I think you'll certainly see more congressional involvement.

Crowley: I think all things are sort of multi-determined. I must say I'm not sure that I even agree with the basic premise of the question, which is that there hasn't been criticism.

I also think that we ought to at least be aware that there are politicians, and I think this goes to your question, there are people in government who do understand that this is beyond politics—it's not only just about our future, meaning the U.S. future, but about the world's future—and who genuinely are working absent a political element. It doesn't mean that there aren't political implications, but there may not be political motivation and that's a different thing. I covered Capitol Hill for a very long time and was always astounded by the nonpolitical motivation of a lot of people that are up there who really do want to make the world better, want to make the U.S. better. So don't come away believing that because there are political implications that there are always political motivations.

Kondracke: I think in times of war there is a natural tendency for everybody to rally together and to support the chief executive and that that inhibits this kind of questioning that you want to erupt. I think you will have a debate over Iraq. I'm a little surprised that there hasn't been more of it up to now, but I think it's going to happen.

16

Public Opinion

P residents often say that they don't govern by polls. That is, of course, the right thing to say, but it rarely reflects the political reality of everyday life at the White House. Polls have become essential tools for measuring public opinion; politicians use them, political science professors use them, the press uses them. The events of 9/11 were followed by a spike in many measures of public opinion, but none greater than the spike in the degree of public trust in big government and big media—a newly reawakened trust that was to dissipate within a matter of months.

Andrew Kohut, director of the Pew Research Center for the People and the Press, visited the Brookings/Harvard Forum twice to discuss his findings. The first time was on November 28, 2001. He was joined by **Jill Abramson**, Washington bureau chief of the *New York Times*, and **Tom Rosenstiel**, director of the Project for Excellence in Journalism and former media critic of the *Los Angeles Times*. Four months later, on March 27, 2002, Kohut returned to the forum. He was joined then by **David S. Broder**, a veteran political reporter and columnist for the *Washington Post*, **Margaret Carlson**, a columnist for *Time* magazine, and **William Kristol**, editor and publisher of the *Weekly Standard*.

Attached to our report on public opinion are excerpts from two press releases regarding a Pew poll done as the first anniversary of 9/11 approached. The first press release (public concerns about the media) was published on August 4, 2002; the second press release (personal reactions to 9/11) was published on September 5, 2002. The year made an enormous difference in respondents' perceptions.

During the first panel discussion, Kohut reported that the public's opinion of the media had significantly improved after 9/11. In the weeks following

9/11, 89 percent of the American people gave the press a "good" or "excellent" rating. Two months later, the percentage had dropped to 77 percent, but that was still seen as "a pretty high number" by Kohut and other professional pollsters. In addition, the public's perception of media accuracy, responsibility, and seriousness also had improved. People appreciated that there was more fact and less opinion in the news. In this positive judgment of press performance, however, there was a negative side, too. Most Americans (about 67 percent) said that the media got in the way of solving the country's problems.

Rosenstiel wondered whether the Kohut poll represented a "permanent, more long-lasting" swing in public opinion favorable to the media or whether in time, "when this war ends," public opinion will return to its earlier negative judgment of the press. "I have grave doubts," said Rosenstiel, "that the news media we have right now is going to remain as serious."

Abramson had a rosier view. She said that the story of terrorism touched people directly, accounting in part for the public's approval of the coverage. "You couldn't find a story," she explained, "that's more relevant to the lives of the people of our country." She spotted two "really healthy trends" in post-9/11 journalism: first, a swing away from opinion to fact-based information; and second, a return to "serious foreign reporting."

At the March 27, 2002 forum, which focused more on personal attitudes than on press performance, Kohut said that in his view 9/11 changed the public's skepticism of the federal government to trust. The biggest change registered among women, who became sudden hawks in the war against terrorism and looked to the government to protect them. Kohut pointed with humor to a poll headline that read "Mothers for Missile Defense."

Broder did not share Kohut's overall view. After visiting many parts of the country and doing "focus groups" in some, Broder concluded that although the public's judgment of government had improved, most people seemed to be "moving back fairly rapidly" toward "a normal political environment where domestic concerns, parochial concerns, are uppermost in people's minds."

Carlson tended to agree with Broder that "out of a sense of fragility and fear," people remained concerned about terrorism, but outside of Washington and New York, where that concern was strongest, many Americans seemed to have returned to their "normal concerns." In the absence of another terrorist attack inside the United States, people went back to their everyday activities, as they were encouraged to do by the administration.

Kristol disagreed with both Broder and Carlson. In his view the war against terrorism remained "the dominant issue" in the country and far from returning to "normal," the American people were prepared to go much further in this bloody confrontation. "Bush's numbers are still high," he concluded. "Terrorism remains a very big issue, . . . that will lead to longer changes in politics and public opinion."

November 28, 2001

Andrew Kohut: I'm here to say that the public image of the press is improving. There, I said it. That's the first time in fifteen years of studying public attitudes  towards the press that I've ever said anything remotely close to that. Now, I'm not so foolish to think that this represents some sea change in attitudes towards the press, nor does the changing attitude toward government represent a complete reversal of distrust of government. I think what it reflects is the way people are responding to these institutions at a time [when] they feel [a] great need to know and [when] they view the performance as pretty good.

The poll shows the public giving the press better grades with regard to performance and with regard to the perceived values of the news media and journalists. As to performance, the percentage of people saying [that] the press usually gets the facts right rose from 35 percent in the survey that we did in September prior to September 11, to 46 percent. That's the best grade that the press has gotten for accuracy in our polling with this question since 1992. Now, that's not much to crow about. Forty-six percent said the press is usually accurate; 45 percent said they're often inaccurate. But it's better than 35/57 a month earlier, but it's not as good as the 55/34 back in 1985 when I first started doing these surveys.

News organizations also continue to get good grades for the way they're covering the terrorism story and the war on terrorism, although not as high as [during] the first weeks of September. Then, 89 percent of the people that we questioned gave the press either an excellent or good rating. That's slipped to about 77 percent in this survey. Seventy-seven percent is still a pretty high number. When we regularly ask people to rate how good they thought the coverage was of typical stories, generally about 50 to 60 percent would give the press positive marks, so 77 percent ain't too shabby.

Now, the biggest rise in positive attitudes towards the press had to do with more people seeing the press as professional, moral, patriotic, and compassionate. The [statement that] leading news organizations "stand up for America" jumped from 43 percent in September to 69 percent in the current survey. Seeing the press as an institution that protects democracy jumped from 46 percent to 60 percent. Seeing the press as moral rather than immoral, we have a 53/23 margin; in early September the margin was 40/34.

I should add that much of the decline in [the] perception of the press in terms of its values occurred during the Clinton/Lewinsky scandal years. That's when the American public began to doubt not only the press's performance and the way it does its job, but began to doubt its basic values. This survey shows some considerable rebounding, at least for now, on these measures. More broadly, just a third say [that] the news media helps society solve its problems, most saying [that] the media gets in the way of society solving its problems. These are clearly not positive measures, but they're better readings than we received in previous surveys both in September and in a very long trend line since 1985. All things being equal, this poll shows—for the first time in a long time—a better opinion of the American news media.

As to why the good grades on a story which sparked an overall image improvement, there are a number of signs in the surveys that we've conducted between September and early November which show a clear link between the coverage and needing the content. When we asked people an open-ended question, Why do you say the coverage is excellent or good? people said, Because it's timely, because it's comprehensive, because it's informative. But it's not only need to know alone that explains the public's positive view of the coverage. I think the lack of contention about public policy and the low partisanship in Washington undoubtedly play a supporting role in [respondents'] liking the way the media has covered the story.

All this unusually good news notwithstanding, the poll finds strong support for government control of news for the sake of national security. By a 53/39 percent margin, the public says [that] it's more important for the government to be able to censor stories that it believes could threaten national security than for the media to be able to report news believed to be in the national interest. These numbers are just about what we found in the Gulf war, with exactly the same questions.

I think they're predicated on a number of judgments that the public made then and are making now about the government and the war effort. First, the public thinks it's been getting a straight story. Eighty-two percent believe that Pentagon officials are disclosing as much as they can and not hiding the bad news. Eighty percent have confidence that the government is giving an accurate picture of the war. And 70 percent believe that censorship is intended to protect the safety of U.S. forces, not to cover up bad news. All of these measures are almost directly comparable to what we found in early 1991.

Finally, despite approval of censorship, there is no appetite on the part of the American public for propaganda. The [poll] finds a solid majority favoring war coverage that is neutral rather than pro-American and an even larger 73 percent margin favoring coverage that portrays all points of view, including those of countries that are unfriendly to the United States, over pro-American news reports. And by a 52/40 percent margin, the public says [that] the press should dig hard to get news and not trust government and military officials.

Finally, there continues to be support for the press's watchdog role, even in a time of national crisis. Half of the public thinks [that] press scrutiny of the military keeps the nation prepared, compared to 37 percent who think [that] it weakens its defense. There was an even bigger margin of support for press criticism of political leaders at this time.

Tom Rosenstiel: What are these numbers telling us? Is there reason to believe that—while as Andy says, he's not so foolish as to suggest a sea change [—]

there are the roots of something that may become more permanent or more structural? Not permanent, more long-lasting. The fact that the numbers are so similar to where they were during the Gulf war might suggest that these things are going to drop again when this war ends. But there are some significant differences between the press outside of war [coverage] in the year 2001 versus the press during peacetime in 1991.

In the research that we've done at the Project for Excellence in Journalism, we've seen a long-term shift away from what journalists would call traditional hard news toward what traditionally journalists call soft news. In 1977, in the twilight of the Walter Cronkite era, hard news made up 70 percent of what was on the evening network newscasts, whereas celebrity and lifestyle coverage made up about 15 percent. By 1997, only 40 percent—less than half of what was on the evening newscast—was hard news and celebrity [coverage] made up roughly a third of the newscast.

That has changed dramatically after September 11. We are back to basically a 1977 kind of mix for news. Today 80 percent of the news on the evening newscasts is hard news, and not all of it war news. And celebrity and lifestyle makes up actually just 1 percent of what people are seeing on the evening newscasts.

How does this pertain to Andy's findings? One of the reasons that people are upset with the press or when they see the press sensationalizing or hyping news is [that] they infer that journalists are doing this to become celebrities, for self-aggrandizement. Even more common, that the press is hyping the news to make a buck. I believe that the root of the credibility crisis in journalism is a question of motive. People have begun to doubt the motive of journalists. If the press agenda becomes more serious and journalists are engaged in more serious work, I think it follows that the public begins to attribute more serious motives to them.

I have grave doubts that the news agenda we have right now is going to remain as serious. In the classic words of the TV hack, only time will tell. I read a quote in the *Washington Post* this week in which the editor of *Vanity Fair* said that the American public were serial-obsessive—they obsess on one thing and then they obsess on another. I find in the research that we've done that he's completely wrong, but that the editor of *Vanity Fair* certainly is a serial obsessor. So are the managers of most news outlets. We are seeing that at this point, and that would suggest that they will obsess again on something else—and it may well be the *Vanity Fair* fashion show if the war ends.

Jill Abramson: I spent a couple of hours looking at Andy's results yesterday. What I found most interesting about them is I think they're reflective of the

nature of the story itself. That the key thing about September 11, the ensuing war on terrorism, the military actions in Afghanistan, the heavy coverage of bioterrorism threats and the anthrax letters, is that this is a story that the public feels impacts their lives quite directly. They feel a strong connection, a very strong need to know. They crave information because they see that information as essential to their safety, to [being able to] turn forward with their lives—to their vision of the country, how strong the country is, how secure the country is, which is something that the public really cares about.

You cited the Monica Lewinsky story as being the apogee of public ill will and resentment towards journalists, and I think that there's a clear reason why that is. The public felt a fundamental disconnect from that story. It didn't matter to their lives, and they felt the press was obsessing on that story and that it was irrelevant to the daily lives of the American public. And their anger mounted as night after night, especially on those twenty-four-hour cable TV channels, there was this nightly drumbeat of obsession on that topic.

I agree with Tom that the questioning of the motive of journalists also became a new thing, but I think there was a very clear frustration that I would find in any forum that I went to. That this was a story that a large part of the public, the Lewinsky story, viewed as irrelevant. September 11 could not [be viewed as irrelevant]. You couldn't find a story that's possibly more relevant to the lives of the people of our country.

I think the more positive feelings toward the press also, hopefully, reflect what I see as the coverage has continued for two months now, to reflect two really healthy trends within journalism. The first is I think it's brought about a shift from opinion to information. There was a shift away from information and reportage being valued that reached an apogee during the blanket Lewinsky coverage [when] opinion became the coin of the realm. And you had the explosion of punditry and this very pointed, very partisan, very bitterly charged nightly debate that really did not usually turn over facts but over how the pundits felt about President Clinton's behavior.

Now I see a devaluation of opinion—even watching some of the same shows, which interestingly enough had some of the same pundits as panelists [who are] now commenting on the war. There's a lot less naked expression of opinion and more discussion of the facts of the day, the actual events—what transpired in the war, what new facts were learned. So I see that as one healthy trend.

The second being that with the shift towards kind of the more entertainment/soft news culture that we had too much of in the '90s there was a shrinkage, in part for cost savings, of foreign news . . . gathering—news gathering resources abroad were slashed by almost all news outlets, except the *New York Times.* The TV networks were busily shutting the doors of some bureaus, where up to that point it was unthinkable not to have correspondents located abroad. I think that was a very unhealthy trend in journalism. Economically these are not the best of times, so it would be premature for me to predict that the doors would be reopened, but there are very few major news organizations who aren't spending what is necessary to cover the war in Afghanistan, and I think it has brought a grudging realization to most news organizations [that it is] a mistake to put fluff above serious foreign reporting. So I hope that's another healthy trend that maybe connects Andy's results.

The results of the poll that I find so worrisome [are] that the public is so willing to accept censorship. While censorship hasn't presented itself as a problem in coverage of the war on terrorism so far, the Pentagon has placed extreme limits on the media on access. There has been very little direct access to the troops. I wish that public support could be a resource on the media side to get more access and have a more open way of covering the war. The press is willing to accept reasonable limits; we're willing to hold stories. The press does not want to put America's troops into danger, but I think the Pentagon has capitalized on the public opinion in your poll where the public is willing to accept a variety of [types of censorship of] the press, and I find that a little worrisome.

March 27, 2002

Kohut: As a pollster whose career began in the sour days of post-Watergate and post-Vietnam, I was truly amazed by the expressions of national unity and patriotism that we saw in the polls right after September 11. The simple fact that the percentage of people saying that they were satisfied with national conditions [went] from 40 percent to 60 percent was an extraordinary thing to me. I think the new relevance of nationhood—of Washington, of the federal government, public officials in Washington—is what stands the greatest chance of remaining.

In campaign 2000 one of the findings of our surveys that really struck me and rattled me was 30 percent of American voters saying that who was elected president didn't really matter so much. That was considerably higher than the percentage we had found even in the early 1990s. I think the September 11 attack stopped those sentiments in their tracks. In our nationwide survey in January, we found double the number of people saying [that] they were interested in hearing what the president had to say in the State of the Union address. In February, Gallup found the highest level of optimism about national progress since 1959.

I think national unity and patriotism may fade, but I think the new relevance of Washington will not. Americans need national government in a way they have not for some time.

I should say, however, the post-9/11 polls haven't found long-standing criticisms of government fading. Our surveys found people continuing to feel that the government was too wasteful, had too much control over people's lives, and nearly half of the public expressed doubts about the trustworthiness of government officials. Yet that poll and every other one has shown an increase in trust in government. It's not the fact that the American public likes government more after 9/11—I think it's the fact that the American public needs government more after 9/11. I think that will stand to prevent a return to the hypercriticism of government and the really very high levels of distrust in government that we saw especially in the early '90s but throughout the decade. It might even boost turnout in 2004 and other forms of civic engagement. I think the public's need for protection is apparent in big bold letters in every poll I've seen. Support for increased defense spending stands at 60 percent—triple what it was four years ago—and funding for homeland defense is just as high if not higher.

I think the biggest change in attitude occurred among women. My favorite headline from one of our polls was "Mothers for Missile Defense," showing a 30-point increase in the number of mothers who felt that missile defense was a good idea post-9/11. Americans have also changed their world views. Rather than retreating to a position of increased defensiveness and isolation, the initial response has [been to] become more committed to U.S. involvement in the world and to take a multilateral approach to things. By nearly two to one, the public said in our October survey that the best way to prevent terrorism was to be active in world affairs rather than not get involved in difficult problems around the globe.

Americans also attach a lot more significance and importance to [the] views and desires of our allies, so much so that more than half of the people who supported the use of force against Iraq said [that] we shouldn't do it if we can't get our allies to go along with us. I should add that the public continues to strongly support the use of force to combat terrorism. We've seen no fall-off in the initial reactions of support from October and November. Our January survey was labeled "Americans Favor Force in Iraq, Somalia, Sudan, and . . ."

David Broder: The general comment that I would make about Andy's survey is that I believe he is right about the sense of nationhood and the role of government when it relates specifically to protecting the country.

But contrary to what I had hoped and to some degree expected after September 11, I think the operative part of his survey says we are moving back fairly rapidly toward a normal political environment where domestic concerns, parochial concerns, are uppermost in people's minds.

One of the things that has struck me since January 1 [is that] people who are actively engaged in politics and civic life are very focused on what's happening in their state, because the states, so many of them, are in fiscal crisis. That's the first thing that they talk to you about. For people who are not so engaged in civic affairs, I think that maybe ironically the effect of 9/11 was to focus them even more on family matters, neighborhood matters, local matters, as far as I can judge.

Margaret Carlson: I find when you leave Washington and you go to some place other than New York, I have the impression that terrorism is a regional mat-

ter. It's almost as if we talk about it here in Washington and people in New York are still involved every day, but, as David says, people outside have gone back to their normal concerns, which are their families and their neighborhoods and their schools. Now, overriding that, in the back of their minds, is a sense of fragility and fear, but they aren't obsessed or narrowly focused the way we are. So I don't think it's going to quite have the effect that it does on us from day to day.

I think I can say, as the only mother on the panel, without any contradiction, women have turned into hawks as a result of this. Because you do turn to government for one main thing, which is to be protected. Government can protect me. Women feel more vulnerable and became much more hawkish in my unscientific survey than the men. I found one big exception. I interviewed Laura Bush in December, and she said, surprisingly, "Like all women, I was hoping the president wouldn't bomb." I said to myself, "Sister, I don't know anybody who's there with you." All the women I know were anxious for some retaliation. Government could have done a lot more during that period, including actually raise taxes and ask people to pay more.

William Kristol: Obviously there's always going to be some kind of return to normalcy, but not only do we have, according to Andy, "Mothers for Missile Defense," but, according to Margaret, we have "Mothers for Bombing." I don't quite buy the return-to-normal argument. Let me argue a bit against the thrust of what David and Margaret were saying. I would argue that people are not focused on domestic policy as usual in Washington. What is the bill that has spurred the most grass-roots activism recently? The immigration bill, on which there was a bipartisan consensus. There's a genuine upsurge of populist activism, which is driven by terrorism. People didn't change their minds about Mexican immigration; they were worried that a loosening of immigration in general and an amnesty in general would sweep in some potential terrorists. That suggests to me that the issue of domestic terrorism has a lot of resonance out there, and I think the war remains the dominant issue.

This is anecdotal, but I think people are very interested in the war. They sense that 9/11 was the beginning of a new moment for America in the world, maybe a new moment at home. I think that's harder to say, but certainly a new moment in the world. That it's not going away, and they're very curious: What's going to happen? What should happen? What are the implications of what's happened so far?

Andy, I don't think you read from the study you did in early March, so I'm going to read it to see if you still agree with it: "The events of September 11th have affected public opinion more dramatically than any event since World War II." Now, I take it what you mean in a sort of literal sense by that is that no other single event jolted various poll numbers as dramatically as September 11.

Kohut: Exactly.

Kristol: It doesn't prove, obviously, that it couldn't be a one-time jolt and that we then go back six or twelve or eighteen months later to [the] kind of the level we were at. But I'm struck six months later that Bush's numbers are still high; that terrorism remains a very big issue. I think that sense will turn out to be true not just as a short-term matter, but that it really will lead to longer changes in politics and public opinion.

August 4, 2002
Pew Research Center for the People and the Press

Public criticism of the news media, which abated in response to coverage of the 9/11 attacks, is once again as strong as ever. The favorable glow from the media's post-9/11 performance has completely disappeared. As the media's focus has shifted away from terrorism, Americans regard news organizations with the same degree of skepticism as they did in the 1990s.

A July survey shows that the public's grades for news organizations have tumbled since November, on measures ranging from professionalism and patriotism to compassion and morality. Just 49 percent think news organizations are highly professional, down from 73 percent in November. If anything, the news media's rating for professionalism is now a bit lower than it was in early September, shortly before the terrorist strikes (54 percent).

Over the same period, the news media's rating for patriotism, which stood at an all-time high in November (69 percent), has plummeted 20 points. While 49 percent say the news organizations "stand up for America," 35 percent believe they are too critical of the country. A majority once again believes news organizations do not care about the people they report on; in November, a 47 percent plurality viewed the press as compassionate. The trend is similar for the public's assessment of the news media's morality, fairness and accuracy, all of which have returned to pre-September 11 levels.

The positive view of terrorism coverage that led to the short-lived boost in the news media's image is still apparent in the current attitudes. The public continues to rate coverage of the war on terror both in Afghanistan and at home more highly than most other news stories.

When the news media's image showed dramatic improvement last fall, roughly half of Americans still viewed news organizations as unwilling to admit mistakes, believed they stood in the way of solving society's problems, and were politically biased. Today, those perceptions are much more prevalent, as all three measures stand at virtually the same point they did just prior to September 11.

Two-thirds of Americans believe news organizations are unwilling to acknowledge their errors, while just 23 percent say they admit their mistakes. There has been less change on the question of whether the news media stands in the way of society solving its problems; still, nearly six in ten see the media as an obstacle. And the number who believe news organizations are politically biased has increased by 12 points, to 59 percent.

Though the public has much lower regard for the media's values, most Americans continue to favor the watchdog role performed by news organizations. If anything, there is greater support than in November, when the media's overall image was much more favorable.

Six in ten Americans (59 percent) say press criticism keeps political leaders from doing things that should not be done, while just 26 percent believe it prevents politicians from doing their jobs. The number favoring the watchdog role is up slightly from November, and is at about the same level as in early September (60 percent).

Americans express more reservations about news organizations criticizing the military; 49 percent say such criticism keeps the nation prepared, while 40 percent believe it weakens our defenses. In November, the same number (49 percent) thought the press' watchdog role kept the nation prepared. During the Persian Gulf War in 1991, more people (59 percent) felt press criticism of the military was worth it, while just 28 percent thought it undermined the nation's defenses.

September 5, 2002
Pew Research Center for the People and the Press

Over the past year, many of the dramatic reactions of the public to the events of Sept. 11 have slowly faded. The spike in trust in government is mostly gone, the public once again is highly critical of the news media. . . . Yet it is also clear that the attacks have left a lasting, perhaps indelible, imprint on life in America as well as on attitudes toward public policy.

In personal terms, all Americans are connected by recollections of the experience—97 percent can remember exactly where they were or what they were doing the moment they heard about the attacks. But the burden and continuing consequences of the attacks are not equally shared. Half feel that Sept. 11 changed their lives, but just 16 percent describe the changes as major. Understandably, the personal impact is much greater in those areas of the country that came under attack.

People living in the New York area report far more emotional consequences than do Americans living in other parts of the country, including residents of Washington D.C. Tellingly, 46 percent of respondents in a survey of the New York area said they knew someone who was injured or killed in the attacks, compared with 21 percent in the Washington D.C. area and 11 percent nationwide.

Concern over another terrorist attack has fluctuated over the course of the past year, but at no point has less than a majority been at least somewhat worried. Currently, 62 percent of Americans say they are very or somewhat worried about the possibility of a new attack.

Despite a declining consensus about the war on terror, two profound changes in American public opinion remain apparent. The public continues to be disposed to use military force in the war on terrorism, and Americans favor the United States taking an active role in the world as a way of preventing future terrorist attacks.

A year after the attacks, the public still believes that the best way to avoid problems like terrorism is to stay engaged internationally. A 53 percent majority currently holds that view, down from 61 percent last October.

At the same time, the public has become much more supportive of a terrorism policy based primarily on U.S. national interests. A 45 percent plurality backs a policy based mostly on U.S. interests, while 35 percent believe that the United States should strongly take allied interests into account. This is a major change since last October when the public, by two to one (59 percent–30 percent), favored taking allied interests into account.

In the post 9/11 era women worry more than men about another attack and this serves to reduce the long-standing gender gap on the use of force and defense spending. Women are about as supportive as men of taking military action against Iraq and suspected nuclear powers, although they are more sensitive to the possibilities of casualties.

While Americans offer that Sept. 11 was a huge event for the nation, relatively few say that their *own* lives have undergone major changes, and many have experienced other events in their lives over the past year that had a bigger effect on them personally.

Similarly, while half of the nation says life in America has changed in a major way as a result of the terrorist attacks, just 16 percent say this is the case in their own personal lives. Instead, 49 percent say their lives are basically the same as before the attacks.

Shortly after the attacks, two-third of Americans considered them more serious than Japan's attack on Pearl Harbor, but that view has changed. Just 37 percent now believe the attacks were more serious than Pearl Harbor, while 43 percent say they were about as serious.

17

Overview

T he "wise men," as a Washington phenomenon, emerged in the tumult of the Vietnam War. During the Tet offensive in early 1968, President Lyndon Johnson summoned a group of former government officials to the White House to consider alternative strategies for ending the war. These officials were dubbed "the wise men," not because their recommendations proved to be brilliantly prescient, but because everyone in Washington needed another perspective on the never-ending conflict in Vietnam.

So, on May 29, 2002, we invited four "wise men" to discuss the war on terrorism, nine months after 9/11 rearranged America's national and international priorities. All four were Democrats, a deliberate choice, since it was clear at the time that Republican "wise men" would feel obliged to echo the White House position and we already had that perspective from the daily briefings. The four were

—**Lloyd N. Cutler**, a Washington lawyer who had served as White House counsel for presidents Jimmy Carter and Bill Clinton

—**Lee H. Hamilton**, director of the Woodrow Wilson International Center for Scholars and a former congressman from Indiana who chaired the House of Representatives Committee on Foreign Affairs

—**Harry C. McPherson**, another Washington lawyer who worked as White House counsel for President Lyndon Johnson

—**James Sasser**, a former U.S. senator from Tennessee and former U.S. ambassador to China.

In terrorism, was the United States facing its greatest crisis since World War II?

"No," said Sasser—not as great as World War II, nor as great as Vietnam, but a major crisis nonetheless.

"No," said Cutler, although he noted the "unique" condition of the United States being absorbed in a war against a "non-state" enemy.

"Not sure," said Hamilton, and he wouldn't be sure unless there was another terrorist attack on the United States. "Depends on how events unfold."

"Possibly," said McPherson. "It is different from anything I have ever experienced." He thought the kind of suicide-bomber terrorism Israel was facing on an almost daily basis seemed "poised" to happen in the U.S.

Hamilton credited President Bush with "channeling" the "anxiety" and "fear" of the American people into an "effective response" to the 9/11 challenge but wondered whether the president was right to convert his effort into the "single focus" of American foreign policy. Hamilton suggested that, as a result, we "may be exaggerating the war on terrorism too much and losing sight of a lot of other important goals."

Sasser's larger worry was that in the struggle against terrorism, which both Republicans and Democrats supported, the administration might end up pushing "a wholesale suspension of civil liberties." Sasser thought that "we're seeing that in some areas, and it's alarming."

When asked "Is this now government by leak?" the "wise men" gathered as one to make two points: one, that every administration leaked information and then denounced the leakers, as though they'd come from another planet; and two, that the leaked stories were, to quote Hamilton, "very, very important to us." The former congressman believed that "leaks are inevitable in Washington—you're not going to stop them, nor should you." At the time, no one on the panel knew that the administration had opened the floodgates for *Washington Post* editor Bob Woodward, from the president on down, providing him with then secret information and insights into the administration's fight against terrorism. All of it became a book-length exclusive.

If there was one issue that especially concerned the "wise men," it was the possibility that the terrorists would acquire and then detonate a nuclear weapon in the United States, killing millions of people. Cutler had chaired a special commission, set up by the Department of Energy, to explore the possibility. Everyone agreed that any nuclear weapon involved probably would have originated in the old Soviet Union, and the commission's recommendation was that the U.S. immediately spend $30 billion to help the new Russia itemize and control its stockpiles of nuclear weapons so that no one could get one. The shame was that neither the Bush administration nor Congress did anything to get the money or push the plan.

Marvin Kalb: *The president has spoken about the period of 9/11 on as a global struggle against terrorism. It's a war. The vice president has said that what happened on 9/11 is apt to be repeated in the United States. The director of the FBI has said that the kind of suicide bombing taking place in Israel almost on a daily basis will come to the United States; he said it's a matter of when, not if. Now, that to me adds up to a big-time crisis. The question: in your judgment, is it the biggest one that the U.S. has faced in modern time?*

James Sasser: It certainly can be described as difficult times and as a crisis. But I would not put it as the same magnitude of other crises we've faced during my

lifetime. Certainly it's not the crisis that we faced after December 7, 1941. It's been seven months since September 11—seven months after December 7, 1941, the whole country was mobilized. We were rationing food, rationing tires, rationing gasoline, and millions of young Americans were being mobilized to fight overseas. I, frankly, doubt that it ranks as a crisis of the magnitude of the Vietnam War. It was the longest war the United States ever fought.

It went on year after year after year and divided our country very, very seriously. Perhaps the United States was the most divided during the Vietnam War that it had been since the Civil War. So I think this is indeed a crisis, but I don't see it as a crisis of the magnitude that we experienced earlier in the twentieth century.

But this is the first time, if memory serves me correctly, since the War of 1812 in which significant casualties were inflicted upon the American population within the continental United States.

Lloyd Cutler: Before we get to enjoy the appellation of being wise men, we need to remember that the judgment of historians and journalists is that the wise

men, at least in the Vietnam War, screwed up. And [former U.S. ambassador to Russia] Robert Strauss likes to say that the way you get to be a wise man in Washington is to outlive your contemporaries and keep your mouth shut.

But I agree very much with Jim. I think that, of course, nothing would compare with the Civil War, but I guess none of us, even we wise men, were around for that. World War II, for those of you who remember it, was the last popular war. It's the war we all wanted to be in. We knew that the fate of Western Europe, which is our cultural motherland, was on the line. We all even wanted combat roles. [Former U.S. attorney general] Elliot Richardson, who couldn't get into the services because he had some sort of physical defect, actually volunteered to be a stretcher-bearer and served on Omaha Beach carrying off the wounded and the dead—he wanted to be in the war that much.

There were many different ways to serve. One way was to have an Office of Civil Defense in every urban community in the United States. I think we had something like 28,000 of them. Apart from those who were in the armed forces, we had 11 million Americans involved in civil defense. We all built bomb shelters in our basements, we bought cartons of tuna fish, we stockpiled water. We didn't have ATM machines in those days, so we stockpiled cash.

But what we have today is unique, unless you go all the way back to the Barbary pirates. We have a war with a non-state at a time when we know we are vulnerable in the homeland. We are going to take casualties in this war; everybody accepts that. And we have to figure out a way to adjust to what may be something that continues for the rest of our lives and perhaps the rest of the century.

Lee H. Hamilton: We can't really tell at this point whether it's the greatest crisis since World War II. If events unfold along the lines that the vice president and the FBI director have predicted—that we're going to  continue to receive casualties or that Americans are going to die on American soil in the future—then it may very well turn out to be the gravest crisis the country has confronted because we know there are a lot of people out there who wish us ill and who want to kill us. But thus far we've had one very, very tragic event, and if we're lucky, and if the FBI director and the vice president are not correct, then I'm not sure it's a crisis that matches World War II or some of the other events.

It is a crisis for sure in the sense that the American people are very uneasy. They feel insecure for the first time in my life. All through my political career, I don't ever recall Americans really having a strong sense of physical insecurity, which they do today, I think, very widely. It is not a crisis if you think about the things Lloyd mentioned a moment ago, where the American people were asked to make considerable sacrifices. Today the advice to us is to proceed with your life normally, to get out there and spend money, cut taxes—no great sense of self-sacrifice that you certainly had during World War II. So, is it a crisis equal to World War II and other events? Not yet. Could be; depends on how events unfold.

Harry C. McPherson: It is different from anything I've ever experienced. I lived about six blocks from the Capitol, which I assume was ground zero, in 1962, and I really didn't worry that we were going to be hit by a missile from Cuba or from Russia. I was not one of those stocking cans and bottled water in the basement. It wouldn't have made much difference in my old brick house on Capitol Hill. It would have been wiped away in a minute anyway.

In the '60s, the crisis was one of spirit, between all kinds, between the university-educated and the non-, between the better-off and the not-so-better-off, between black and white. It tore us up. It made us extremely distraught in our spirit. But it was not like this. I do sense in people a degree of apprehension that I have not experienced before. Today there is this sense, this apprehension, that the next twenty-four hours, the next forty-eight hours, may produce something. And it's because of that unforgettable experience of watching those towers get hit. It's the sudden staggering shock of violence and death coming into America, and our feeling that it can happen again.

And, looking at Israel, watching the willingness of young people to take their lives and many others, innocent though the world might think them to be, that just seems as if it's something that is poised to happen here. At least that's something that is very much in people's minds at the moment.

Kalb: *Am I right in saying that none of you believe that the president is exaggerating the threat currently facing the U.S.?*

Sasser: Well, that's difficult to know. But I do think that when you have at the same time questions being raised about the administration's handling of the intelligence prior to 9/11, and as the Congress begins to talk about having a commission and there's some thought of second-guessing what happened with regard to information the administration may or may not have had—it's not a coincidence, in my mind, that a day or two afterwards, you have the secretary of defense saying that this will happen again. You have the director of the FBI saying it will happen again. You have the vice president saying it will happen again—as if they're trying to defend themselves in saying, "Now look, we're warning you it's going to happen again." If it doesn't happen again, well, great. But if it does, they can always say, "Well, we told you it was coming." So I think there's an element of sort of politically covering yourself in some of these statements.

Hamilton: I think the president's success—and it's an important success—is that he took the anxiety of the American people, maybe the fear of the American people, and he channeled that into an effective response against the events of September 11. That was a considerable political achievement, and he deserves credit for that.

I don't think he's exaggerated the problem of security. I don't have that sense at all. I do think, however, that there is an exaggeration with respect to the war on terrorism in making it, if he does, a kind of a single focus of American foreign policy. The war on terrorism is important. It's terribly important. I don't want to be misunderstood here. But it cannot be the sum and the substance of American foreign policy. There are a lot of other interests out there that we have as a country, and you must not see all of these interests through the prism of the war on terrorism.

And I don't know [whether] that's a criticism of the president or not, but sometimes, when he speaks about the war on terrorism as being the defining moment of his presidency and dividing the world into the good guys and the bad guys, the evil and good, I get the sense that we may be losing sight—maybe exaggerating the war on terrorism too much and losing sight of a lot of other very important goals: nonproliferation, human rights, environmental concerns, and many, many others.

Kalb: *You know the Hart-Rudman commission. On the day that [its report] was put out, it was not reported in the* New York Times *nor on three of the major networks that night. As you look back upon it and the importance of the press in serving as the middleman between the government and the people, what should be happening now? Did the press do us a favor by not focusing on terrorism on that day when the Hart-Rudman report came out? I can't imagine that it did.*

Hamilton: What I detect among people is [that] they want to know what they should do in their personal lives. You put out a warning by the vice president or by the FBI director and say, "We're going to be hit," and it raises the level of apprehension. But if you go out and talk to people in Indiana and you ask them about it, they say, "Okay, we're going to be hit; but what do I do in my family? What kind of steps do I take?"

So one of the things the media has to do and one of the things the government has to do is to try to help people, ordinary people living ordinary lives, get through this crisis and tell them what they do in their lives. That's what's meaningful to them. And I don't think either the government or the media is doing a good job of that, although I think generally the media has done a pretty god job explaining the war on terrorism.

Stephen Hess: *Something else has been happening with the press that I think you gentlemen can throw some light on—and that is the sudden surge of leaks. Now, leaks may have a bad reputation, but they do play sort of a lubricating*

role in this society, in this culture, [indicating] how government responds, what
government is doing, what government is hiding, how Congress picks up on it.
What's happening here now? Is this a good thing, a bad thing? And can it be
stopped? Should it be stopped? Is this now government by leak?

Cutler: It's really déjà vu all over again. Every president I can remember tried
to stop leaks. It never works, and I guess that we're all very lucky that it doesn't.

McPherson: I don't recall an administration in my time that was more
obsessed with keeping material out of the public eye than this one. I don't
recall any one that has been so buttoned up—and in all of its agencies, starting
at the White House—than this one.

I mean, in the Johnson White House, in the Kennedy White House, in the
Carter White House, people talked a mile a minute, everybody did, to the
despair of the president and of many of his aides. Everybody wanted to let on
what was going on. I was an absolute sucker for [newspaper columnists] Evans
and Novak. As long as they would take me to a French restaurant across the
street, I felt that I was obliged to pay for my lunch by giving them what they
wanted.

Kalb: *Well, turn that around for a second. If the administration is right that*
this is a new kind of war that we are dealing with, a new kind of enemy, who is
to argue, then, with the administration's case that we can't put out the kind of
information that you might have done in the Johnson administration because
the threat is entirely different?

Sasser: Well, we have a right to know certain facts. This is supposed to be a
democracy. And in a democracy, you need to have an informed electorate.
Now that's the ideal. I think we miss that by quite a bit, quite frankly. And this
administration is the most buttoned-up that I've seen. And I think they were
buttoned up prior to 9/11. And I think they're using 9/11 as a pretense for bat-
tening the hatches even tighter.

Kalb: *Dan Rather, who is the main anchor at CBS News, has stated that he*
fears that the press is buttoning up itself out of concern that they may be labeled
unpatriotic.

Cutler: Now I don't really see how you can maintain that argument. If you
were a reader of the *New York Times* or the *Washington Post*, they are getting
leaks. They are seeking leaks. They are reporting leaks. You have to go all the
way back to the Bay of Pigs, when [*New York Times* Washington bureau chief]
Scotty Reston had some advance information which he was talked out of using,

and he regretted it for the rest of his life. I really think the press is doing what it's supposed to be doing, and it is literally impossible to stop leaks. LBJ thought he had a monopoly on leaks.

Kalb: *And that's part of my point. A lot of these leaks are deliberate. It is information that the administration wants out and gives to the* New York Times, *the* Washington Post, *because they get the biggest circulation.*

Cutler: The people who come into the White House—they're not like a team of General Electric managers who've worked together for twenty years. They come from different state campaigns. They all think they deserve to be chief of staff, at least the deputy chief of staff. And the one thing they will never do, because it's so embarrassing to them, is to admit that they don't know the answer to a question. So you always give an answer, even though it may be a wrong one.

Hamilton: Let me make this observation that runs a little counter, maybe, to the other panelists. There are reasons to keep many things secret. It's important to recognize that there are national security secrets, there are operational secrets, there are sources and methods secrets that are a very important part of the national security of the United States.

Now, the problem comes when this administration, or any administration, moves to the point of saying, "Trust us, we can handle this problem. We know the full facts; you don't have to know them." I think a healthy skepticism is always important for members of Congress, for the American public, and certainly for the media. We would not understand today as well as we do—and we don't understand it perfectly—the problems in the intelligence community had it not been for these leaks that Steve was talking about a moment ago. Those leaks are very, very important to us.

There is an attitude in the national security community that says, in effect, "We can handle this. Just let us handle it and everything will be all right." I don't think we should accept that attitude. Now, where you draw the line is always difficult. And the question of leaks in Washington: leaks are inevitable in Washington; you're not going to stop them, nor should you.

Sasser: But we are talking about something very fundamental here, and that is about the deprivation of civil liberties outside of what we perceive to be the rule of law. Now, we may look back on these days that have occurred since September 11 years from now and compare them to the taking of the Japanese and putting them in internment camps, Japanese-Americans, after December 7, 1941. Or we may compare it to the Palmer Raids of the 1920s. Amnesty International is doing that already. I don't see this crisis as so severe that we should have a wholesale suspension of civil liberties. And I think we're seeing that in some areas, and it's alarming.

Question (from the audience): *My question relates to the risk of a nuclear device being detonated in the United States. Do you agree that there is this risk? Or is this overstated? And if it is a risk, do you believe that the administration's actually working very hard to avert this in ways that we can't see?*

Hamilton: I believe it is the most serious risk to the national security of the United States that the so-called loose nukes would get into the hands of the terrorists. And certainly, the result of that, if [they were] detonated, would be devastating—perhaps more devastating than what happened on September 11. I was on the Hart-Rudman commission. We agreed that Americans would die on American soil far before September 11. And it was a unanimous view of all of the commissioners with very different perspectives. Now, "What do you do about it?" is a very tough question. But the biggest problem in the world today is Russia. Lloyd Cutler headed up a commission at the Department of Energy with Senator Baker that put their fingers, I guess I should say, on this problem of the loose nukes. And we all agreed—Lloyd, what was it—$30 billion?

Cutler: We thought $30 billion could usefully be invested in getting control of the Russian nukes, helping them literally to guard the nuclear material they had and helping them literally to count the number of weapons and quantities of highly enriched uranium and plutonium that they had.

Hamilton: We're not putting nearly enough resources into trying to collect, analyze, account for, secure these weapons. And I think it's a major flaw presently in our national security policy. A lot of members of Congress agree with what I've just said, and I think the administration is moving here in the right direction—not quickly enough, from my standpoint, but they're moving in that direction.

Question (from the audience): *My question is what do you say to the critics that would say that we are violating our own ideals and our own way of life more than any terrorist has?*

McPherson: Well, it's always been a dilemma, how to be safe without being repressive. We don't have in America what some countries have; we don't have an internal intelligence apparatus. I was very aware of this in the '60s, when there were riots in Detroit and a number of other major cities, and there were rumors that some communists had played a role in stimulating activists into starting these riots. When you tried to see what the truth was, you realize that the intelligence apparatus for a president, the internal intelligence apparatus, the one inside America, is composed of bureaucrats, politicians, business guys, labor leaders, citizens who come in, many of them, with an ax to grind.

But it's always been difficult for us as a nation, and we've largely chosen not to empower anybody, any agency, including the FBI, with the reach to invade all of our lives to the extent that they are invaded in many other countries, even in democracies.

Question (from the audience): *Each of you in varying degrees has been critical of what you regard as the shortcomings and the failures of the administration to act to confront the terrorist challenge. How do we get the government to do more? What to do to translate your impatience into active policy?*

Hamilton: Well, I think you're beginning to see the process work. After September 11, there is a rally around the president, rally around the flag; patriotism asserts itself. We're all very, very reluctant to make any criticism, because we genuinely want to see the president succeed in the war on terrorism. And that remains, I think, our overwhelming feeling.

But as you move beyond phase one of the war, which was the fight against the Taliban in Afghanistan, the objectives and the implementation of the war on terrorism become a little less clear, murkier, and you begin to see some problems in the conduct of the war on terrorism. And you begin to see that there are choices or alternatives that can be made on the military side, the political side, the humanitarian side, the intelligence side, the civil liberties side of the war now. All of this is beginning to come out now and to circulate and people are getting a better understanding.

I think the process is working, although working slowly. So what do you do about it? Well, you have to get these matters out into the public. You have to begin to discuss them and criticize the president. The president should not be above criticism in his conduct of the war on terrorism. That doesn't make any sense in a democratic society. You have to be both a partner and a critic, and it's not always easy to carry out those two roles. You want the president to succeed, you want the country to succeed in the war on terrorism; but at the same time, you see things in the war on terrorism that you think run counter to your sense of values and you have to speak out on them and see if others agree with you on it. You're beginning to see that process in the Congress and in the country.

PART SIX

9/11 and Beyond

18

Running toward Danger

O ne year after 9/11, a book entitled *Running toward Danger: Stories behind the Breaking News of 9/11* was published. Written by Alicia C. Shepard and Cathy Trost, it was a song of praise to the reporters who covered the terrorist attacks on the United States, a remarkable story that this generation of journalists may regard as their Pearl Harbor.

On September 19, 2002, the last of our twenty panels was convened to honor the book and the journalists—and to look beyond 9/11 to the brief "spike" in public approval of American journalism: the dramatic rise following 9/11 and then the precipitous fall a few months later, when reporters seemed to return to their pre-9/11 pursuit of the trivial and their absorption with scandal and sensationalism. Our panelists were

—**E. J. Dionne Jr.**, a former *New York Times* reporter who migrated to the *Washington Post*, where he is an op-ed page columnist, and to the Brookings Institution, where he is a senior fellow

—**John McWethy**, chief national security correspondent for ABC News, whose beat includes wars and terrorism

—**Alan Murray**, Washington bureau chief for CNBC and *Wall Street Journal* columnist

—**Alicia C. Shepard**, author and frequent contributor to the *American Journalism Review*.

The book highlighted two facts: first, that many American reporters, when faced with the crisis, rushed to the nearest telephone booth, changed, and emerged as journalistic Supermen and Superwomen, no questions asked; and second, that they exhibited a sure and solid patriotism that, for a time, bound journalism and government together as they joined forces to find and defeat the common enemy. One might have imagined that as long as the United

States was engaged in this war such collaboration would likely continue. But it did not continue. Within months, the press was back to criticism and skepticism, much of it justified, and the government was back to a jaundiced view of the media, much of it justified too.

McWethy stated that Defense Secretary Rumsfeld, a very popular figure at the time, regarded "the press as the enemy," creating "a real danger" for journalists covering American forces. During the Afghanistan war, McWethy said, the Pentagon imposed severe restrictions on journalists, and he predicted that during a war against Iraq, if one were to materialize, such restrictions "will be as bad, if not worse."

Murray agreed with McWethy's sharp and bleak judgment but disagreed with his belief that journalists should show no favoritism toward the "home team"—for example, by wearing an American flag pin on their lapel. "I do not believe that being a patriot is somehow inimical to being a good journalist," he said. McWethy responded: "When you are on television, you are a symbol for your network. I would no more wave an American flag while I am trying to report in a nonbiased way about conflict overseas than I would a Canadian flag or a British flag if I were a citizen of those countries. I'm a reporter." Patriotism for a journalist was clearly a tricky proposition.

Shepard tried to reduce the emotional quotient, explaining that immediately after 9/11 journalists seemed human and therefore vulnerable to the public, but after several months they began to look once again like institutional performers and therefore no longer worthy of the public's support and sympathy. "Seeing them as patriots made them seem more human," she said. Seeing them as "just some sort of institutional function" robbed them of popular esteem, especially when they began to criticize the government and question its policies. Dionne added that many people believed the press should be subject to tighter legislative constraints, especially in war. He cited a poll published in the *American Journalism Review* saying that "freedom of the press" had become the least popular right in the First Amendment.

Alicia Shepard: On September 11, 2001, because of the hideous attacks, there was another strange phenomenon that happened in the United States. Everyone in the country, whether they lived in Ketchum, Idaho, or New York City, was suddenly startled out of their daily routines and focused on the exact same event. If you think about it, how often does that happen? Maybe when the Challenger blew up in January 1986, definitely when President Kennedy was killed in 1963, and yet in all of those three events, it's inescapable to note that the very first place nearly every member of the public turned was to the news media.

They learned about the first plane hitting the north tower at 8:46 a.m. only minutes later from television and from the Dow Jones wire [service] that broke the story first because of its proximity to the World Trade Center.

Peter Jennings said, "There's never been anything like this. Not a single event in a single moment in a single day. I realized that we had a very special job." And on this day of unimaginable tragedy and terror, journalists acted on instinct. They literally ran toward danger.

It's my opinion that that's just what journalists do. It might even be in their DNA, although as of yet there's no scientific evidence of this. We saw journalists at their best, determined to get to the scene and report the facts.

And just getting to the crash sites of the World Trade Center, the Pentagon, and also rural central Pennsylvania was a logistical nightmare. Bridges and tunnels were shut down at 9:21 a.m. in New York City. That was after the second plane hit. After the Pentagon was hit at 9:38 a.m. roads around D.C. were shut down. In Pennsylvania, reporters didn't even hear about the crash that occurred at 10:10 until almost 10:45. They didn't know where it was. It was in a rural strip mine. Many of them listened on radios and followed the directions that were being given to rescue workers, and they just got in and got behind fire trucks.

What was remarkable to me was that journalists commandeered taxis, they hitched rides in cars, they jumped on boats, they rode bicycles, they walked miles, and some of them even sprinted just to get to the site. It didn't matter if they were pregnant, terrified, jogging on a treadmill, sitting in a barber shop as the managing editor of the *New York Times* was, or home asleep—or even, like John McWethy, sitting at their desks inside the Pentagon. They had to get there. They had to get the story and report it to the world.

I listened to Maggie Farley, who is a New York–based correspondent for the *Los Angeles Times* and was also eight months pregnant at the time. She said, "I felt this journalistic desperation to get to the scene." En route to getting to the Brooklyn Bridge to get into the city, Maggie Farley ran into her husband, Marcus Brauchli, the national news editor for the *Wall Street Journal*. He looked at her and said, "Don't even try." He was heading back to their Brooklyn home, where he would then go on to coordinate a lot of the coverage that day using BlackBerries [wireless handheld e-mail system] and the Internet. He said, "I don't want you to go." Maggie said, "But I felt like I had to try. I went to the Brooklyn Bridge and there were thousands of people coming across like a parade of refugees. Suddenly the stream of people turned into a throng that looked like *The Night of the Living Dead*. I tried to find people who were coherent enough to interview. Though I had a police pass, the police wouldn't let me get on the bridge because so many people were coming from New York to

Brooklyn. But I was in the reporter mode, and I felt the journalistic desperation to get to the scene."

Maggie didn't get there, but she didn't go home either. Like many others who weren't able to get to the scene, they went out and found other stories. She went to the mosques, the hospitals, the restaurants in her neighborhood. I think Maggie's determination and drive embodies what all journalists felt on this seismic day. They want to know, they feel a deep responsibility to share that information with the public, and they strive to do it fairly and accurately.

It's the journalist's job to document history, whether it's in words or photographs, and journalists that we talked to were keenly aware of their social responsibility to calmly and reliably explain what was happening to a public that was desperate to understand. There was no star system. There was no competition. Whoever got there, whoever had the best information, whoever could provide the best photographs, the best videos, that was what was viewed. I think in that sense it was truly a unique day for journalism. One audience all wanting the same story and all journalists acting as one trying to deliver it.

I think I'll stop there, and I will let Jack tell his really dramatic story because he happened to be sitting inside the Pentagon when the plane hit at 9:38.

John McWethy: I don't know how dramatic the story is. Like everyone, we all know exactly where we were at that moment. I was watching the World Trade Center scene, and ABC tends to come to me when there are potential terrorist threats. They wired me up. I was ready to go on a small camera in my booth with them yelling in my ear, "Are you ready? Are you ready?" and me yelling back at them, "But I don't know anything." Which often doesn't stop them.

Then I felt the jolt in the Pentagon. About a third of the way around is where the aircraft hit, and because of the oblique angle it hit, much of the explosive impact went in one direction around the hallways of the Pentagon.

Almost immediately the place was full of smoke and chaos. But as many military officers will tell you: if anyone is going to strike at the United States, this is a good place to strike, because the military folks know how to deal with this, and they did.

I got out of the building, made my way around, and tried to get as close to the crash scene as I could and determine what had happened. One of the first people I ran into was a reporter from *USA Today* who was one of the eyewitnesses, who had been commuting down the highway. We were all trying to get it straight, what was it that hit the Pentagon, and he said, "I saw American Airlines right above my head." Then I interviewed a taxicab driver who watched it clip off the light poles as it came in low and careened into the side of the building.

We all just wanted to get the story that day. It was a dramatic day. Communications were awful, as everyone remembers. The cell phones were totally jammed. I commandeered a pay phone at the CITGO station across from the Pentagon. It was just minutes after the place had been hit, and they were worried about a fourth aircraft coming in. They were yelling at us, "Clear the area, there's another airplane in-bound to Washington. This is a potential target. This gas station."

I had finally gotten on the phone to ABC, and I wasn't about to give up this pay phone. Some rent-a-cop came along and started to make like he was going to pull his gun on me, and I just looked at him and said, "Look, I'm a reporter. I have to report to my network. Shoot me." His eyes sort of glazed, and he ran on yelling at other people, threatening them.

It's the kind of scene that you run into again and again. In some ways, thank God, it was in this country. I've been threatened many times with guns in other countries in war zones, and I tend to take them a lot more seriously than I did this young man who was getting ready to threaten me. But it was an amazing day.

Alan Murray: I said to my staff at the *Wall Street Journal* at the time that it was both the worst day of my life and one of the most exhilarating days of my life.

 The worst day for all the obvious reasons, all the co-workers [in New York City] who were in the building right across the street [from the World Trade Center], and we didn't know what had happened to them. My wife had family who lived in the building immediately behind the *Wall Street Journal* building who were separated from [their] young kids for most of the day. You were working with reporters who just were doing what reporters do. All of them. It wasn't a love of danger; it was just sort of a lack of regard.

Let me just take you quickly through the story of that day, and I think you have to put this in context. Remember that the big story of August of 2001 was Chandra Levy. We only got a brief break from that when the fellow dove into the water and pulled his son's leg out of the shark's mouth. That was the kind of journalism that was capturing national attention before September 11. On that Tuesday morning, at about 9:15, I got a call from the paper's managing editor, Paul Steiger. At that point we knew about both planes, and he said "We're leaving. We have to get out of this building. We're going to head over to South Brunswick, New Jersey," where the paper's corporate offices are. He said, " I don't know how long it's going to take us to get there. We're going to try and put out the paper from there, but in the meantime, you have to handle the coverage, put together stories so when we finally get things up and running we can put together a paper."

I called together the staff. I think everybody instantly recognized [that] this was one of those days. This was our generation's Pearl Harbor. The world was changing before our eyes. I cannot remember a single incident during the course of the day when somebody said, "Hey, I've got to get home to my family, I have to leave, I can't stay here." I'm sure people dealt with those things over the course of the day. I'm sure people did have to get home to their families. Schools were dismissed. People dealt with all those things. But the only thing I remember is reporters walking into my office saying, "What can I do? What can I do?"

The front page of the *Wall Street Journal* won the Pulitzer Prize for breaking news that day. Four of the six stories on the front page were compiled and written in the Washington bureau. But the most compelling of those, other than probably the first-person account by John Bussey, was pulled together by Brian Gruley. It was a first-person account of what was happening in New York.

For those of you who aren't reporters, I will let you into a little secret, which is reporters don't get to the office very early in the morning. So at 9:15 most people weren't there. They were walking into the office. A lot of them were getting off the subway stops, walking down the street when they saw this specter unfold in front of them. Then, of course, the communication systems went down. Many of these reporters in New York never had any contact with their editors, had nobody to tell them what to do. They just couldn't communicate with anybody, so they did what reporters do. They took out their notebooks, and they just started writing.

Later in the day when they finally got to some place where they could at least get a phone line, plug their computer into their phone line, they just started filing these accounts into the ether. They didn't know who to send it to, because there was nobody in New York organizing coverage. In fact what you had at the *Wall Street Journal* was this totally chaotic situation, where people are running around just taking notes, looking, seeing, and then they just filed into the ether. There's an e-mail address that goes to virtually everybody at the *Wall Street Journal*, and Brian Gruley sat here and just pulled these incredible stories down from the e-mail and put them together in what I think has probably got to be the most fascinating account of that day that anybody put together. Again, done without any direction, any top-down management, just reporters doing what reporters do.

I remember reading these things as they were coming in. There was one incredible account written in the third person about someone trying to get onto the boat to New Jersey after the towers had collapsed. You had this incredible concentration of dust and grime chasing people down the street. Again, this account written in the third person talks about how this person was trying to get onto the boat and he fell into the river and had to be lifted out of the river back onto the boat. And only when you got to the end of this account did you realize that the person involved was the reporter.

Shepard: Many of the photographers who were in New York took pictures, and the police or the people who were the subjects were saying, "Why are you taking my picture? What's the matter with you?" And several different photographers said, "We have to document this. We need to tell this story. This is an important story to tell." In each case the people agreed instantly. The police backed away. So I think that was one of the remarkable things—that this story, this event, whether you were in Pennsylvania, New York, or aboard Air Force One or in D.C., it was happening to the journalists at the same time. It wasn't that they were there dispassionately covering it.

E. J. Dionne, Jr.: Actually, I wanted to make that point too, about photographers. The day before I went to Lebanon for the first time [for the *New York Times*], I had never covered a war and was absolutely pet-

rified. The late Flora Lewis, who was then a columnist and had actually given me my first job as an intern, knew I'd be scared and took me out to dinner. She gave me some advice on how to cover war for the first time. The first piece of advice was, "Stay away from the photographers; they have to get a lot closer than you do." It was excellent advice. My favorite story from Lebanon was of a photographer/TV cameraman talking to a group of marines, the marines who were later blown up in that terrible attack. But the photographer describes what he does for a living, and here this big tough marine says, "You guys are nuts. We would never do anything like that." I think it's just an indication of what they do.

[Another] point that I think is often overlooked: editors are actually very concerned about the lives of their reporters. The one story I have to tell about that was in my first week in Lebanon. I will never forget this man. It was Bill Borders, who was then the assistant foreign editor. I was going to go up into the mountains to report on the fighting. I'd been there a week, so I was a really experienced war reporter. Borders gets me on the phone and said, "You're not going up there." He said, "You are at your most dangerous stage. You've been there long enough to think you know what's going on, and you're too dumb to know that you don't know how to do this yet." I'll always love him for that. I think it's important that editors do that in these circumstances.

Murray: Just to reinforce that, having lived through the Danny Pearl episode, which was a really tough one for all of us, and I sat in on daily phone conferences with the chairman of the board and the editor of the paper, and I can tell you that every single decision that was made was made with only one concern in mind, which [was], What we can do to get Danny out?

Shepard: How about in terms of when you were talking about the story before he was kidnapped? Was there a "Danny, don't do this?"

Murray: No. Danny actually was one of these reporters who did not throw himself into an incredibly dangerous situation. He didn't want to go to Afghanistan and cover "the war." I don't think either he or his editors appreciated the danger of the situation that night.

Dionne: What also comes through from how reporters covered 9/11 is the sense of good fortune you have to have in a situation like this. In Lebanon I had the experience of going up the mountain the day after the USS New Jersey shelled Druze positions, and by sheer chance in a little town ran into a Druze American who had gone back to the mountain during the war, happened to read some of my stories, and took me all the way to see the guys who had been shelled that day. If I had not run into that guy and he had not read the stories—what are the chances of that in a little town in a mountain of Lebanon? So I think all of us who have been in this line of work say a prayer for luck because it's very important. Then you try to make the best of it.

Stephen Hess: *E. J., how do you explain "the spike," the remarkable U-curve from a very low public assessment of the press on 9/10, to overwhelming approval for a while after 9/11, to the current return to the low approval ratings?*

Dionne: A couple of theories. First, I think everything about 9/11 coverage was visible to the people in the country. At some level it wasn't any more complicated than that. It was so raw. You [couldn't make every transition seamless], so it actually looked extremely honest to people the way the press was trying to report that.

I am told, and I never want to look it up—as a journalistic concept too good to check[—]that Hegel, of all people, said the job of journalists is to convey information and hide ignorance at the same time. On that day we were actually quite honest about information and ignorance, [about] what we knew and what we didn't know.

Then there's the second question about what happened in the days after. The press did become, if you will, red, white, and blue. I don't think that was put on. I think reporters got affected by this in much the same way as the rest of the country did. It was the first attack on the mainland of the United States since 1812 and the first attack on the United States since Pearl Harbor. In that sense reporters were no different than people in the country, which may surprise others. So I think there was a kind of red, white, and blue quality to the coverage if you looked at the coverage of President Bush on that first day, which was his shakiest day in the whole business. There was enormous restraint.

We did look red, white, and blue patriotic in that period, and I think a lot of people who had been hostile to the press as a sort of critical agency—always tearing down the government and whoever was in it and other institutions—saw us in a different light. And I think as well [that] there was a kind of a partisan element of this. The polls from Andy Kohut asked a very interesting question: When covering the war on terrorism, journalists should "dig for hard news or trust officials?" Liberal Democrats said dig for hard news, 60–33. Moderate conservative Democrats, dig for hard news 56–37. Moderate to liberal Republicans were on the same side, 53–42. But on the other side, conservative Republicans said trust officials, 55–38 percent.

I think in that period what you had was a sense that the press was in fact being more trusting of officials, or at least we conveyed that sense, and that it took a while for the press to make a turn back to more critical reporting. I think it's perfectly normal for the country to like [the press] in a sense when we seem terribly nice and to dislike it when we become critical again, but it is the natural role of the press eventually to turn to digging for information that makes public officials uncomfortable.

Murray: There seems to be an undercurrent to what you're saying—that the public liked the press more because they weren't, in your view, doing their job as well.

Dionne: No, I don't think it's so much doing their job. I think first of all the job to be done, especially in that immediate period, was so clearly an information-gathering role, not about what went wrong. We weren't looking at, "My God, what did the CIA do or not do, what did the FBI do?" We were trying to collect raw factual information, which always makes us popular. But I think in the second instance, . . . whether under Clinton or under Bush . . . some segment of the public doesn't like it when we become critical. The segment of the public that doesn't like an administration at the time loves a critical press. The people who support that administration hate a critical press. The people in the middle probably lean towards a little skepticism of criticism.

So I think in that period it was because we were behaving in the ways we did, in some ways I think quite justifiably, but I think in retrospect we may pose some questions about it. There was a kind of artificial spike where we picked up people who were normally critical of us, and it's not at all surprising that when we returned to behaving the way we normally behave those numbers flipped around.

I think there is one element that is purely about the success of the press that day in doing its job and some of it was genuine admiration for the work. Another piece of it was indeed the shift from a sense of us as a critical agency to us as a fact-gathering, more patriotic agency, and it would be intriguing for somebody to look at these numbers to figure out which was which and why, to explain this fantastic U-curve, because the numbers are almost identical today to what they were a year ago. It is almost a perfect U, and I think that's an intriguing question for us to ponder.

Hess: *Let me get back to Jack McWethy, for several reasons. First of all, we go from 9/11 to Afghanistan. You were there briefly. Afghanistan was a remarkably difficult exercise for the press. It was the most dangerous war—*

McWethy: More reporters died in the early days than soldiers.

Hess: *Yes, eight reporters died. But the war was mostly explained to us by Secretary Rumsfeld in Pentagon briefings. The public loved him in a very special way. He became the patriot, and what were the reporters?*

McWethy: The dynamic begins on the day of the event. I have never felt such a thirst for the information and the perspective as I did in the five days that ABC News took over the network and we just did it for five days straight. There was an unbelievable thirst and connection that I felt in being a journalist, a very special trust.

But the worm began to turn as the issues turned: Are you an American? Or a journalist? Those two issues immediately began to be debated within my news division. The issue of [whether] you wear an American flag lapel pin on the air. ABC decided no. You're a journalist first, though you are an American. That's undeniable. The greatest criticism of the American press during this period is that international journalists saw us as being nothing more than cheerleaders for the administration. We walked a very delicate and difficult line, especially those of us that cover national security. We were immediately in disagreement with the administration over how we cover this war and what steps we are going to be allowed to take—what steps we took, even though we were not being allowed to take them in terms of providing the American people with some perspective as to where the United States was headed. And it continued to be a very delicate and interesting debate among those of us that cover this sensitive subject area, which is not just the Pentagon, but . . . what the CIA is doing and what other parts of the government are doing in trying to cover the aftermath of 9/11.

Don Rumsfeld has become what I regard as C-SPAN's greatest daytime soap opera. When he takes to the air, C-SPAN's numbers go right off the charts. He is enormously popular. If you watched any of his hearing yesterday, the members of the House Armed Services Committee acted as though they had a TV star in their midst. They were so excited to be in Don Rumsfeld's presence. He has a persona now.

The press in dealing with him, in trying to get answers to very difficult questions: alternately we hold our heads up high and sometimes we are made to be fools in the daily briefing. Rumsfeld, in my opinion, is a very skilled communicator. He slam dunks the press with great regularity. And he has begun doing it with such regularity that I have called it to the attention of Torie Clarke, the assistant secretary for public affairs at the Defense Department, because I see a danger.

When Rumsfeld goes out and talks to the troops and basically portrays the press as the enemy, which he does to a degree, I feel that it has implications far beyond just a debate. It has implications for the safety of reporters who deal with the military in combat zones. And when soldiers are told by the highest-ranking man in a civilian suit at the Defense Department that we are in essence an enemy, it creates a real danger and a perception among the troops that I feel is something that needs to be corrected and dealt with.

We began pushing in the very early days for answers to some of the things that were unfolding before our eyes in the war in Afghanistan. What kind of commitment was the United States making to governments who had suddenly decided to allow the United States to put their troops on their soil? Many of them are countries that the United States would not have touched with a ten-foot pole prior to this, and it was very much [a matter of] marriages of convenience. But to this day I do not feel that the United States public has a very good idea of the financial, the moral, the ethical, and the legal commitments that the United States has made to these various governments for which we have now a very deep and abiding relationship. There are not answers to those questions, and those are important questions.

To this day the public has absolutely no idea how many civilians were killed in Afghanistan, not a clue. There are classified estimates. The military argues, and there's some validity to this, that they have no way of knowing. And that's true to a degree. They don't have a way of knowing accurately, but they do have estimates and they do know about collateral damage, and these are issues that the press did not push on hard enough. I didn't. But I began pushing, and it became a very difficult issue.

A third [question] is how close are reporters going to be allowed to be with the troops when the troops go into the field? There has been a constant debate within the Pentagon over the decades of various wars about how close reporters are going to be to the front line and to the forces that are conducting the combat.

This was a war that was very different. It was conducted primarily by about 200 to 250 special forces soldiers on the ground. There were no reporters with those soldiers until after the fall of Kandahar, until the war was essentially over. There were no eyes and ears, and that's the way the Pentagon wants it. They make absolutely no apologies for it. Reporters were allowed on aircraft carriers to watch planes take off, and that's about as close as we got. There were reporters later who got to go with the marines as they established rear bases, but the marines fundamentally didn't do anything. The war was over by the time the press got close enough to actually cover it.

To this day, we do not have a good idea, other than the rudimentary routes that were taken and some of the aspects of the political and military things that happened on the ground. To this day we do not have a good outline of what occurred during the two months of intense combat that overthrew a government and defeated an army in Afghanistan. It continues to be a very troublesome aspect of the issue right now as the United States prepares to deal with yet another conflict in Iraq, and I feel the exposure and ability of the press to cover that conflict will be as bad or even worse than it was in Afghanistan.

Hess: *Part of the reason that Don Rumsfeld became so popular is that no one else in the administration was available to tell the story. Ken Walsh, who is the White House correspondent for* US News and World Report, *was giving a speech this week, quoted in the* San Antonio Express News, *and he says that "the White House is now much more secretive than it was under his father," under George [H. W.] Bush. "Today, it's hard to get people to talk, and when they do they're all saying the same thing. You get the same rhetoric over and over."*

It strikes me that the degree to which these people have been buttoned down has serious consequences for how much information we get and also for how the press will respond when ultimately the administration slips on a banana peel, as all administrations do.

Murray: I think that's absolutely right. I agree with everything that John McWethy just said, but there's one point I want to make. I disagree with the decision of the networks to not allow reporters to wear flags on their lapels. I do not believe that being a patriot is somehow inimical to being a good journalist. We are Americans. My publication probably more than most has something of a global audience, but it's small compared to the American audience; our readers are Americans. I think for us to pretend to deny that is a huge mistake.

It doesn't mean that you can't ask the tough questions. I was frustrated because I was asking my reporters every day, What about civilian casualties? What damage are we doing? We have to know that. We have to report that. It doesn't mean you can't ask the tough questions about civil liberties. What's more American than civil liberties? In the process of this war, what are we doing to American values and American civil liberties? It doesn't mean that you can't try to understand what's going on in the Muslim world. The great tragedy, to me, of Danny Pearl's death is that he was one of the few reporters out there who was really doing sympathetic reporting about how the Muslim world viewed the events that were going on here.

So you can do all the things you need to do to be a good or great journalist and still love your country and care about your country.

McWethy: It's like waving a flag. When you are on television you are a symbol for your network. I would no more wave an American flag while I am trying to report in a nonbiased way about conflict overseas than I would a Canadian flag or a British flag if I were a citizen of those countries. I'm a reporter.

Dionne: I don't want to get too sidetracked on this, but can I ask John a question? It was my understanding that one of the reasons for that policy was that people can be equally patriotic but some may want to wear the flag and some may not, and that reporters at the network were running into difficulty: "Well, I believe the guy that has the flag on, but I don't believe the person who doesn't have the flag on." So the decision was made that either you had everybody wear the flag or nobody should wear the flag. Was there any of that?

McWethy: To be quite honest I had no participation in management's decisionmaking on this. I've never worn flag lapels. I've never worn any designation for anything on my suit, whether it indicates what my religion is or my nationality or anything else. I think I need to be dressed in a way where I am not a distraction.

Shepard: On 9/11 I think the public really saw the press as human beings who were scared, who were terrified, who were trying to do their job in tremendously dangerous situations. Think about photographers who ran when the first building fell and then went back to photograph more. You're saying that seeing them as patriots made them seem more human, and I think that is probably one of the key reasons why you then had the drop. The public sees the press not as human beings but as just some sort of institutional function.

Hess: *E. J. explained the spike in part because all of the conservatives that hate you suddenly love you and then they start to hate you again, which is very interesting but it doesn't answer the question about why the conservatives hate you in the first place. Gene Weingarten, a very funny columnist in the* Washington Post, *this Sunday had his ten "hates." Hate number ten was the "fact that the general public—afloat as it is in its reactionary, bigoted, Neanderthal self-interest-posing-as-conservatives—thinks all journalists are sanctimonious liberals." As our representative of the liberal persuasion, E. J., what's going on this past year?*

Dionne: Two points I want to make. I cited that piece of data, but there's some other data that suggests that there was an up and down among all groups. I don't want to overrepresent that. I think that data is interesting, and that's why I raised it. But there was an up and down across all groups, and that's why I think it is more complicated than just a conservative-liberal thing, although I do think that's fair.

I think it's obvious that going back to the days of Spiro Agnew there has been a concerted effort on the part of conservatives—quite successful from their point of view, very intelligent—to put the press on the defensive, to say "the press are a whole bunch of liberals so don't believe them, believe us." I think that's continued, it's had an effect, it's entered deep into the conservative movement.

My own view is that the biases of the press are not so much liberal or conservative; they tend to be the biases of the educated upper-middle class. Therefore on social issues such as abortion, you probably do have a more liberal bias. That is not true of economic issues, such as trade or budget balancing.

Hess: *The* American Journalism Review *in the current issue has a new poll on the First Amendment. The least popular First Amendment right is freedom of the press. Forty-two percent say that the press has too much freedom. Maybe it's just that "they" don't understand "you" or what your role should be?*

McWethy: What we do is sometimes difficult for the public to deal with. For those of us that have spent a lot of our careers overseas doing things, the most profound difference that I observed and that people I run into overseas observe about the United States is freedom of the press. There is no country that has an institution like this, and we as journalists sometimes abuse it, and we as journalists sometimes honor it tremendously.

I think one of the points of great tension since 9/11 is the issue of classified information and how much journalists find out about military operations and secrets of the government. We walk on very shaky and difficult ground, especially those of us that come into contact with classified and secret information every day. Don Rumsfeld would like to throw the people we talk to into jail. He has made absolutely no bones about it. But for those who know anything about classified information, a lot of it is the same stuff that's in the *Wall Street Journal* every day, and they classify it.

So there is an inherent conflict and tension I think with journalists, and there is also a blurring of the lines [between] serious journalism [and] what other people do—Geraldo, Oprah. Those are all considered to be journalists, and to a degree I suppose they are, but they are not some of the dinosaurs that you see sitting up here, whose view of great reporting is [that it deals with] issues of great significance.

Shepard: There is definitely a tendency to see "the press" as monolithic and to not distinguish between the *New York Times* and the *National Enquirer*, and I think that's very frustrating for a lot of journalists because it's always the squeaky wheel that gets the attention. And so much of the good reporting that goes on every day and the journalists with integrity and honesty and dedication are just overlooked, and it seems to me very unfortunate.

Hess: *We have representatives of various segments of that media here today, all of whom may have to answer some tough questions. Alan Murray, who escaped one of the great newspapers, at least as a bureau chief, has become the bureau chief of a twenty-four-hour-a-day cable news channel. Shouldn't we serious people have some worry about stations that go on twenty-four hours a day and when they only have one hour of news fill the other twenty-three with people shouting at each other or retired generals pointing their sticks at maps of the world? You made a big move; defend yourself, Murray.*

Murray: I don't think you can blame the medium. I think there is good journalism on television and there is bad journalism on television, just as there is good journalism in print and bad journalism in print. And in both mediums there is probably more bad journalism than good. It is a very different medium. I wouldn't be terribly happy if I didn't have a weekly column in the *Wall Street Journal*. I mean, I love what I'm doing for CNBC. I'm having a great time. But I am constantly amazed at how little depth you can achieve even with a full hour of television to play with every night and with a pretty sophisticated and intelligent audience relative to the average TV audience. I'm amazed and frustrated and shocked at how much more I can do with an 835-word column.

So it's a medium with limitations, and it is a medium that requires you to be visual. Does it require crazy people shouting at each other? I don't think so. In fact, I think you can see a bit of a turnoff with that kind of television going on right now. You look at somebody like Aaron Brown on CNN cultivating an image and some success by being the opposite of that. So I think it's a reflection of the face of the people watching television, not a reflection of the box.

Hess: *McWethy works for a broadcast network that after the Berlin Wall came down closed up all its bureaus around the world, or almost all of them. America seems to be interested in the rest of the world again, if only in self-defense. Are you going to open any bureaus? Are you going to go back to the good old days of Murrow's Boys?*

McWethy: It's been an interesting ten or fifteen years since the Wall came down. ABC and all of the networks closed many of their overseas operations, and it was a straight line function of economics. I believe a lot of newspapers have closed their overseas operations as well. Is it because the American people don't want to know about what's going on? Maybe. I think the network has an obligation to continue to report what is happening out in the world. I am proud to say that ABC, especially World News Tonight with Peter Jennings, does more overseas coverage than any other evening broadcast, which is still not enough for my taste.

But I take these periods of conflict—as someone who has covered them intensively for several decades—as wonderful opportunities for this powerful medium, what I call teachable moments for our many millions of audience. When there is a conflict in Afghanistan, the network goes and teaches people who couldn't care less about Afghanistan all about the ethnicity, the religion, the economics, the history, the geography, the theology—all of that gets put before an audience in small bites, but it's done again and again and again. The same was true with Bosnia, the same was true with Kosovo, with Somalia, Haiti, you name it. Those are the teachable moments when the medium for which I work is magnificent. We pour resources into it, and we explain in ways that [allow] people who may not have an abiding interest in it [to] learn an incredible amount. For that I am so grateful. It is a powerful communications tool, and it's very effective in those teachable moments. And when we're left with Chandra Levy and the O. J. Simpson trial, I just go mute.

Dionne: In some ways I'm happy that it is only 42 percent that seem not to be wild about the First Amendment, because you can really take a bunch of components and say it's pretty easy to build up to that number. There are some people who use their democratic right to support whatever administration is in power, and some of them will be unhappy about what they see. Over a long period of time of a number of conservatives distrusting the press on general principle, that builds up that percentage. Then you have people seeing reporters as people who go to others who are suffering, put a mike in their face or get out their notebook and say, "So how does it feel to have been . . . " Or they say, "Some people think that's awful what you guys do; why do you do that?" Then, there is the component of journalism where we go off and cover Chandra Levy. And this sentiment is shared by a good segment of the public. Then the blurring of the lines. I sit here as someone who personally blurs the line, since I spent seventeen years as an old-fashioned journalist and now nine years in opinion. But I think it gets even worse now because you don't know who is what any more, and a certain segment of people love people yelling at each other on television. You put all that together, and you have a lot of skepticism about what is called journalism. But fortunately most people still would say, Let's keep the First Amendment, and thank God for that.

Shepard: Can I just add that I had the fortune to go to Botswana and Swaziland, two small countries and burgeoning democracies in southern Africa. They were at that time thinking of restraining and licensing reporters. So they asked me to come over and speak to government officials about the First Amendment and how it worked. They couldn't fathom the idea that we didn't have government control over our press. And this was during the time that Bill Clinton and his escapades with Monica Lewinsky were in the front of the news.

I said to many different legislators that I bet my life that if Bill Clinton, who hated the coverage he was getting, had a choice between getting rid of the First Amendment or not, that he would be one of the most vigorous champions of it. And they were just in disbelief that a government official, a president of a country, would actually defend what was embarrassing him. And I think we are really fortunate to have the First Amendment. And I think that figure would change if there were any talk of getting rid of it.

Question (from the audience): *My name is Monique Chu, a reporter with the* Taipei Times, *which is an English-language daily in Taiwan. I know that Torie Clarke has held various regular briefings with all these bureau chiefs. To what extent do you think these meetings are actually helpful to reporters?*

McWethy: The bureau chief meetings I think were marginally productive. They helped in some of the nuts-and-bolts coverage of things. I was drafted to go to some of them and found them numbingly boring, and they have stopped doing them because they're not terribly productive anymore.

Murray: I had the same experience. I went to the first couple, and [they were] sort of trying to be helpful, but you're still dealing with an administration that really isn't terribly interested in being terribly helpful. So they were frustrating. And add to that the fact that . . . I had to go across the river and get into a secure building to go to them, and I stopped going.

Hess: *Can I pursue that a little, if you'll forgive me, because Torie Clarke asked Brookings early on if we would organize a session with her public affairs people and the bureau chiefs, and they came here in early November. Two things happened at that meeting that I thought were interesting. One was the reporters badgered her with nuts-and-bolts questions.*

Now it struck me that this was an opportunity at least to ventilate, at least to expose these questions in what was a systematic way. No matter how boring they may have been, that certainly distinguishes it from other countries where the defense ministers probably are not being exposed to those sorts of questions. And maybe indeed they could have an effect.

The other thing was when Tom DeFrank, the bureau chief of the New York Daily News, *got up and said, This is all very nice but this problem is insoluble. You people think that we're in the way. You people want to get rid of us because you want to fight a war and we're getting in your way. And this is all very nice, but let's be sensible about it, we just have different institutional needs. That was challenged by some of the admirals there.*

Murray: You have to understand the nature of these meetings. These were not meetings to say, Hey, I want to get this reporter on this ship. These were meetings to talk generally about the issue, and they all covered the same issue. It was the reporters saying, "With each successive war, access to the battlefield is getting more infrequent, scarcer, harder to do, and you guys clearly don't want us around," and them saying, "Well, no, we're trying to help you, embed you in this and embed you in that."

There was, as Tom DeFrank said, no solution to the problem and so going to meetings every two weeks to hear it hashed out again didn't seem like a terribly productive use of time. I think Torie has worked with news organizations and tried to work things out. John knows this better than I do. It seems to me it's sort of a combination of the nature of modern war plus the natural penchant of this administration—reflected very clearly by Don Rumsfeld or by John Ashcroft or by the president himself—to not be terribly helpful to the press that creates the problem.

McWethy: The truth of the matter is you could not satisfy reporters' questions no matter how much you told us. I mean that's a reality. You can reveal to us the entire war plan of every war there is, and it's not going to be enough. So there is an inherent tension between what the government does and what the press does, which is what makes this inherent tension so interesting. It is a living organic line that moves back and forth on different issues, whether it is dealing with the Justice Department on detainees or whether it is going to war.

The fact of the matter is, and Torie will argue this again and again, Don Rumsfeld has had more press briefings than any secretary of defense in history, and he has. He has been out there talking to us. Now does moving his lips and saying the words mean that he is communicating? Well, yes he is communicating, but he's communicating a very strict and well-thought out message.

Shepard: Over and over, right?

McWethy: We discussed it earlier. Message control is the way that this administration is trying to communicate what it is trying to do. Reporters don't like message control because we know that the government, that democracy is sloppy, that there are debates within the government and people disagree, and we love to write about the disagreements as they are coming to a policy formulation. So there is this inherent tension.

I'd say a couple of things about the way war goes today in the modern battlefield. Never before has the military faced the kind of challenges they now face in trying to conduct a war given the technologies that are available to us as reporters. We have civilian satellite images of bases that they are operating in, and we drive them crazy. During the war in Afghanistan, the Pentagon bought up all of the output of these satellites, but they realized it's not going to work because other companies outside of the United States are putting up their own satellites, and we're buying the images and we can tell that things are changing.

International satellite phones, believe it or not, work in Afghanistan. There is the Internet, which we discovered in the air war in Kosovo. We couldn't get people on the ground in Kosovo, but all of us had Internet conversations with people in the cities that were being bombed, and there was all of this communication going on.

Then there are other television networks, the famous al Jazeera example, where images are coming out whether the U.S. government likes it or not. Their challenge is to figure out how to respond to images of 120 dead bodies stacked up, and they say, "We didn't bomb the village." Well, something happened there, what was it?

So the whole notion of them trying to figure out how to conduct a war and us trying to figure out how to cover it I think is changing, and in fairness, both sides are struggling with how to come to grips with this. No military plan for a major military campaign is absent a plan to deal with the press. In one way or another they do factor it in. Now it may be that their idea of accommodating us is not satisfactory for us, and usually it's not, but it's always part of their plan.

Dionne: When I was in Lebanon a gentleman named William Buckley was kidnapped. We journalists covering the story that day looked at his resume, and it was very clear to us that he had been in the CIA. I went back and looked, and as far as I could tell not a single journalist—American for sure, I don't know about the rest of the press, but I think it was true abroad as well—just to show how smart we were wrote in our stories, "Looking at his resume, he's probably CIA." Why didn't we do that? Well, we didn't do that because we weren't sure it was going to serve any function in addition to just saying what the guy had done, but we did not want to put him in any more danger than he already was. Whether that's patriotism or a simple respect for an American who's serving the country whose life was at stake? Now it turns out unfortunately that they already knew from having captured documents at the embassy in Iran in '79 that he was in the CIA, and he was tortured and he was killed, but none of us wanted to be responsible for making that happen.

The flip side of the patriotism question, the marines on the ground in Lebanon knew how vulnerable they were and the military used the press in a very smart way by opening up to us entirely. They told the marines to be completely honest about how [they felt] about this. A bunch of us wrote stories about how vulnerable they felt in the situation they were in. [Clearly their commanders let them speak freely] to send a message back [to policymakers in Washington]. That was in September; in October they were blown up. That is a case where journalists doing their job of gathering information that parts of the government [the State Department, some in the Pentagon] didn't like were in effect trying to protect the soldiers on the ground [by letting others know about their vulnerability]. And those two things were not incompatible.

Hess: *Alicia, we've about come to the end. You wrote the book. Any final thoughts on journalism at this moment in history?*

Shepard: It's a thought that I've had and continue to have as a media critic, which is that one of the keys to improving public credibility of the media would be for the media to talk more about how it does its job. You just heard several examples of John McWethy saying that if lives were at stake they would hold back information. The public doesn't know that. They only see when information is released. E. J. mentioned William Buckley and the press making a responsible decision to protect his life, to not mention the CIA. The public doesn't know that. If journalists and especially editors and network heads would say more, would explain more how they do their jobs, the tough decisions they make, why they put something on the air, why they don't, I think the public would have a much greater respect for the media.

Hess: *My final comment comes from a very wise journalist, Jack Fuller, the president of the* Chicago Tribune, *who wrote, "It is often said that a society gets the press it deserves. I'm not sure about that, but I know that in the end it gets a press no better than it wants. If the public is led to accept shoddy or dangerous goods, the public will prevail. So it is up to newspapers to make news values compelling enough that people will see in them their deeper interests." Let us expand that thought to all the media.*

Postscript

As the United States was preparing for a second war in Iraq, ABC's John McWethy, one of the most experienced national security reporters in the business, went out on a limb to predict that Pentagon restrictions on press coverage would be "as bad, if not worse" than they were in Afghanistan. The *Wall Street Journal*'s Alan Murray agreed with McWethy's bleak judgment. But within a few months, with war on the near horizon, the Pentagon inaugurated a new press strategy, based on embedding hundreds of reporters with American and British military units. Never had the press been presented with such access. Reporters had to promise not to compromise the troops or the mission, but, as far as we know, none had that in mind anyway. The upshot was that the American people got unparalleled coverage of the conflict, and the Pentagon took a big step toward restoring a degree of confidence and trust among reporters in its relations with them, which had been shattered during the Vietnam War. Next time, it will be difficult for the Pentagon to reimpose the strict restrictions McWethy properly feared. Although it may, a positive precedent has been established.

Index